'In Mastering the Infinite Game *Charles Hampden-Turner and Fons Trompenaars continue their campaign to transcend reductionism in Western thought. This time they link economic achievement in the information age with circular thinking and complementary relationships. This book swoops through data and concepts with aplomb. This writing is the kind that entices rather than pummels you with ideas; it leaves you feeling intelligent, not just informed.'*

Milton J. Bennett
Director, The Intercultural Communication Institute, Portland, Oregon

'A timely call to Western managers . . . to inspect their ideological assumptions about business and to open their minds to the Asian reality. Although controversial . . . successful managers will pay heed because the alternative is decline.'

George C. Lodge
Jaime and Josefina Chua Tiampo Professor of Business
Administration Emeritus
Harvard Graduate School of Business Administration

'A highly original insight into Asian management from a cross-cultural perspective.'

Professor Malcolm Warner
Fellow, Wolfson College, University of Cambridge

'The authors demonstrate an understanding of the Asian tigers that is second to none in the world. Anybody doing business in that part of the globe must read this book.'

Dr Ronnie Lessem
Academic Director, Management MBA
City University Business School, London

'With its unique insights into the success of East Asian economies this is a provocative yet strangely reassuring book. For after blowing us out of our comfortable mental boxes the authors reconnect and reframe the facts. With Eastern and Western management cultures illuminated and the opposites unified, perhaps this time Charles Hampden-Turner and Fons Trompenaars really have squared the circle.'

David K. Hurst
Speaker, writer and consultant on management
Author of *Crisis and Change: Meeting the Challenge of Organizational Change*

MASTERING the Infinite game

How East Asian Values are Transforming Business Practices

Charles Hampden-Turner and Fons Trompenaars

CAPSTONE

The right of Charles Hampden-Turner and Fons Trompenaars to be identified as the authors of this work has been asserted in accordance with the Copyright, Designs and Patents Act 1988.

First published 1997
Reprinted 1997
Capstone Publishing Limited
Oxford Centre for Innovation
Mill Street
Oxford OX2 0JX
United Kingdom

British Library Cataloguing in Publication Data
A CIP catalogue record for this book is available from the British Library.

ISBN 1 900961 083

Designed and typeset by Forewords, Oxford
Printed and bound by T.J. International Ltd, Padstow, Cornwall

This book is printed on acid-free paper

Contents

Acknowledgements

This book began when R S Moorthy, Director of the Center for Culture and Technology at Motorola University, sent one of us a copy of *Finite and Infinite Games* by James P Carse. Without this timely communication several years of our thinking would not have been so clearly distilled. Even then, this book might not have happened if Richard Farson had not invited the British author to address the Aspen Design Conference, where he received considerable encouragement, especially from Professor John Kao, who chaired the conference, and from Stewart Brand, another featured speaker.

Thanks to such encouragement we both took the concepts explored here to Singapore. The Dutch author shared a platform with Lee Kuan Yew and the British author addressed a seminar kindly convened at the Institute for Policy Studies by Tommy Koh. We were both encouraged to persevere.

Philip Merry, who represents the Trompenaars Group in Singapore, was an unfailing source of support. We are also acquainted with Ed Schein, and his research on the Economic Development Board of Singapore had an important influence on us.

Earlier we had been fortunate to meet Madame S K Ko, Managing Director at Motorola's facility in Penang, and P Y Lai, then managing director of Intel Penang. Our admiration of East Asian management was confirmed during our meetings with them. Bill Wiggenhom, President of Motorola University, has also been an invaluable ally, as has Robert Textor, recently retired from Stanford University's Department of Anthropology. His wide knowledge of East Asia guided and sustained us. Pat Canavan, VP for Global Leadership, was another invaluable ally within Motorola.

In Britain, support for this thesis came from Geoff Mulgan, President of DEMOS and editor of *Life after Politics*, who was kind enough to publish a *very* tentative draft of our central thesis. Support was also given by Angela Dumas of the Design Council. Professor Malcolm Warner, Professor John Child and Nick Oliver, of the Judge Institute, were very helpful.

In the USA we were supported, as always, by the Global Business Network, especially Napier Collyns, Peter Schwartz and Lawrence

Wilkinson. Amanda Young typed innumerable drafts of this manuscript, so greatly improving on our spelling and punctuation that reading it became a pleasure instead of a reproach. She even divined the words we had omitted.

Our publisher Richard Burton of Capstone has been an enthusiastic supporter of this book from the outset. Joe Spieler, our agent, kept our nerves for us. Bob Garratt acted as valued friend.

To all staff at the Trompenaars group in Amsterdam, we remain deeply appreciative. They are too many to name, but their friendship and support helped to make this book possible.

Charles Hampden-Turner
Cambridge University
Judge Institute of
   Management Studies
Trumpington Street
Cambridge CB2 1AG
UK
Tel: +44 1223 339645

Fons Trompenaars
The Trompenaars Group
AJ Ernststraat 595D
1082 LD Amsterdam
The Netherlands
Tel: +31 20301 6666

Executive Summary

The research that underpins *Mastering the Infinite Game* was conducted via a 58-item questionnaire, among 34,000 middle and senior managers from some 58 countries. There were nearly two million responses. The Trompenaars database is believed to be the world's largest contemporary store of information on global business culture issues.

The rapid economic development of East Asian 'tiger economies' is unprecedented in economic history. Singapore, for example, has grown almost 100% since 1990, overtaking the USA and Britain in GDP per person. Such feats are seen to originate in the values of East Asian public and private managers. We measure values by means of a Dilemma Questionnaire, which puts values like *cooperating versus competing* in conflict with each other to see which managers choose. We range our research results along seven dimensions:

Specific criteria (e.g. profitability)	Diffuse criteria (e.g. knowledge)
Winning/compromising	Negotiating consensus
Individualism (e.g. competing)	Communitarianism (e.g. cooperating)
Inner-directed (steered-from-within)	Outer-directed (steered-from-without)
Status achieved (success is good)	Status ascribed (the good should succeed)
Universalism (rule by laws)	Particularism (unique and exceptional)
Sequential time (time as a race)	Synchronous time (time as a dance)

On all the dimensions above, North American and most West European managers prefer the left-hand column and most East Asian managers prefer the right-hand column.

It is *not* our case that the column of preferences on the right are somehow 'better' than those on the left. It *is* our case that East Asian cultures learn Western values when they play host to Western corporations, when they utilize Western technologies and when they allow free competition. In doing these things they *reconcile* their values with ours. For example, they reconcile specific profits with the development of diffuse knowledge, individuals are reconciled with the communities of their membership, and so on. Taoist, Confucian and Buddhist traditions teach the complementarity of all processes.

This means that while East Asian managers prefer the right-hand column, they can *include* the left.

Unfortunately the same cannot be said for many Westerners. They champion the left column but tend to dismiss the right column as inferior. One result is that we find ourselves playing Finite Games in which individuals win or lose by specific criteria in universal contests. Achievement consists of beating others in an imaginary 'race'. One result of East Asian adherence to the right-hand column (and the fact that they define these values inclusively) is that they are playing Infinite Games with rules which are adapted by the exceptions they encounter, with contests from which all players learn cooperatively.

In a Finite Game improvement comes from the fiercer competitor rising to the top in a battle which favors the 'survival of the fittest'. In an Infinite Game improvement comes from the game itself developing 'survival of the fitt*ingest*', players self-organizing more effectively.

East Asian economies have succeeded, we argue, because of seven major integrations, explained in Chapters 3–9. East Asian tiger economies have moved . . .

- Beyond the scarcity of *specific* things, like profits and property, to the abundance of *diffuse* processes, like knowledge generation.
- Beyond the 'level playing field', where one side vies with the other, to clusters of players whose joint contributions improve the 'game', or industry, for all players.
- Beyond *competitive* rivalry towards cooperative competing, a process in which all players learn *cooperatively* from studying the better plays.
- Beyond straight-line reasoning in which persons reach logical 'conclusions' (and hence stop!), to reflecting after the fact, to create a process of continuous and infinite improvement, in which reflection feeds back on reasoning in a cycle of eternal return.
- Beyond achievement to discovery of and inquiry into what is most worth achieving and *then* achieving it. Of all technologies originating in the West or East, which best educates employees and citizens?
- Beyond strict adherence to contract terms to a dynamic reciprocity of relationship. Here one partner does more than the contract specifies and obligates the customer to do *more* also, so that favors escalate on both sides. In this way actual performance

may far exceed prior agreement. Contracts are finite, relationships infinite.

• Beyond time and (sequential) motion, wherein finite games are won by the fastest mover, to redesign of the game itself so that all sequences are synchronized *just in time*, thereby shortening 'the racecourse' and initiating infinite improvements.

The seven cultural integrations help to account for East Asian economic prowess. Such lessons are well known by Western corporations that operate in this region and which are part of this dynamic—companies like Motorola, Intel, SGS Thomson, Advanced Micro Devices etc. What they have learned we must learn before it is too late.

Introduction

Economics-as-Usual or a Transformation in Values?

Economic growth rates in East Asia are truly astounding and without precedent in the history of development. Most observers watch these trends through their accustomed Western economic mind-sets. What we are seeing, they claim, is more of the same speeded up. There is nothing there to afflict our comfort. Other nations want to be like us and now they are hurrying. Which only shows how right we are and always were! It is all about economics now and in this we excel. Gerald Segal recently pronounced 'Asian Values' to be a myth.[1]

Our view is that these extraordinary growth rates have their origins in the cultures of that region, that they are growing so fast because they *differ* from us and that their values represent a challenge to our whole way of thinking. Our economics is not the solution but part of our problem. However painful it may be to learn from former colonies, we must start to do so. We do not have much time. The pendulum of economic advantage is swinging eastwards at momentous speed.

In this introduction we pose three questions.

- How fast are the tiger economies of the Asia Pacific region growing relative to other economies, mature or newly industrializing?
- Are the routine explanations of this growth credible?
- Why are we so keen to explain away this phenomenon, rather than come to terms with it?

Table 1 shows the world growth-leagues for 1996, the latest available figures taken from *The World in 1997*. Gross Domestic Product per

Table 1 GDP per head growth for 1996

1	*Vietnam*	9.7%		26	Australia	3.6%
2	*China*	8.7%		27	S. Africa	3.0%
3	*Malaysia*	8.5%		28	Portugal	2.5%
4	*Singapore*	8.0%		29	Finland	2.3%
5	*Thailand*	7.7%			USA	
6	Chile	7.3%		31	The Netherlands	2.2%
7	Turkey	7.0%			UK	
	Czech Republic				Spain	
	Jordan			34	Greece	1.9%
10	*South Korea*	6.8%			New Zealand	
11	Irish Republic	6.6%		36	Sweden	1.8%
12	*Taiwan*	5.8%		37	Canada	1.7%
13	Slovakia	5.6%		38	Iran	1.6%
14	*Philippines*	5.5%		39	Hungary	1.5%
15	India	5.0%		40	Italy	1.3%
16	Poland	4.9%			Argentina	
17	Norway	4.6%		42	Denmark	1.1%
	Pakistan			43	Bulgaria	1.0%
19	Romania	4.5%			Austria	
20	Mexico	4.2%		45	France	0.9%
21	*Hong Kong*	4.0%		46	Belgium	0.8%
	Israel				Germany	
	Colombia			48	Switzerland	0.7%
24	*Japan*	3.9%		49	Saudi Arabia	0.3%
	Egypt			50	Venezuela	0.4%

person is the comparison. Economies of the Asia Pacific regions are in italics.

From this we see that *all* of the top five performers are tiger economies, while six out of the top ten, or nine out of the top fifteen, are from the Asia Pacific area. All Asian countries are in the top half of the table. The slowest growing economy in the region is Japan, which leads all of Western Europe with the exception of Norway and the Irish Republic, and all of the G7 including the USA and Canada.

Of course, just one year's growth can mislead, so it might be fairer to ask about growth over the last seven years. These figures are indicated in Table 2.

Once again the tiger economies occupy no fewer than eight of the top ten places. With the exception of Pakistan no Asian economy is in the bottom twenty places. Eight tiger economies have grown over 50% in the last 5 years. China has grown 136% and Indonesia 124% from very low bases. Obviously something is stirring of vast consequence.

Table 2 GDP per head growth

1	China	136.0%	21	Japan	26.8%
2	Indonesia	124.0%	22	Norway	26.6%
3	Chile	117.1%	23	South Africa	25.7%
4	Singapore	99.8%	24	Poland	25.0%
5	Brazil	85.2%	25	USA	24.8%
6	Thailand	84.3%	26	Belgium	23.9%
7	Hong Kong	68.8%	27	Pakistan	22.4%
8	Malaysia	64.9%	28	Spain	21.0%
9	Philippines	61.1%	29	Australia	20.6%
10	South Korea	55.9%	30	France	20.5%
11	Irish Republic	53.6%	31	UK	18.5%
12	Greece	49.3%	32	Germany	18.4%
13	Turkey	41.9%	33	Switzerland	17.9%
14	Taiwan	40.9%	34	Italy	12.8%
15	India	40.7%	35	Hungary	12.7%
16	Israel	33.2%	36	Sweden	1.9%
17	New Zealand	35.3%	37	Mexico	0.4%
18	The Netherlands	34.0%	38	Venezuela	0.2%
19	Portugal	33.9%	39	Canada	−1.2%
20	Austria	29.5%	40	Saudi Arabia	−11.5%
			41	Finland	−15.7%

But is it in any way unprecedented? These are some of the standard explanations.

Newly industrializing countries often develop fast, but when economies mature they slow down

There is something to this. As economies grow rich a consumption ethic often takes over, which distracts them from working so hard. People in these economies have bought their 'basic stuff'—i.e. refrigerators, TVs, stereos, autos. So long as people feel deprived of the idealized Western lifestyle, they will work together with great unanimity to achieve this. But there is less focus on common goals once this has been achieved.[2]

The problem with this thesis is that the anticipated slow-down does not always arrive. In the case of Singapore, the GDP per person has, since 1991, overtaken the USA, the UK, Germany, France, Austria, Australia, Belgium, Finland, France, Italy, The Netherlands, Sweden and Canada. Projecting current growth rates, Singapore will overtake

Table 3 Comparative GDP per person, with 1996 versus 1990 rankings

Rank 1996 (1990)	Country	Total	Rank 1996 (1990)	Country	Total
1 (1)	Switzerland	$42,350	21 (22)	Israel	$16,980
2 (2)	*Japan*	$38,120	22 (20)	Spain	$15,522
3 (5)	Norway	$35,710	23 (23)	*Taiwan*	$14,090
4 (6)	Denmark	$34,620	24 (25)	*South Korea*	$11,910
5 (17)	*Singapore*	$32,878	25 (26)	Greece	$11,900
6 (7)	Germany	$30,300	26 (27)	Portugal	$9,700
7 (9)	USA	$29,600	27 (39)	Argentina	$8,470
8 (3)	Sweden	$29,209	28 (24)	Saudi Arabia	$6,800
9 (10)	Austria	$27,804	29 (36)	Chile	$5,680
10 (12)	France	$27,600	30 (29)	Czech Republic	$5,570
11 (18)	*Hong Kong*	$27,130	31 (33)	Brazil	$5,450
12 (11)	Belgium	$26,380	32 (28)	Hungary	$4,724
13 (14)	Netherlands	$26,000	33 (35)	*Malaysia*	$4,543
14 (4)	Finland	$25,030	34 (32)	Poland	$3,930
15 (13)	Italy	$22,900	35 (29)	Slovakia	$3,870
16 (15)	Australia	$22,115	36 (–)	Lithuania	$3,700
17 (16)	UK	$20,900	37 (38)	Russia	$3,550
18 (8)	Canada	$20,690	38 (30)	Mexico	$3,340
19 (21)	Irish Republic	$19,670	39 (40)	*Thailand*	$3,250
20 (19)	New Zealand	$18,020	40 (31)	South Africa	$3,130

Norway and Denmark by 1998, Japan by 2002 and Switzerland a year later to head the growth leagues.

Both Singapore and Hong Kong give the lie to the idea that already developed nations slow down. Singapore moved from 17th to 5th, growing at the astounding rate of 99.8% between 1990 and 1996. Hong Kong moved from 18th to 11th, growing at 68%. Japan held 2nd place but closed upon Switzerland, knocking almost $2,000 off the latter's lead. Tables 1–3 show that Taiwan, South Korea, Malaysia and Thailand all either climbed up the table or held their places with well above average growth rates.

Pioneering capitalist countries invent new technologies, while catch-up economies need only implement what is already available

It is believed that invention and origination are relatively slow processes, like building a road, while simply using these technologies is a relatively fast process, like driving along a road once it is completed.[3] Plausible although this argument sounds, it will hardly do. The inventor of any technology or process has a sizeable lead (not to mention patents and licenses) over someone coming upon this technology in completed form. If following fast is so easy and quick, why do European and North American economies not do this? All economies are 'ahead' or 'behind' in certain industries. If being behind has secret advantages why are these not being seized? Why are not Australia and New Zealand in hot pursuit of their Pacific neighbors?

East Asian economies are taking ruthless advantage of their low wage costs, their lean and inexpensive governments and the resulting low tax-burden

The final argument used to explain why we cannot develop as effectively as East Asian 'tigers' is that they have 'once only' advantages over us. This argument makes common cause with right-wing politics in Europe and North America and is therefore not so much an accurate description of tiger economies as a way of sharpening domestic political axes. We would not expect it to be accurate and it largely misreads the realities.[4]

Japanese wage costs are not low at all. Next to Germany, they are the second highest in the world. Singapore's average wage is over *fifteen* times that of Vietnam. So, far from low wages being a policy, Singaporean employers who pay below levels the government deems sufficient—$800 per month—are subject to a levy(s). The money is used to finance skills upgrading, thereby raising minimum wages. 'Tiger' governments do not see the issue as one of high or low wages *per se* (wages have been allowed to rise), but as the need to raise skills faster than wages so as to enhance the wage/quality ratio. Competitive edge is created by the delivery of high quality, high complexity goods at the best available price. Low wages by themselves too often mean low skills. As for the effect of taxes, Japan's 'glory days' of 8.0–10% growth per annum were achieved with an 80% top tax rate.[5]

It is true that governments of East Asia are smaller and disburse less welfare overall. But the reason is not in a willingness to dump their less productive citizens in the gutters to sink or swim, but the availability of social provisions from other sources. The two main sources are businesses and family networks. Businesses tend to take a broad view of the work bargain. If workers are provided with free bus services, free child care and English Language tuition adjoining the work place, sports facilities and adult activity centers, then this increases their obligation to 'repay' the company through cost-saving initiatives, loyalty and ingenuity. In this way social provision is less an up-front entitlement than a reward for service, less a right than a desert.

The second major source of provision is intact nuclear families and the survival of some extended families, especially family businesses. It is a source of shame to have a family member dependent on the public purse, so families provide for their own. Unlike many Western economies, then, social provision is integrated with earned livelihoods: you get something for something, not something for nothing.

But why are our pundits so desperate to belittle and explain away Asian prowess? Why do they seek to dwell on the negative? For example, *The World of 1997*, published by *The Economist* from which all the figures in this introduction come, presented the growth figures for Singapore, adding the comment:

In the wake of disappointing election performance, the ruling PAP may crack down on the opposition . . .

Is that all we have to say? Few readers can have missed reports about the 'collapse' of the Japanese economy, its 'now permanent recession'—all of which was anticipated in *The Sun Also Sets* and *Japan Not as No. 1*. Column after column of disparagement, much of which was written on Japanese word processors and printers, has deluged the broadsheets. Japan has certainly had its troubles. Its economic fortunes are worse than most of us can remember. But before we get carried away by vengeful satisfaction, let us compare Japanese 'failure' with our own performances. Tables 1–3 show that, despite all her crises, including an earthquake, Japan grew faster than North America or the EEC in 1996 *and* over the last seven years on average. Japan has retained her second place in GDP per person and is likely to overtake Switzerland within the next five years.

Because Japan is already such a large and rich economy her 3.9% growth in GDP per person for 1996, and her total of 26.8% growth since 1990, has actually *increased* her lead over most other economies.

The UK, for example, would have to grow at over twice Japan's annual percentage growth simply to stay the same distance behind. With the exception of Ireland, Greece and Turkey, Europe is still falling behind Japan, year by year. If Japan's current 'failure' takes her ever further ahead of most Western economies, one shudders to think what her recovery might do! It is time, we believe, that experts begin to provide *answers* to the inexorable advance of tiger economies, not excuses and not wishful predictions of looming catastrophe. It is time we faced up to the Singaporean view that the West is, in some respects, decadent, that its values belong to a retreating phase of Capitalism (Figure 1).

We are not as convinced as most Western economists that breaking the laws of their 'science' brings the terrible retribution they keep anticipating, and if not now, soon! The view taken in this book is that it is *our* paradigms that will have to change, that two centuries of talking down to Asians is due for reappraisal. We doubt that the burgeoning success of Pacific Rim economies is explicable within our customary frameworks. That the world of business now speaks English does not mean that the formulations of English-speakers are

Figure 1 The crumbling edifice?

necessarily the best. Rather than witnessing 'more of the same speeded up', we are confronting alternative patterns of thought, which we should have the humility to learn from. As we shall see in Chapter 1, Sino-Japanese perspectives turn our conventional world upside-down.

Figure 1 represents a Singaporean view of the West's arrogant posture and rhetorical certainty, even while its own values are crumbling beneath it. Kishore Mahbubani, Dean of Singapore's Civil Service College, writes

Most Western journalists travel overseas with Western assumptions. They cannot understand how the West could be seen as anything but benevolent. CNN is not the solution. The same visual images transmitted to living-rooms across the globe can trigger opposing perceptions.   (Mahbubani, 1993)

Chapter 1

East Asian Values: A World Turned Upside Down

If East Asia can master industrial skills and yet retain its cultural values, it will be in a position once again to create a civilisation greater than any in human history . . . Of course we have no ambition whatsoever to bring the West under Asian dominance. In keeping with the fundamental principles of Eastern philosophy we seek only . . . co-existence and co-prosperity.

M. Mohamad and S. Ishihara, *The Voice of Asia.*

Are East Asian values crucially different from Western values or is this simply a fashionable claim by some Asian elites? If there *are* major differences does this matter in any way to economic development or to business? Traditionally, neo-classical economics has regarded values as purely 'subjective'. There is no reason, claimed Lionel Robbins, to regard carrion as a disutility and caviar as a utility.[1] If vultures had money, the former might soar in value. It is all a matter of subjective taste. 'Pushkin is as good as poetry' wrote Jeremy Bentham, better if it leads to higher economic demand.

Values become objective when they register themselves as economic demand in the market place. It is at this point, and not before, that they enter economic science. Insofar as values are seen as relevant at all to business these are generally disapproved of. Economic development arose, said John Maynard Keynes, 'out of nothing so much as avarice, usury and precaution, none of them genuine values'. Yet we had to go on 'pretending to ourselves that fair is foul and foul is fair' so as to pass through 'the economic tunnel of necessity'.[2] If there *are* spaceless, timeless economic laws holding good for all societies, then values whether Asian, Western or otherwise are simply irrelevant.

Mastering the Infinite Game argues that, on the contrary, the creation of values underlies wealth creation. Cultures earn their livings, and produce and develop effectively that which their members most value. To believe that a particular task is valuable is the necessary prelude to doing it well. This process begins in values, is woven through and through with values and constitutes much of the meaning of our lives and our work. Of course, not everyone's life *has* much meaning. But even this dire condition ramifies upon us, as we shall see. We can escape neither the richness of our values nor their poverty. Economic stagnation and chronically slow growth are rooted in failures of valuing.

In the opening chapter we explain both why East Asia joined the world leagues of economic development so late *and* why it is now so well adjusted to 'late capitalism', that it is growing much faster, even to the point of pulling far ahead of us. East Asian values are not a 'myth', as George Segal has recently asserted.[3] Rather, they pattern everything the tiger economies do, their choice of products, their business strategies, their customer relationships, their levels of investment, their propensities to learn.

So in what ways do the values of East Asian economies differ from our own? Even here the picture is not simple. There are major differences *between* the tiger economies, as we shall trace in the chapters which follow. However the East–West differences are far wider and more significant than the intra-Asian differences. Here are some historical roots of value differences.

- Supernatural religion versus secular humanism and enlightenment
- Belief and faith versus paradigmatic assumptions
- Cartesian dualism versus The Way of Complementarity
- Values as things versus values as wave-forms
- Cultures and values as mirror images
- Pioneer capitalism versus catch-up capitalism
- Finite and Infinite Games

Supernatural religion versus secular humanism and enlightenment

Values in much of the West have their origins in the commandments of supernatural beings and their sanctions for good or bad behavior in an after-life. Our concern here is *not* with the moral validity of Judeo-Christian beliefs. There is much that is both wise and beautiful in these precepts. Our concern is with their purported *origins* 'above' or 'beyond' this world in a celestial realm.

The problem is that belief in the supernatural and in heaven and hell are waning as science advances. Where values are authenticated by appeals to another world they suffer where the existence of that other world is doubted. Takeshi Umehara, the Japanese philosopher, has argued that the West is caught in a spiritual crisis as belief in supernatural authority and an after-life declines.[4]

This is not helped by the attitudes of Western scientists to religion. Science has historically advanced by skepticism, by believing nothing which cannot be tested and potentially falsified. Faced with anti-scientific belief-systems like Creationism, science has declared itself 'value free'. While such claims are extremely dubious (since when is skepticism not a value?), the effect has been a general loss of respect for valuing processes, leading to the 'moral crisis' of Western societies, much proclaimed of late. Trapped between the certainties of sectarianism and the neutrality of science, value systems are assailed from both sides. If mainstream religions secularize, they lose popular appeal; if they evangelize, they become obsessed with single issues and intolerant excitements.

The value systems of East Asia have proved more durable and tenacious in their appeal. Marriage and family have not eroded to the same extent. Respect for authority remains high. Salaries are generally more equal. Educational attainments at primary and secondary levels are higher and crime rates are, with some exceptions, substantially lower.

The value systems most influencing East Asia are of mixed origins, but for the most part their wisdom is secular, practical and of this world. They are 'humanistic' in the sense that they aspire to improve the human and social condition, and failure in this leads to criticism and re-appraisal. Confucianism, for example, is a philosophy of wise leadership, state-craft and good government through learning. Ceremony and worship are minimal and atrophied. Taoism, literally 'the way', is an earthly set of disciplines for living in harmony with the ecosystem. Buddhism has been accused of retreatism and of teaching inner-immigration, but its promise to mitigate the miseries of material existence is potentially verifiable *in* this world, into which its adherents are periodically reborn.[5]

Perhaps the most supernatural religion is Shintoism, which is largely confined to Japan, but this is really a nature religion, with gods as personifications of natural forces: wind, rain, sun, river, rice, etc. It is up to worshippers to entrap and pacify these seething elements within cultural artefacts designed to enshrine them. Whether gods are as destructive as typhoons or as benign as blossoms depends upon the offerings by the faithful of objects of habitation. Hence the shrines and cylindrical objects with *torii* gates which shore up earth and sky. Shinto gods demand ceaseless human construction and cultivation to keep them benign. The solutions lie in human craft and ingenuity.[6] East Asian philosophy and religion strives for human improvement and spiritual discipline.

Belief and faith versus paradigmatic assumptions

In the Judeo-Christian tradition it is good to have faith and it is bad to doubt. Faith moves mountains and sustains you 'through the night of doubt and sorrow'. Skepticism is not an aid to truth but its sworn enemy. To believe in a good God *against* the testimony of suffering and chaos all around you, is the mark of true virtue. John Bunyan put it well in his famous hymn:

No hob-goblin, nor foul fiend
Shall daunt his spirit
He knows he in the end
Will life inherit . . .

Clearly what is being described is an *adversary* system between belief and doubt, between Eternal Life and the everyday reminder of death. Those expressing doubt in the hearing of the Pilgrim are foul fiends and dismal story-tellers, who only make the Pilgrim *more certain than ever* of his righteousness and their wickedness.

In direct contrast, the values of East Asia are largely *paradigmatic*; that is, they describe a general approach to inquiry about the universe by trying to answer the question, *what should we assume when setting out to learn?* Since it is not humanly possibly to rid the mind of pre-conception, we need an awareness of the orientation which we have taken for granted. The view taken by Asian philosophy is of a state of harmony in the universe, made up of contrasting elements which are complementary to each other.[7] It could be said that this is a fairly risky assumption, but no more so than assumptions made by Western philosophy. We assume the world to be random and unrelated until such a time as discrete 'objects' or 'facts' reflect themselves in the retinal mirrors of our dispassionate observations. We then manipulate these objects in predictable ways to establish an order amongst them. This orientation *also* involves massive pre-suppositions, omitting phenomena which do not fit the paradigm. Amongst these omissions are values, as we shall see.[8]

Cartesian dualism versus The Way of Complementarity

Early on in Western scientific history there arose a schism between mind and body. The mind did the seeing. The body or bodies *were seen*. The result of this schism was that Western science set out on a long journey to accumulate facts, of which our bodies were examples but our minds were not. The original motive was probably religious piety. The mind was the seat of the immortal soul, thought for many years to be the pineal gland in the brain. The mind was therefore to be left to the church, while accumulation of external facts was the province of scientific investigation.

The dominant paradigm of East Asia is 'The Way of Complementarity'. It is a framework not so much for accumulating facts but for elevating human nature, a far more ambitious project. Much of the new technology is likely to originate in the West for the foreseeable future but more and more of the capacity to create valuable products and services will come from East Asia.

The complementarity paradigm is traceable to Lao Tzu, the Chinese originator of Taoism in the sixth century B.C. The Tao means 'The Way of the Universe'. The Tai Chi, or Diagram of the Supreme Ultimate, is depicted in Figure 1.1.

There are differing accounts of its primordial origins. Yin (dark) and yang (light) meant originally 'the dark and sunny sides of the hill'. Others claim the reference is to the ebb and flow of mountain mists of contrasting color. Yin has been used to depict earth, female, valley, steam, night and yielding, while yang symbolizes sky, male, mountain, rock, day and forcing. There are serious implications for gender equality in such schema, softened somewhat by the Taoist insistence that yielding is a form of strength and all values are achievable by indirection, by going with the rhythms of the universe, the flow of events.[9]

Figure 1.1   The Tai Chi.

Among the subtleties of the Tai Chi is the belief that every polarity or extreme contains the seed of its opposite: the strenuously righteous are haunted by guilt, the bully is a coward, the tough boss is running scared, the great individualist is really lonely, the glamorous film-star is a nervous wreck and so on. There is no need here for a theory of the unconscious. Paradox lies in the heart of the universe. 'The more he talked of his honour, the faster we counted our spoons.' When President Johnson started to pray, the Vietnamese were wise to duck. Indeed, the praying and bombing were connected.

Nothing better characterizes the difference between West and East than Aristotle's division between A and not-A, now part of the computer's binary code of 0 and 1, and the insistence of Asian philosophy that opposites are complementary and potentially reconcilable through harmony.

Harmony (or *wa*) is not simply a Sino-Japanese value, it is a value of values. Prince Shotku in eighth century Japan pronounced that *wa* was the supreme value of all civil societies. Values are not good or bad *in themselves*, but are good when they harmonize with other values and bad when they clash or fight with other values. Buddha, Kung Fu-Tsu (or Confucius) and Lao Tzu are depicted in a *Dialogue of Sages* although it is extremely improbable that they were, in fact, contemporaries. No one could accuse these three philosophies of being alike. It is their diversity which creates their unity, their combined contributions to elevating the human condition. In Box 1.1 we see how this tradition translates into Thai culture, according to its former Minister of Education.

There was much merriment in the pages of *Encounter* a few years ago on the 'rabid anti-intellectualism' of Japanese students. Asked

Box 1.1   Buddhism and Development in Thai Culture

Thai people have a long history of openness to other cultures and mutual tolerance. Even before the modern era they learned from Indians, Chinese, Khmers, Mons, Burmans, Indonesians and Malays. Today they are learning extensively from Japan.

Logically their way of thinking is 'both–and' as opposed to 'either–or', with a preference for harmony over dichotomy. Although this is common among East Asian cultures, it is more pronounced than usual in Thailand. Many Thais espouse *both* Christianity and Buddhism, and Buddhists accept this synthesis as Buddhist. Non-exclusivism is the rule. The Thai Buddhist way of 'knowing' *(ruu)* is much broader than what Westerners mean by knowledge. It includes cognition, but also extends to intuition and emotion: heart to heart, heart to society, heart to nature . . . and psychometrics too! The knower is not detached from the known. Integrating and synthesizing old with new is much admired. You must be open to change but harmonize with it.

Thai society is seen as self-equilibrating, self-correcting. New technology must harmonize with the social and natural environment. The watch-word is 'sufficiency for all'. The Buddhist 'middle path' *(madchima patipathaa)* is the way to development, with no 'great leaps' and enough time to adjust. Even Singapore is too fast and too dramatic.

Development needs participation by the peoples' own values. No generation should be sacrificed to the next. Thailand's change has been independent, evolutionary and gradualistic, with people borrowing voluntarily that which they admired. The capacity to envision whole scenarios of the future is the essence of social choice. The future lies latent within us. Buddhist 'development monks' have made progress in fusing economic with religious values.

Source: S. Ketudat and R. B. Textor (ed.) (1990) *The Middle Path for the Future of Thailand*, East-West Center, Honolulu, Hawaii.

whether they were Marxist, capitalist, humanist, existentialist, pragmatist, idealist, statist, etc., they tended to tick all or most of these! The accusation was that they did not know the difference and/or that they were eager to placate all convictions.[10] A less hostile interpretation is that all these philosophies are benign when they work together and are pathological when in conflict. All this happened before a Marxist-capitalist economy (China) began to grow at an average rate of 10% per annum over more than a decade!

In the past 40 years there has arisen a quite extraordinary vindication of the Tao and of the world as a set of complementarities. As theoretical physicists began to study minute entities in the sub-atomic world, it became impossible to prevent the investigator from altering the nature of what he observed. This was brought about by the very small size of electrons, protons, neutrons, etc. and the proportionally gross nature of scientific intervention, which consists of firing particles at very high speeds and observing the scattering effects. Scientists have now had to confront the reality that *to investigate nature is to disturb it* and the manner of our disturbance has two contrasting consequences.

We see the sub-atomic realm either as particles or as wave-forms (see Figure 1.3), so that there is a fundamental bifurcation and complementarity at the root of all sub-atomic investigation. None of this would be of any surprise to the culture of China and the Pacific Rim. They have believed for over two thousand years that discourse takes this form.[11]

The reason this problem did not arise in nineteenth century physics was that the phenomena being investigated were dead and too large to be affected by human methods. The moon does not alter its

Particles   Waves

Figure 1.2 The wave and particles complementarity represented by the Tao.

substance because a telescope is trained upon it. It remains an object, hence objectivity, a trained dispassion which respects the separateness of things. And science began in the heavens, where things are very far away.

The problem today is less the smallness of phenomena than their *reactivity*. Sub-atomic phenomena react when we attempt to observe them, but *so do living systems*. The problem here is not smallness but aliveness and seeking to remain so. If I try to cross a river via stepping stones, I had best ensure that none of these are alligators or snapping turtles who react to being stepped on. This is even more true in the social realm. If we approach a subject with clipboards and a blank expression, we will be answered in kind. If we approach with a topic of shared interest and smiles we will get another reaction which reflects our own inputs.

No less an authority than Niels Bohr, the Danish physicist and Nobel Prize winner, has incorporated the Tao into his coat-of-arms (see Figure 1.4).[12] Warner Heisenberg, his student, has proclaimed 'physics is conversation'. Theoretical physics was faced by giant paradoxes in this century, which have been solved by dialog between contrasting viewpoints, a position championed in his last years by David Bohm.[13] *Mastering the Infinite Game* contends that *complementarity applies to all domains where 'objects' of study react to that study*, a situation encountered in psychology, anthropology, sociology, management studies, economics and most *especially* human values and ethics.

In short, East Asian cultures have an ancient framework for comprehending the complementarity of values, which most Western cultures lack. What we see depends on how we look and what our values are. For years we have dismissed Asian philosophy as 'metaphysical' or 'metaphorical'. We can do so no longer. Complementarity is at the roots of scientific inquiry.

The concept of complementarity is also at the roots of wealth creation and values creation. What makes a product valuable are the values reconciled within its design and production. 'Value added', a phrase used by economists, is a misnomer. Values do not add up that easily. In any complex product they have to be 'designed in' or reconciled. Take an automobile. We want it to be high-performing, comfortably sprung and of premium quality. Unfortunately we also need it to be safe, to corner well and to be as low cost as possible. Any engineer or designer will tell you that to reconcile high-performance

Figure 1.3   'Opposites are complementary' reads the inscription over the Tao.

with safety, comfortable rides with easy cornering and to make premium quality cheap is quite a challenge![14]

That is not all we want. We want 'intelligent' braking, steering and gear-changing, yet *we* want to be in charge of the driving. We want fast acceleration and economic fuel consumption. The car must be standardized to lower costs, yet distinctive to attract consumers. All such value-pairs are *in tension*, that is potentially in conflict, yet potentially reconcilable, through design and production excellence. All this is the world of the Tai Chi.

There are many other examples. Computers grow ever more complex yet need to be 'user friendly'. Foods need to be of high quality yet we want them ready-to-serve so as to save valuable time. We design buildings to provide community and privacy, esthetics and utility. The list of synthesized attributes could be extended indefinitely. Our contention is that cultures in East Asia have always thought this way and are busy weaving values together while we pile them up precariously, fact on fact, a heap of 'goods' (good things) 'added' to each other.[15]

Values as things versus values as wave-forms

'What is Courage?' asked Socrates. Twenty-four centuries later the West is no nearer to an answer. Why? Because the implication of the question is that *values are things*, which is equivalent to seeing the world as composed of particles. 'Is this a good thing?' our moral philosophers ask, and then they get hopelessly bogged down.[16] Good for whom? Good for what? Value judgements have no 'testable meaning', the positivists tell us. They are merely 'exclamations of preference', relativistic noise. One man's 'courage' is another man's 'recklessness' or 'fanaticism'. It all depends whose side you are on! Allies and compatriots are 'courageous'. Enemies are 'reckless'.

But there *are* answers to these questions, if we think of values as wave-forms which either harmonize or clash with one another. Harmony should be distinguished from unison. When we sing in unison we are belting out the same tune. When we sing in harmony we have blended esthetically *different* tunes—there is a unity of diversity. The concept of harmony requires members of a culture to be different, yet create from those differences esthetic wholes. *The Book of Music* (Yueh) was one of Confucius' six classic works. The sage leader was a gentle person who cultivated melodious waves, rippling to the far corners of the kingdom.

Edward de Bono has argued that what Western thought lacks is a 'water logic'.[17] Let us re-frame the question of Socrates 'What is courage?' to ask 'How can we risk ourselves (courageously), while securing ourselves (cautiously)?'. Imagine if you will, an expanse of water, depicted in Figure 1.5.

Suppose two stones have been dropped at top left and bottom right, causing interference waves to cross and to qualify one another. Suppose the wave-forms constitute risking (courage) and securing (caution). Positive value lies in *harmonizing* such waves at the top-right of the diagram, as both propel the swimmers forward. You *risk yourself to make things more secure*, a good description of the growth of a business. Show courage so as to return to a life of relative caution, thereby exemplifying the maxim 'discretion is the better part of valor'.

But there is nothing automatic about harmonizing these contrasting

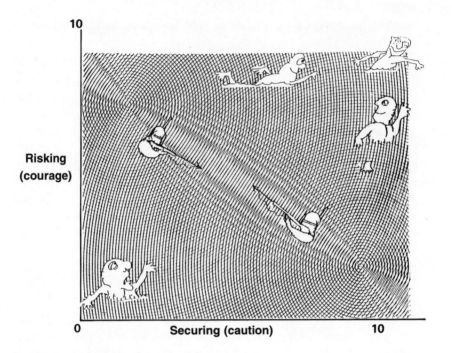

Figure 1.5   Water logic.

values. You *could* get caught in the 'adversary zone' of rival scuba divers in the middle of the picture. Here risking and securing combine in *destructive interference*, the waves canceling each other out until one or more exhausted loser is washed out of the pattern at the bottom left, trapped between 'recklessness' and 'cowardice', the names we give to *disharmonious* values.

The probability of getting trapped in adversarialism is obviously much higher if values are conceived of as solid things, rocks of righteousness or colliding billiard balls. While waves *can* harmonize, solid missile-like objects cannot. Courage has to 'conquer' caution to prevail. Fundamentalism and single-issue imperialism stalk the land in many Western economies. As W B Yeats put it:

> The best lack all conviction, while the worst are full of passionate intensity.[18]

Yet could it be that we are at war with our mirror-images, yin against yang?

Cultures and values as mirror images

If values are indeed wave-forms then it follows that these are mirror-images of each other. Courage and caution, risking and securing, loving and correcting are like reflections of each other in the water, with the image reversed. The implications of this complementarity are of great significance. It means that *no culture is wholly strange to us*. While values differ as between cultures, these differences are neither random nor arbitrary. They are orderly complements of our own preferences. All cultures, for example, need to make rules and find exceptions, need to analyze and synthesize experience, need to build communities and nurture individual members, need to equalize opportunities yet rank successes, need to have arguments and reach agreements. Where cultures differ is in the *relative salience* they give to one or another complementarity. Hence Anglo-American cultures extol individuals more than communities. East Asian 'tigers' extol communities more than individuals.[19] To visit such cultures then is to discover your own 'lost values', the community necessary to the nurture of genuine individualism, the harmony that allows individual views to register.

For East Asian values are not simply different from ours, but largely the *obverse* of our own. At first, this seems frightening—they are contradicting us! They negate our precious individualism with their collectivism. But not if the seeds of individualism lie within the community. In that case they may restore to us the origins of what we most value. What we find in China, Japan and East Asia is our own world turned upside-down, like the reflection in a pool of trees standing on its far side. This is not only reversed left to right like a mirror, but top to bottom with the branches at our feet and the trunk in the sky.

This effect has been famously portrayed by Escher, who skillfully contrasted the 'object world' of leaves and fish with the 'image world' of culture. Mirror images are reversible. We look in the mirror and observe that Satan is left-handed! What a terrible person this is, who reverses all I believe in!

But in fact these mirror images are every bit as coherent and internally consistent as is our own cultural world. For example, it makes as much sense to say—with Adam Smith—that pursuit of individual self-interest leads to customers being served and the public being benefited as it does to say the opposite: that serving customers and seeking to benefit the public will lead to the satisfaction of individual self-interests. The larger truth is probably the whole Tao. Adam Smith saw only half of it, the yang. Once we admit that our economic icons are reversible then we begin to see why these 'upside-down' economies work as well or better than our own. For among the reversals of the way we think are our very different experiences of capitalism. We, the English-speaking cultures and Northwest Europeans, pioneered capitalism, while they are catching up. It makes a lot of difference in what form success comes.

Pioneer capitalism versus catch-up capitalism

So far we have assumed that there is one global economy in which Western nations and East Asian 'tigers' compete. But in fact, the experience of cultures which have *pioneered* capitalism is very different from the experience of cultures which have come from behind to *catch up*. There is an enormous difference between the values that were necessary to create the first industrial revolutions and those necessary to select the best technologies to develop an economy.

No explanations of East Asian values are adequate unless they solve a crucial issue. Why were the UK, the USA, Australia and Northwest Europe so adept at pioneering, while Asia stagnated? And why today are several countries in East Asia growing at such alarming speed? What repelled them from joining the capitalist path of development for over a century and why are they suddenly so successful? Table 1.1 tries to answer these questions.

Countries who pioneered had to defy the aristocratic, rural, mercantilist elite of their time. Industrializing required strong assertion by the middle class *against* the orthodoxies of their times, typically championed by governments, acting as a brake on economic progress. In the social disturbances following rapid industrialization, governments acted as regulators, reformers and referees.

Knowledge was useful in creating new industries, but it was rarely possible to say which knowledge might be subsequently applied to industry. Everyone felt in competition with everyone else since all innovations competed for limited funds from investors and consumers.

Labor relations were often poor, because when leading industries felt competitive pressures, they often tried to reduce wages to match

Table 1.1

	UK, USA, Australia, Canada, New Zealand	China, Japan, 'The Little Dragons'
1. Development strategy	Early industrializers Innovate piecemeal.	Late industrializers Follow selectively.
2. Role of government	Governments seen as ignorant of technology and foolish about business.	Governments seen as well informed on world technological trends.
3. Type of intervention and social policies	After-the-fact to regulate and to reform. Referee.	Before-the-fact to manage and to facilitate growth. Coach.
4. Educational policies	Stress on 'pure' knowledge, which is subsequently 'applied'.	Stress on successful technologies and industrial processes.
5. Fundamental orientation	Competitive individualism.	Cooperative communitarianism.
6. Labor relations	Poor, because wages come under pressure when other nations catch up.	Good, because wages increase steadily as nation catches up with leaders.
7. Development philosophy	*Laissez-faire*, empirical. No-one knows what will succeed so don't pick winners.	Managed competition. We *do* know what succeeds so let's pick the best teachers.

lower wage rates abroad. Life at the leading edge was so unpredictable that businesses favored *laissez-faire* policies in which they could find their own directions. No one knew what might succeed next, so trying to 'pick winners' was disparaged.

For most of the twentieth century, the nations of East Asia, with the exception of Japan, saw so little to admire in these values that their economies stagnated. Encouraged to grow economically by America, which opened its markets, and inspired by Japan's example, East Asia began to catch up and found that this required quite different values from those of the pioneers.

Instead of innovating new technologies, they could choose to adopt some of those technologies already developed in the West and follow selectively. For example, choosing electronics not heavy industries.

Having had a decade or more to study technological trends, their governments were usually well-informed and acted as facilitators or coaches to their national champions. Educationally these governments stressed skills and training in the technologies they had chosen, keeping wage costs down by ensuring that skilled labor was abundant.

The process of catching up was plotted jointly by government, educators, unions and/or workers, banks, research institutes and industries. They were able to cooperate in shared purposes, e.g. build a multimedia complex.

Labor relations were generally good because wages grew with the economy, but not faster than productivity. Hence the fruits of competitive advantage were shared among employees. In this way competition was managed. The fastest-growing, most profitable technologies were used to inform and upgrade the whole economic infrastructure.

Finite and Infinite Games

Competitiveness in capitalist countries is non-lethal. We may wish to destroy our opponents economically, but we do not seek to destroy them physically. Hence competing stops well short of outright war. It is, however, a form of mock combat. As such it is a game in which war-like encounters are simulated, yet real consequences follow. These include one party bankrupting another and eliminating it from the game.

Now most games are partly competitive and partly cooperative. The competitive element lies in the contest for scarce resources and in outright victory over opponents. The cooperative element lies in a respect, even a love, for the game itself, for the fact that one improves the culture of the corporation by mastery of the game and that valuable goods and services are supplied to customers.

The thesis of this book is that Anglo-American capitalisms and the capitalisms of East Asia contain *varying blends of competing and cooperating*. These correspond with what we call Finite Games and Infinite Games. The Finite Game leans toward competitiveness as its major ingredient. The Infinite Game leans towards cooperativeness as its major ingredient. Yet each type includes both values. The distinction between these types was first made by James P Carse.[20]

The two types of games include many of the distinctions made earlier in this chapter. For example, the Finite Game is decreed by external authorities. The Infinite Game is agreed by players attempting to improve their human condition. Finite Games are divided between spectators and contenders. Infinite Games assume a complementarity among all who enjoy the plays. The game is the Way, the Tao, mastered for common enlightenment.

Finite Games are separate 'things' or episodes with no necessary connections. Infinite Games are joined together like harmonized waves. Each is the mirror image of the other. In Finite Games you compete, the better to cooperate. In Infinite Games you cooperate better to compete, but because cooperating is foremost, every game is one in an infinite series joined to the Way itself. These are the differences that inspire this book.

Chapter 2

Finite and Infinite Games

The spread of European modernism led to two world wars, making the twentieth century the bloodiest ever. Thankfully the era of mass slaughter is finally drawing to a close. We need some new paradigms and ways of thinking about how countries can relate to one another. That is easier said than done. In a multi-cultural world the spread of ideas can be a zero-sum game, where one set of beliefs triumphs at the expense of others . . . We should begin our search by agreeing to abandon the old paradigm.

We must renounce European-style international relations that have turned warfare into a sacred endeavour, thus ridding the world of sovereignty infused with belligerency . . . the sheer stupidity of the old approach is evidenced by nuclear arsenals, built at enormous cost and unusable.

M. Mohamad and S. Ishihara, *The Voice of Asia.*

Two symbols will be used throughout this book to stand for the Finite Game and the Infinite Game. The Finite Game is shown in Figure 2.1.

Figure 2.1 The Finite Game.

Here two serpentine forces struggle to be uppermost. As one rises the other falls. What one gains in profits the other loses. Their sales graphs move in opposite directions. The logics by which they think are adversarial and linear. 'I cause you to lose.' The game is zero sum, with gains and losses canceling each other out. Competition is for scarce or finite resources.

Yet there is progress for society in this process, harsh though it is and relentlessly combative. Progress comes from scarce resources moving from losing 'snakes' or contestants to winning ones. This means that the more competitive will drive out the less competitive, the tough will exclude the tender, the efficient will displace the inefficient and all contestants, lured by the prospect of victory, goaded by the fear of defeat, will work harder. Valuable resources, land, labor and capital, pass away from the incompetent into the hands of the competent. People watching this process and wanting to survive bend their minds and their efforts towards winning. And this, of course, benefits customers.

There is, over time, a general increase in the prowess of winning managers so that the necessity for heightened performance never ceases. Such a system, then, improves the effectiveness of combat. It is rather like a demolition derby, in which winning automobiles are allowed to acquire the pieces and the wreckage of losing cars they have eliminated from the contest through collision, to the delight of spectators. That said, the system certainly generates wealth, accompanied as it is by the 'natural selection' of the leanest and meanest competitors. It is significantly more successful than, say, command economics or statist systems, and the defeat of communism by finite game players was always a matter of time. The Cold War was very much an extension of the Finite Game metaphor and helped to define it ideologically as the West won.[1]

Yet the West is challenged today, both internally and externally, by the metaphor of the Infinite Game. We say 'internally' because there are companies playing Infinite Games in the West as well as in East Asia. It is less foreign, or specifically East Asian, than an advanced form of capitalism which is more readily grasped in East Asia, because it is consistent with the ways they think. But it is also manifest in several multinational enterprises, as we shall see (see Figure 2.2).

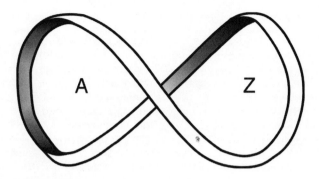

Figure 2.2   The Infinite Game.

Here two helices join into something akin to an infinity loop, which symbolizes that the game does not end but continues indefinitely. The reader can create a similar effect by cutting a thin strip of paper, twisting it 180° and gluing the ends together. If she then holds this in the middle, between thumb and forefinger, something very similar to the double loop illustrated above will emerge.

Another name for this is the Mobius strip, called after the German mathematician Thomas Mobius. The effect of twisting the paper is that 'the back' becomes 'the front' and 'the end' becomes 'the beginning'.

The image is both circular and paradoxical and flows forever to and fro in the image of Tao. Like the Tao it stands for many different complementarities of values.

But what is the difference between finite and infinite game playing? What are the consequences? We argue that the Infinite Game also creates wealth and in so doing incorporates most of the processes of the Finite Game plus major additional advantages (see Table 2.1).[2]

Before we consider this list of distinctions there is an important qualitative difference between the two columns of Table 2.1. Most of the characteristics of the Finite Game necessarily exclude those of the Infinite Game, or at least impede them For example, if the purpose of the game is to win, little time or energy remains to improve the game itself. If winners exclude losers, how can they teach them better plays? If winners-take-all then winning plays and the rewards of winning cannot be widely shared. You cannot be narrowly focused on short term decisive contests *and* engage in a long term generative process.

But the characteristics of the Infinite Game can be so defined as to include many finite episodes along the way. You can continuously improve the game by drawing intelligent conclusions from who won

Table 2.1

Finite Game	Infinite Game
The purpose is to win	The purpose is to improve the game
Improves through fittest surviving	Improves through game evolving
Winners exclude losers	Winners teach losers better plays
Winner-takes-all	Winning widely shared
Aims are identical	Aims are diverse
Relative simplicity	Relative complexity
Rules fixed in advance	Rules changed by agreement
Rules resemble debating contests	Rules resemble grammar of original utterances
Compete for mature markets	Grow new markets
Short term decisive contests	Long term

Adapted from James P. Carse.

and who lost successive rounds. You can knock out losers from one or more of these rounds, then invite them back to teach them better plays. Winning can be widely shared if knowledge from winner-take-all episodes is widely acknowledged and widely distributed. The long term includes many short term events and contests whose outcomes informed *all* the players.

In other words, the Infinite Game, as its name implies, consists of many Finite Games connected to each other. With this inclusive characteristic in mind let's look at the contrasts, before asking ourselves whether this model is genuinely from East Asia or just our own wish-fulfillment. Box 2.1 summarizes two well-known academic games, both finite. Each supposedly reflects Western culture.

To win the game versus To improve play

In the Finite Game who wins and who loses is the whole point of playing in the first place. The spectators, the money markets, the media want a result. It would be hard to imagine a more unpopular outcome than an announcement that 'both sides won'. The sheer *contrast* between winning and losing is what all the interest and excitement is about. Giants of yesteryear are cast down. The media, which had a high old time extolling the winners and building them up, now enjoys itself even more in breaking them down. IBM, for example—'Big Blue'—becomes 'Big Blues' or Bureaucratic Blues.

Box 2.1   Zero-Sum and Prisoner's Dilemma: Do These Games Model Capitalism?

There are at least two Finite Games widely used in academic research in the West to model behavior in capitalist economies. One is called the Zero-Sum Game, which is straightforward competition in which the loser's losses are subtracted from the victor's gains to equal zero. Lester Thurow in *The Zero-Sum Society* argued that US society increasingly resembled a zero-sum game.

The second form of Finite Game, much touted for its 'co-operative' nature, is called the Prisoner's Dilemma Game. Its name derives from two imaginary prisoners under arrest but being questioned separately. Each prisoner, A and B, has two choices which will lead to four possible outcomes. The pay-offs range from 5 to 0, which we can think of as 'years off your sentence'. The outcomes and pay-offs are as follows:

Both co-operate (remain silent)	Each gets 3 points
Both defect (confess)	Each gets 1 point
A defects, B co-operates	A gets 5, B gets 0
B defects, A co-operates	B gets 5, A gets 0

Let us consider what this tells us about the values of Western capitalism. The best of all outcomes is to defect and betray someone who trusts you (5 points). The worst of all outcomes is to trust your partner and *be* betrayed (0 points). A compromise is for both of you to trust each other (3 points). This is much better than both of you betraying each other (1 point).

The volume of literature over the last thirty years on Prisoner's Dilemma would fill a multi-volume encyclopaedia. We have the spectacle of thousands of academics playing, but few, if any, inquiring into what is being modeled. Are we all prisoners trapped in an unchangeable, rational cage by a phantom police chief? Does morality consist of compromises made to avoid being betrayed by partners? Is cooperative behavior always inferior to the successful exploitation of others, yet preferable to *being* betrayed? Some writers refer to Prisoner's Dilemma games, played for hours or days, as 'infinite'.

This is *not* what we mean by Infinite Game in this book. We refer to a game modifiable by those playing it and continuously improvable and ever more challenging and fulfilling for its players. No 'iron laws' of economics or phantom police chiefs

---

Box 2.1   Continued

prevent the games consensually evolving or the players learning. Zero-Sum and Prisoner's Dilemma games are cultural artefacts of our own alienation.

Source: A. Rapaport (1966) *Two Person Game Theory*. Ann Arbor, MI: University of Michigan Press.
A. Rapaport (1969) *Strategy and Conscience*. Boston, MA: Little Brown.
A. Axelrod (1984) *The Evolution of Co-operation*. New York: Basic Books.

The purpose of the Infinite Game in contrast is to improve the Way (the Tao). There are many such 'ways'. Shinto, Aikido, Kendo, Bushido and Judo are all 'ways of', e.g. archery, swordsmanship, gentleness, etc. This has come to include industrial processes: the way of automobiles, the way of electronics, the way of desalinization.

Almost no traditional Japanese 'ways' are primarily spectator sports. Judo, Bushido and Aikido are forms of spiritual mastery, personal improvement, heightened discipline. The purpose is to improve plays, to perfect the game itself. While contestants win and lose against each other, this is largely a way of monitoring progress, *not* an occasion for screaming fans or wagering on results. The ideal is for the Way to absorb the individuals, so that all merge in heightened excellence and infinitely expanded consciousness.

Survival of the fittest versus The evolving game

We must not ignore the fact that the capitalism of finite game playing involves improvement. This comes about by the familiar Neo-Darwinist process of the fittest surviving and forcing out the weak. This is very much to the advantage of consumers, because they will be served only by the best. The lazy, the incompetent, the unmotivated must put up their shutters in the high street and their place is taken by a more enterprising unit.

It is to our *benefit* that Finite Games inflict defeat on losers, otherwise they would take up space and handle money better managed by others. Now there is clearly something to this. The genius of capitalism is that resources are channeled selectively to where the talent is. Those who operate at a profit get to expand fast. A virtuous circle operates. China's switch to open markets has unleashed a whirlwind.

But is this the only way, or even the best way, that economies improve? There is surely another source of improvement, *the evolution and improvement of the Game itself*. The problem with the Darwinist metaphor is the assumption that the unit of survival is the individual, whereas in the reality of today, rather than the nineteenth century, the unit of survival is the individual-in-the-game-being-played.[3]

It is technologies and whole industries which survive, informed by human heads and hearts. The game is not a static institution, but improves and co-evolves with its players. Better games infinitely improving are what transform an economy and lead to fast growth. Who wins and who loses are of minor importance compared with the development of products and processes themselves. If we focus on the infinite improvement of the game itself, the better players will recommend themselves.

Winners knock losers versus Winners teach losers

We have already seen that the Darwinist metaphor involves losers 'not surviving'. This may be less harsh than it seems. While there is some displacement *downwards* into societal garbage heaps, in the form of record prison populations and welfare roles, there is also displacement *sideways*. The carpenter may discover that he is better suited to pottery. Without competitive standards people would not find the best job for their potentials.

Nonetheless Finite Games, like knockout contests, work by elimination of the less 'fit'. Sometimes, as in the Great Depression, the 'unfit' comprise a majority of the population and nations turn against finite game playing itself. Capitalism becomes subject to many controls and restrictions. But today losers are a minority and increasingly consist *of* minorities. We are progressively losing patience with them.

Part of the problem is that welfare burdens and the percentage of the economy consumed by governments is much lower among our East Asian competitors. We believe that to remain competitive parasitic 'losers' must cost less. Hence the pressure is building to punish the poor in various ways. The problem, of course, is that while we have knocked them out of Finite Games, we have *not* eliminated them from society. They are still huddled on the sidelines, sheltering in cardboard boxes and generally disgusting us with their helplessness and hopelessness.

With Infinite Games, losers are not so much eliminated or knocked out of the workplace, but are *invited to learn from winners*. For example, Motorola, one of America's most enlightened corporations, took an inventory of the skills and educational attainments of its own blue-collar workforce and was appalled by the educational deficits. Clearly the taking of greater responsibility by work teams was going to be seriously impeded by illiteracy and innumeracy. But the corporation decided that all workers willing to attend remedial classes would thereby protect themselves from lay-off. The small minority which refused were liable to lay-off. There is no right to ignorance in a complexifying world.[4]

One of the puzzles about East Asia is the sheer extent of domestic competitiveness. China, for example, has one thousand pharma-ceutical companies. Sixty companies making pagers have arisen in just the last five years. Perhaps a shakedown is coming, but perhaps not. Japan, for example, keeps a very large number of competing companies in play.[5] A feature of *all* 'tiger economies' is vigorous domestic competition and an unwillingness to reduce the number of contestants, who are often 'down' but seldom 'out', by reason of cross-shareholding by customers, suppliers, banks, etc. Rather than being *eliminated* from the game, contestants keep playing and keep *learning* how to improve the game.

Is this effective? Probably it is more effective than being eliminated. Consider a company employing three thousand people. It must have made many good decisions to have reached that size. Should it be eliminated or taken over because it made one serious mistake? If allowed to survive, its future decisions could be excellent. It might even improve the game for everyone else.

But in any case it helps to improve the game if there are *many* players, and a greater diversity from which new ideas and better plays arise, to be learned by all players. In contrast, Finite Games tend towards fewer players in which one or two dominate as oligopolists. This brings regulation and litigation in its wake.

Winner-takes-all versus Winning widely shared

What prevents losers learning from winners is an increasing tendency towards *The Winner Takes All Society*, to cite a recent book.[6] The cultures and media of English-speaking democracies increasingly hype 'the winners', even where they won by inches or a puff of wind. Moreover the winner can get rewards a thousand times greater than highly competent persons who were bested by quite insignificant margins.

We see similar patterns in the USA, Canada, Britain and Australia, who have first-past-the-post electoral systems, giving all the power to those who routinely attract less than 50 percent of those voting and around 30 percent of the electorate. Such countries are now ruled by organized 'winning' minorities who argue that their fortunes 'trickle down' upon the rest of us and have become widely unpopular.

There are many problems with winner-takes-all finite game playing; a vast number are mobilized by the hope, not the likelihood, of winning. Their aspirations are inevitably dashed. Their efforts are misdirected, their genuine talents under-rewarded and obscured in the darkness around the spotlights. This skews national resources and celebrates inequalities. It reduces the number of, say, electrical engineers and magnifies ambitions to become multimillionaire plaintiffs' attorneys, playing Finite Games in court rooms to the strains of *LA Law*.

All this appeals to the psychology of the casino, since winning margins are so tiny and the rewards for winning so disproportionately vast. What is *really* being sold is the contrived and fleeting excitement of Finite Games. 'Let them eat hope', a million hearts thumping as the lottery balls tumble. It even turns talent into a lottery, and brings to mind the warning of John Maynard Keynes: 'when the operations of capitalism come to resemble those of the casino, ill fortune will be the lot of the many . . .'

Where business is an Infinite Game, 'winners' are any or all of those whose participation, suggestions, contributions and commitments were incorporated into the large game. Mitsubishi reports an amazing twenty thousand implemented suggestions per year.[7] All these contributors 'win' when their convictions and recommendations become a part of the Infinite Game.

But what really makes the Infinite Game a better model of democracy is that inputs are *too diverse to rank order*, and too qualitatively different to quantify. To this critical difference we now turn.

Aims are identical versus Aims are diverse

It is crucial to a Finite Game that contestants have the identical aim, namely to win and to wrest profits from rival players. Unless we all want the same things, there is not a genuine contest. Unless we all agree that three goals, or three million, are better than two, the game will not yield a clear result, with agreement on who won and who lost.

The insistence that all aims can be reduced to money means that we never feel we earn enough. Someone is always getting more than we are, thereby eclipsing us on this yardstick. CEOs want more, shareholders want more. 'Enough' is what others are getting. Hence Lee Iacocca, when head of Chrysler, earned *thirty six times more* than the head of Honda, although in that period Honda fared better commercially.[8] Finite game playing escalates executive rewards to obscene levels, much as it boosts the salaries of football and baseball players.

What characterizes the Infinite Game is that the players' aims are often diverse. One believes that the personal computer will win the day, another that the network computer will. One sees the future of automobiles as lying in superior mechanics, the other in superior electronics. The truth is that *both* approaches could improve automobile engineering or computer networks. The Infinite Game draws its strength from the *complementarity of diverse aims*, from other ancient traditions of the East which seek unity amid diversity and hence growing complexity . . .

Relative simplicity versus Relative complexity

Finite game playing is in the end too simple-minded. The atmosphere of the 'jock' and the locker room pervades the culture. You listen to the obscenities and petty rivalries of President Nixon around Watergate with amazement. Like all exciting simplicities, Finite Games become addictive. Stock markets go wild selling stocks in companies of which they know little and care less. Money, which comes to symbolize everything it can potentially buy, thereby becomes a substitute for that variety, a huge pacifier restricting the vision of those who suck.

You get the same feeling discussing 'serious money' with the financially astute. Playing the market requires a massive reduction in the subtlety and complexity of the companies being traded. Reduced to simple commodities, measurable in quantities only, our minds run like rats in straight lines and non-communicating pathways. It is a world of 'low context', as anthropologists put it; that is, a world of highly quantified yet highly restricted information. In such worlds you can be clever but not catholic, smart but not wise. The very fact that there is a game that can be 'psyched out' and 'won' suggests a highly restricted universe, 'global' in scope, yet only an inch deep.

In contrast, the Infinite Game expands indefinitely to combine multiple inputs, any one of which could transform the whole. The fusion of nano-technologies with medicine so that tiny molecular engines could be inserted into blood vessels to target diseases opens up a kaleidoscope of possibilities, as does a world powered by solar cells and renewable energy. It may be 'smart' to make a killing in the financial markets but it is wise to put yourself at the places where streams of knowledge cross-fertilize and complexity reigns.[9] It is only when you realize that possibilities are infinite that you are strategically best placed.

Rules fixed in advance versus Rules changed by agreement

It would not be a Finite Game without rules. Rules prevent players cheating and injuring one another. Since only the rules stand between contestants and such excesses, these have become very important and largely replace morality. All is fair in business if it is not expressly illegal. You never give a sucker an even break. Competing must be as fierce as the law allows.

Because laws must be enforced there grows up a Finite Game between law avoidance and law enforcement, with the regulator as one's opponent. Millions of dollars are siphoned off into this epic struggle which benefits the economy not at all, but is a cost of doing business and of governing.

What has happened, most especially in the USA, is that both the strictness of regulations *and* 'heroic' feats of escaping regulations have escalated on each side. Right wing politicians extol deregulation, only to engulf the economy in a new wave of scandals and floods of sleaze, with the result that regulations are further heightened and become more elaborate. In the USA, where competitiveness is probably more fierce than anywhere else in the western world, the rules are *also* more strict, more numerous and more *detailed*, since any ambiguity is immediately exploited. The Federal Register has 5,000 plus pages. The 'land of the free' is the most regulated on earth. Cutting loop-holes in the law and stringing the net ever more tightly becomes a finite contest in itself.[10]

All of which becomes a serious problem for an economy and industries seeking to develop quickly. Innovation makes old laws obsolescent and calls for new ones. One reason that Finite Games change slowly and grow slowly is that old rules encumber them. One reason that the players of Infinite Games develop faster is that rules are made and altered by agreement among players. For example, one secret of Germany's rapid growth between 1870 and 1914 was that its industrial associations set up joint training councils, changing their requirements as technology changed.[11] They also suspended patent laws among one another. Instead an industry prize was given to all important innovations to reward creativity, but the invention was copied at once, not after an interval of years. Key German industries had caught up Britain by 1914. Singapore has deliberately created industry clusters in several industry parks, where players in, say, the multimedia cluster agree their own rules and standards. These rules are not designed to stop players doing what they want, they are attempts to discover the rules of development itself.

Rules of a debating chamber versus Rules of grammar

In a debating contest the rules are quite separate from the content of what is being debated. You give a forceful and articulate exposition of your own position. Because you are asking judges, the audience and/or member of the House to side with you, there is a strong tendency to clarify this choice by polarization and to demonize opposition. Britain's mother of parliaments was the first to substitute words for swords, but the use of words *as* swords has lingered ever since. The two parties face each other across an aisle *two sword-lengths wide* to discourage a lunge at Honourable Members opposite. The Finite Game is enshrined in Westminster, Washington, Canberra and Ottawa at the legislative pinnacle of these societies. Prime Minister's Question Time is screened on US Television for *entertainment*, which is what it really is, a joust between word-smiths. Despite its name, few if any questions to which the asker does not already know the answer are ever posed. And the information content is vertically zero. Moreover each side remains determined to resist influence and advice from the other.

All this leaks into business relationships and the media into the Battle of Underarm Deodorants, or more importantly into the 'two sides of industry', each of which attempts to find an alliance with political parties so that ideological cleavage in government replicates itself across industries, dividing consumers from producers, industry from environmentalists and so on. The rules are to ensure that the confrontation is fair, that each side gets equal time to fire sound-bites at the other. Nothing as complex or boring as a possible *solution* sullies the entertainment. Indeed, the only solution sought is the victory of one side and its deliberately polarized ideas.

But this is not the only form, or even the best form, which rules can take. Nor do rules *have* to be apart from content. They can be embedded within it. When we speak to each other in grammatical sentences these obey rules, yet they may be original to the speaker, even to society. We call those who invent their own syntax and grammar schizophrenics.

What applies to spoken sentences applies also to the ways products and services are created, developed, produced, refined and distributed. All such processes are lawful. All are elements of an Infinite Game. The rules within the process of creation are not restraints upon a shouting match, but ways of reconciling values so as to create a more attractive synthesis of values. What is being searched for is the process of origination itself, and this will vary with disciplines being fused.

Take, for example, the environmental crisis and compare the approach to this problem of finite and infinite game players. Should we have a non-stop debate in which industry is shamed and abused until such a time as it absorbs costs of clean up? Or should pollution control technology become part of what industry creates and sells, so that development *itself* is sustainable and the economy actually benefits by pollution control? This Infinite Game strategy is being pursued by Japan, Singapore, Malaysia and others. Germany was able to tell the Reno summit that its production had increased by 80 percent while emissions had fallen by 40 percent.[12]

It is perhaps not surprising that Infinite Games are preferred by cultures which dislike confrontation, prefer conversation to debate, are shy and respond indirectly to questions, and believe in the values of harmony. This includes China, Japan, Indonesia, Thailand and most of the economies managed by the Chinese. In the West we tend to regard anything less than a public clash of wills as undemocratic.

Compete for mature markets versus Grow new markets

The Finite Game has an affinity for mature markets, in which products and services are well on their way to commoditization. In this view the market is a piece of machinery, hence 'the Market Mechanism', which becomes the impersonal arbiter of those playing the game, taking away resources from some contestants and allocating them to others. No one is supposed to have any power in this situation. The market is *not* something we have made, but a supra-human 'It' (see Figure 2.3), where demand meets supply and everything is so simple that information on prices and products is 'perfect'. Leaving on one side the suspicious similarity of 'the Market' to a faceless, Calvinist God, we may note that it envisages millions of finite acts of demand and supply, which average out and 'clear'. Neo-classical economics insists on the separateness of each transaction and hence on its sterility and disconnection from other acts. The Dismal Science is barren of procreative connections.

In contrast, infinite game players see the market as 'Us' rather than 'It', as something *we* are making between us as a gift to customers. Such attitudes are typically present in new fast-growing markets. Steve Jobs offered every high school in California three Apple computers if they would buy another three each. The legislature took him up on his offer. This was extended to the whole nation but got bogged down in the Senate Education Committee who saw it as subverting capitalism.[13] But of course if was part of the Infinite Game, an inestimable, long term advantage to a company who, at that time, *was* the PC market. Imagine a whole generation learning largely on one's own products. Apple customers are devoted to this day.

If a market is an 'Us' not an 'It',[14] then it is *not*, after all, an impersonal mechanism, an aggregate of isolated episodes. Rather, the market is in part our own passionate commitments to what we have wrought, a new way of engaging customers, our own dedications writ large. To the extent that our attentions turn to mature, obsolescent 'it' markets, away from new, growing 'us' markets we are surely

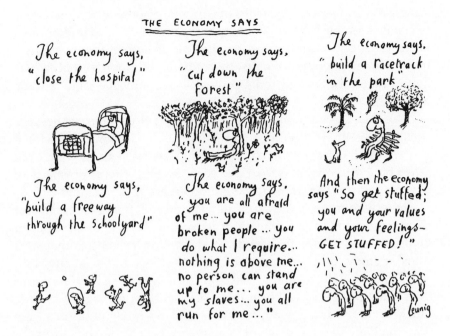

Figure 2.3 The Economy depicted as 'It' rather than 'Us' in the discourse of Western nations, an impersonal Calvinist task-master, the Dismal Science rapport. Source: M. Leunig *You and Me*. Ringwood: Penguin Books.

impoverished. No wonder that the Eunuchs of Mechanism are losing out to the Masters of the Infinite Game.

Short term decisive contests versus Long term generative processes

The Finite Game is the origin of our much lamented Western short termism. The quarterly or half-year report to the shareholders has to please Wall Street or the City of London, if major reductions in share price are not to occur. There is no objection to long term profitability, of course. Indeed it is valued, *provided* it consists of regular increments of short term profitability which add up to long term success.

Unfortunately a large number of things can happen to a corporation which will boost the short term value of shares which have nothing to do with its longer term prospects of survival and growth. It may 'downsize' and lay off thousands of workers, dispose of various assets, sell and lease back its downtown company HQ, be identified as a takeover target or a leveraged buy out, or be subject to 'green-mail'. It may offer to buy back its own shares, announce that it has appropriated the surplus in its pensions fund, unveil a joint venture, retire debt.

In all such cases and many more, the share price jumps, *not* because such policies are effective long term but because assets have been freed up for distribution to shareholders. With stocks now held on Wall Street on average for less than one year, the longer term prospects of any *one* company are of increasing indifference to capital markets.[15]

Those who manage the assets of large mutual funds are hired and remunerated for anticipating short term finite 'plays'. If they inform themselves well over thousands of short term exigencies they will move money out of companies making losing plays and into companies making winning plays, and the average performance of their share portfolios will beat those of rival asset managers. Despite much wizardry and legendary acumen, many funds perform worse than the Dow Jones average. It is a game where as much is lost as is won.

The last thing that such fund managers would do is leave their funds long term in particular companies, since this effectively reduces the occasions on which their judgement is exercised. Money is made from churning stocks and recognizing peaks. That these are of brief duration is part of the fun. You get in fast and out fast. Every smart move is a Finite Game. Box 2.2 asks if Finite Games are not cultural fixations.

What makes Infinite Games different from Finite Games is a logic, joining all your different plays, which *transcends the making of money*. Such logics include the science and technology of the developing industry, the social process of getting the products to people and the learning necessary for people to use the product properly.

Nor can we reasonably expect every element in the system to be so profitable in itself that shareholder interest peaks. There may be intervals of low returns as the larger system is assembled. Pay back may be years away where a whole new 'game' is being designed. What you need are investors who know, care and will wait for their returns.

You can get this kind of 'patient capital' where companies are more 'highly geared' (have a greater ratio of bank debt to equity). This is because banks find it easier to be patient, have deep and detailed

Box 2.2 Finite Games as Cultural Fixations

Is America somehow addicted to Finite Games? These are, of course, spectacular, exciting and attract millions of fans (fanatics). Portraying social, political and economic events like a metaphorical Super Bowl delivers large audiences, but is somehow reminiscent of The Roman Circuses.

American culture habitually construes every problem in terms of a finite struggle. The War against Poverty, the War against Crime/Drugs, 'Just Say No', 'Alcoholism. You can lick it', say the postage stamps. But are not poor people *already* the casualties of economic struggle? Is it not obvious that white, middle class consultants are going to win this war too?

The late Gregory Bateson argued that alcoholism was the *consequence* of finite mental games. Alcoholics were out 'to beat the bottle', to prove that 'will power' could conquer 'weakness'. Indeed, dosing your body with alcohol is an attempt by the Mind to conquer the Body. 'Relax, damn you!' Prohibition was a thinly disguised attack on newer ethnic groups via their tipple. Drug 'wars' occurring on our streets only raise the price of drugs and sponsor re-supply. Helicopters and defoliants war against Third World growers. The War against Crime pursued by J. Edgar Hoover spared organized crime but amassed information on the sex lives of politicians who might one day dismiss him. Robert Kennedy's inclinations had a thicker file than the St Valentine's Massacre.

Metaphorical wars spawn real wars hot and cold. Mutual Assured Destruction (MAD) held that arms 'succeeded' only if never used and therefore wasted. The Vietnam War, inspired by the 'Dominoes Theory' (another game), wreaked incredible destruction on a peasant society, now growing faster economically than any other nation, although still communist. And recall the Red Scares and Communist Conspiracies in a culture with fewer communists than anywhere else in the world! One cell was found to contain only FBI informants reporting on each other.

Finally we have hot-shot CEOs, hired guns and Grand Acquisitors, who lay off thousands so that shareholders and managers with share options can 'score' at their employees' expense. This includes at least one self-styled 'Killer CEO' who calls himself Rambo and poses for photographers in battle fatigues and ammunition belts.

Sources: G. Bateson (1974) 'Towards a Theory of Alcoholism', in *Steps to an Ecology of Mind*. New York: Ballantine; 'Bastard in the Boardroom: A Dunlop Soldier of Fortune', in *The Bulletin*, Sydney, October 1996.

knowledge of their customers' future plans and in most of East Asia *may also invest* in those customers. Indeed, cross-shareholding, common among Asia's tiger economies, means that customers, contractors, suppliers, banks, townships and joint-venture partners may all own shares in each other's corporations and may have a long term interest in their prosperity and growth.

Is this the way that the economies of East Asia think?

So far we have used the Infinite Game to explain how the economies of East Asia think and act. Is there, in fact, any evidence that it is real? Have we simply projected our own fantasies upon the Orient, like thousands of travelers before us, seeing in these unfamiliar climes what we wanted to see?

In fact the 'Double Swing' model of Japanese thinking was proposed by Muneo Yoshikawa, a Japanese professor at the University of Hawaii as early as 1980. He sees it as embedded deep in Japanese historical tradition. Yoshikawa proposes four modes of inter-cultural encounter; ethnocentric, scientific, dialectical and dialogical (or double swing). These are contrasted in Figure 2.4.

Despite Japan's long historical isolation from the rest of the world and its formidably different language, its own culture is harmonized by 'double swing' or dialogical concepts. The foremost of these are listed in Figure 2.5.

We see from Figure 2.5 that the Double Swing model accounts not simply for traditional Japanese thought, but for the way Japan has been learning from the West. Western technology (*yosai*) is to be reconciled with Japanese Spirit (*wakon*). Japan seeks to select (*erabi*) its own path to economic development yet accommodate (*awase*) itself to the rest of the world. While accepting foreign models (*katu*) it seeks to preserve its own form (*katachi*). Harmony (*wa*) is only possible because of separation (*ri*) between harmonized elements. Such harmony occurs at two levels, official politeness and etiquette (*tatemae*) and true empathic feeling (*honne*). The first is a pathway to the second as relationships deepen.

Finally, the infinity sign is itself a strip twisted once at 180°, as explained earlier in this chapter. This makes the inside (*soto*) into the outside (*uchi*) and vice versa. All are manifestations of *yin* and *yang*.

Since Yoshikawa cites the Buddhist logic of *soku* and the *Tao* as major

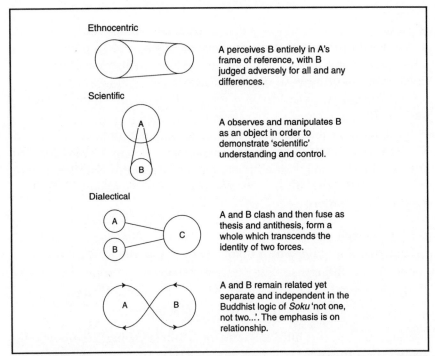

Figure 2.4 Four modes of intercultural encounter. Source: M. Yoshikawa (1992) *Communicating with the Japanese*. Portland, OR: Institute for Intercultural Communication.

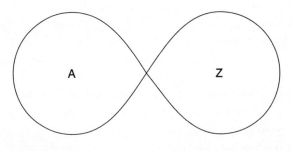

A. *Jomon* (forest culture)	Z. *Yayoi* (rice culture)
A. *Wakon* (Japanese spirit)	Z. *Yosai* (Western knowledge)
A. *Katu* (mold or model)	Z. *Katachi* (shape or form)
A. *Erabi* (selection)	Z. *Awase* (accommodation)
A. *Wa* (harmony)	Z. *Ri* (separation)
A. *Tatemae* (official stance)	Z. *Honne* (true feelings)
A. *Soto* (outside)	Z. *Uchi* (inside)
Yin	*Yang*

Figure 2.5 Japanese 'double swing' concepts.

sources of his model, and sees it as symbolizing the Unity of Diversity, it is at least probable that his model also exemplifies the thinking of cultures influenced by Buddhism and Taoism, which includes all the tiger economies, large and small. The slogan 'Chinese learning for fundamentals, Western learning for practical needs', dates from the late nineteenth century.[16]

More recently the then Prime Minister of Singapore Lee Kuan Yew justified his nation's policies of bilingualism, teaching all Singaporean students English *and* their ethnic language, Mandarin, Tamil or Malay. In this way they would see as Westerners *and* as Asians, with 'two eyes' rather than one.

> From my observation, the monolinguist is more likely to be a language chauvinist and a bigot. He only sees the world through one eye . . . Bilingualism gives a more balanced and rounded view of the world. The Bilinguist sees both sides. If we are to modernize and industrialize we must be bilingual . . .[17]

The model of the Infinite Game or 'Double Swing' resembles the 'two-eyed' approach Lee Kuan Yew is advocating. This is the model of East–West dialog of which the tiger economies may be the more apt pupils. The one-eyed, single-language 'bigots' with their finite plays are recognizable too!

To summarize: it is vital to grasp that our Western Finite Games are not so much wrong as incomplete. Finite games are organizable within a larger, more inclusive Infinite Game which is represented by Katsuchika Hokusai's classic woodblock print, *The Great Wave* (Figure 2.6).[18]

What can be observed from the overall pattern of this print is that the shape of the whole is repeated many times within the larger design; see especially the pincer-like depictions of foam at the crests of the wave. This organic type pattern is found in nature and is called *fractal*. Trees, branches, twigs and the patterns within leaves are fractals. Similarly the Great Wave symbolizes the hidden order discoverable within seeming chaos. Order and Chaos symbolized by dragons and vortices are also favorite subjects of Chinese art. What concerns us here is that a myriad of Finite Games are integrated within the Great Wave itself, the infinity of the ever rolling sea. It is this capacity to harness or capture 'disorderly' elements within a larger whole or game, which distinguishes the leading economies of East Asia. It was Schumpeter who described modern Western capitalism

Figure 2.6 *The Great Wave*, by Katsushika Hokusai, c. 1831. From the Honolulu Academy of Arts. The James A. Michener Collection (HAA 13.695).

as a 'gale of creative destruction', very similar to the Great Wave which dwarfs the tiny human craft beneath it. What our East Asian competitors have discovered is a pattern and order in these turbulent seas, the social equivalent of catastrophe theory. Schumpeter argued that socialism would ultimately win the political contest because capitalism was too harsh, too wild, too ungovernable. We now know that socialism, at least in its anti-capitalist forms, could not civilize a dynamic it so disliked. But might the esthetic visions of Asian capitalism render capitalism more benign? Might an understanding of the Infinite Game tame our finite factionalism and internecine struggles? The seven major manifestations of Infinite Games are the subject of the next seven chapters:

- Beyond Scarcity: Knowledge as a Perpetual Feast
- Beyond The Level Playing Field: Catalysts and Clusters
- Beyond Competition: Competing Co-operatively to Learn
- Beyond Reasoning: Cycles of Eternal Return and Continuous Improvement
- Beyond Achievement: The Discovery of What is Worth Achieving
- Beyond Contract Compliance: Dynamic Reciprocity
- Beyond Time and Motion: Designing with Time.

Chapter 3

Beyond Scarcity: Knowledge as a Perpetual Feast

People are, and will always be, our most precious resource. More than anything else, it is the effort of Singaporeans, with their drive and talent, that has made the country what it is today. Overcoming great odds as a newly-independent nation without natural resources, we have turned our city-state into a thriving and modern economy.
Singapore: The Next Lap. EDB Yearbook.

The advent of 'The Influent Society', as it has been called, of The Knowledge Corporation which learns for its living at an ever accelerating pace, is by now widely heralded. At this level of rhetoric, peans of praise for learning are unavoidable East or West. Unfortunately many who extol learning in the workplace do not believe that this requires them to change habitual ways of thinking. So accustomed are they to the capitalism of physical property, a Finite Game in which material resources are wrested away from rivals, that 'learning' becomes an advertisement decorating the race-track. Competition is now so fierce that *of course* you train the contestants!

While everyone is all in favor of 'learning' nowadays, not everyone knows how to run a corporation, much less a nation's economy, in such a way that fast learning results. Learning and the intensification of knowledge within product portfolios grow out of special combinations of objectives. Most Western economic thinking and business practice cannot grasp anything so broad or elusive as knowledge. Hence learning is given much lip-service but little real attention. Britons, North Americans and Australians tend to see knowledge as something inside the heads of hunted individuals, recruited from skill markets, not as an organizational or national infrastructure deliberately nurtured and enriched.

The argument in this chapter is as follows:

- Knowledge relationships are Infinite Games in markets of Finite Games.
- East Asians may have a readier grasp of knowledge because they think more broadly and diffusely. For such reasons they deploy . . .
- The strategy of knowledge intensification, which operates by concentrating knowledge within products to make these scarce. A good example . . .
- Singapore's successive stages of development, a process which is liable to . . .
- Western misconceptions about this strategy.

Knowledge relationships are Infinite Games in markets of Finite Games

Jay Ogilvy of the Global Business Network recently showed how information transforms economic exchange.[1] Suppose that Tricia sold to Tommy a bar of candy, in the school playground. At once the laws of economics operate. Tricia can keep her candy *or* take Tommy's money, but she cannot have both. For Tommy the bar of candy competes with all *other* uses of his money, including the option of keeping money in his pocket. Moreover the greater the supply of candy bars the lower the 'marginal utility' of each subsequent bar. In any case Tommy's appetite for candy is limited. The fourth bar may make him nauseous. Neither the human stomach nor the human house are insatiable. They get full.

Let us change this scenario slightly while changing its significance totally. Suppose Tricia were to sell Tommy information for 50 cents. Tricia receives her money as before but gives *and keeps* her information. Nor is Tommy the victim of declining utility. The information he receives may well make sense of data he already has. His fourth piece of information may illumine all the rest. The human mind is insatiable. The more it holds the more it wants.

In short, the transition from materialist economics to informational economics is a move from finite game playing to the Infinite Game. Let us first model the Finite Materialist Game.

The lure of the candy competes with and overcomes...

The attraction of rival purchases and the utility of retaining the cash...

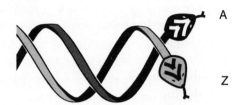

A

Z

An either/or choice has been made by Tommy to forgo money and acquire candy instead, also to acquire candy and *not* other consumables. Tricia has made a similar choice to forgo her candy and acquire money. It is scarcity which makes such choices exclusive.

But the exchange of information for money transforms the situation, for both Tricia and Tommy, into one of potential abundance, not scarcity:

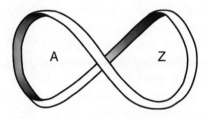

A. The generation of information is offered...

Z. For money which then funds and sustains...

The generation of needed information allows Tricia to share information while gaining money. The former scarcities are diminished. Entropy is reversed. Sharing partly replaces exchanges. We cannot now draw a line between what Tommy and Tricia know and hence 'own'. Information and money have generated each other. By recombining finite resources these have become infinite. These children are in the process of emerging from what John Maynard Keynes called 'the tunnel of economic necessity', which so darkens and narrows our vision.[2]

But before we get carried away, let us concede that not *all* scarcities have been transcended. Tricia still has 50 cents more and Tommy 50 cents less. If Tricia's information had not been new and hence 'scarce' Tommy would not have paid her for it. The market place remains an arena for the exchange of scarce resources. We need to distinguish between markets as external environments in which we trade and *relationships of potential abundance among actors in that market.* Actors in markets can join corporations, form networks, create partnerships, develop supply-chains, form clusters, research jointly, share ideas, and so on. Just as information within the mind of an entrepreneur is generative and creates abundance, not scarcity, so knowledge within self-organizing groups and networks grows spontaneously, and is *then* traded on open markets.

Abundance created by the co-generation of knowledge is *internal* to human relationships. Yet where this knowledge creation is successful that very knowledge becomes scarce in the *external* market. It is analogous to a desert, dotted with oases, many of them joined together. Trade between these oases is generated by the lushness and greenness of the oases themselves and their success at pushing back the desert. So once again we confront paradox and complementarity. The abundance generated by knowledge shared between economic actors allows them to engage successfully the scarcities of markets.

Yet many in the West see markets as an unlimited good which should pervade all corners of the culture and colonize our minds. If our minds are 'markets' rather than integrities of values, then value will fight value within our divided souls. If public service bureaucracies create 'internal markets' every department gets into a Finite Game with every other, rather than saving lives or serving the public with improved knowledge.

Just as abundance within and scarcity without sustain each other, so abundant knowledge is nearly always embedded in scarce materials of some kind. Books have to be printed, software designed, computers manufactured. It follows that knowledge and materials interweave. You can look at a book and see information and knowledge, or see an inscribed object. It is a question of cultural perception.

This helps to explain how the West has been able to persist in its materialist mind-set and beliefs in pervasive scarcity. If wealth is thought of as goods, literally good things, then these will always be scarce, will always use up the world's finite resources. But it is equally legitimate and much more conducive to national morale to see wealth as streams of knowledge, capable of informing products and services, whose intelligence can tap into renewable energy resources like sunlight. This is the viewpoint of the Pacific Rim and much of East Asia.

East Asians have a readier grasp of knowledge because they think in broader and more diffuse ways

It has proved beyond our capacity so far to measure the extent to which different cultures embrace the Knowledge Society. The problem is that knowledge, like motherhood, is something everyone now favors and it upgrades the status of all occupations to say this is 'knowledge work'.

So we looked instead at the cultural preconditions for taking knowledge seriously as an economic and national goal. An important precondition is to think broadly, diffusely and holistically, as opposed to narrowly, specifically and analytically. Since knowledge ramifies diffusely and in all directions, you need highly inclusive ways of thinking to capture all these advantages. Exclusive and specific criteria of judgement are likely to see knowledge as an 'externality', something outside economics and hence irrelevant. Specific thinkers tend to say 'What is the bottom line? How much profit will this product earn?' Diffuse thinkers tend to say 'what will making this product teach us, our suppliers, distributors, customers and the nation? What more might we discover while developing and supplying it? What new opportunities will open up?' The more diffusely you think, the more valuable learning and knowledge acquisition becomes.

We can see this in the two metaphors that inform this book. A Finite Game depends crucially on keeping score. Crowds only go wild with enthusiasm if goals or touch-downs are clearly defined, and decisive for victory or defeat. Criteria are finite when these are specific, countable, precise. In an Infinite Game, the benefits of learning to play better, evolving the game itself, perfecting processes and continuously improving are extremely diffuse, even vague. Crowds would not know what was happening. Learnings are too subtle.

We would expect, therefore, that cultures thinking diffusely are more oriented to knowledge acquisition and intensification than are cultures thinking specifically. To that end we posed three dilemmas to managers, obliging respondents to choose between broad and narrow definitions of work. For example, we offered the view of the company as a system, 'designed to perform functions and tasks in an efficient way. People are hired to fulfill these functions with the help of machines and other equipment. They are paid for the tasks they perform.' This is virtually a checklist of specifics, tasks, function, pay, machines etc.

In contrast, we offered a more diffuse perspective. 'A company is seen as a group of people working together. The people have social relationships with other people in the organization. The functioning of the company depends on those relationships.' We expected East Asian cultures to score more diffusely and they did, although not all. Seven in the top twelve were East Asian. Only Hong Kong, possibly influenced by British specificities, scored at the specific end.

We also asked for the definition of 'a good manager'. Does he 'get the job done' and 'take care of information, people and equipment for the execution of tasks' (specific) or does he 'get a group of subordinates working well together, guiding them continuously in solving problems, like a father might' (diffuse)? Here the East Asian cultures form a salient subgroup at the diffuse end. Ten East Asian cultures take the top ten places. Belgium is 8.0 percent below Thailand. It might have been the hint of family and fatherhood which repelled so many Europeans. Singapore is three times higher than the USA.

A third question has to do with the detection of errors, a crucial aspect of learning fast from experience. Is the person who caused the defect specifically to blame, or does responsibility and hence learning diffuse to the whole group? Nine East Asian nations score in the top twelve. Employees learn even from mistakes made in their vicinity. Responsibility diffuses fast. The Finite Game known as 'who's to blame?' is twice as salient in Australia as it is in Indonesia.

For ten years, ending in 1994, we asked whether 'the only goal of the corporation is profit' (specific) or whether 'the company, besides making a profit, has a goal of attaining the well-being of various stakeholders' (diffuse). We dropped this question because those seeking 'profit only' were falling steadily. Nevertheless the results are highly significant although only six East Asian countries were questioned in sufficient numbers to make valid comparisons. Profit maximization, the most specific of all specifics, is clearly getting in the way of knowledge. Objections to profit maximization have been rehearsed elsewhere. Among the problems are the following. The logic of what is profitable is not a coherent science nor a body of learning. Profits typically evaporate as newcomers enter the market. Knowledge has lasting themes and accumulates. Profits are mostly opportunistic and short term. While rare knowledge and skills form one important path to profitability, profits on their own point nowhere in particular. In contests where you seek profits only, and your opponent knowledge which is profitable, you will be left with the simpler and the dumber stuff.

But an important caveat is in order. Simply thinking in diffuse

Table 3.1 Diffuse styles of thinking

Question 1: '*Company as social relationships*' (not specifics)
% agreeing

Thailand	70.37	*Philippines*	57.14
Norway	65.98	Australia	56.74
New Zealand	64.47	Belgium	54.84
Korea	63.58	*China*	53.73
Ireland	62.68	Spain	53.39
Japan	61.62	Germany	52.84
Taiwan	60.55	Italy	52.01
France	59.96	Canada	51.26
Indonesia	58.55	Sweden	49.47
Singapore	58.35	United Kingdom	48.89
Malaysia	57.59	*Hong Kong*	48.21
Brazil	57.35	USA	44.82
Switzerland	57.20	The Netherlands	43.77

Question 2: '*Gets his group of subordinates working well together . . . helps them solve problems . . .*'
% agreeing

Singapore	55.50	Australia	26.40
Hong Kong	55.36	Italy	25.29
Japan	53.95	United Kingdom	24.43
Philippines	53.85	Spain	24.35
Korea	47.67	Ireland	23.40
Indonesia	46.69	Germany	22.51
China	42.86	Sweden	22.40
Malaysia	41.12	New Zealand	21.86
Taiwan	40.27	Norway	20.62
Thailand	39.90	The Netherlands	19.73
Belgium	31.61	Canada	19.27
Brazil	30.74	USA	16.10
France	29.96	Switzerland	15.87

Table 3.1   Continued

Question 3: *'Mistakes are the whole team's responsibility'*
% agreeing

Indonesia	83.28	Norway	59.76
Thailand	76.44	Malaysia	57.82
Singapore	69.35	Belgium	56.76
Japan	67.99	The Netherlands	56.73
Italy	66.76	Ireland	55.40
Brazil	66.16	France	54.76
Hong Kong	64.29	Spain	53.88
Germany	63.79	United Kingdom	51.65
China	63.10	Canada	50.89
Philippines	62.07	New Zealand	48.28
Taiwan	62.01	USA	47.25
Korea	61.27	Switzerland	41.60
Sweden	60.54	Australia	41.00

Question 4: *'Attaining the well-being of various stakeholders . . .'* (rather than profit) (up to 1993 only)

Japan	92.42	Belgium	74.90
Singapore	89.19	The Netherlands	73.88
Malaysia	87.01	Sweden	72.50
Korea	86.26	Italy	71.42
France	84.20	United Kingdom	67.21
Indonesia	81.74	Canada	65.34
Taiwan	79.20	Australia	64.31
Germany	76.12	USA	59.62

Source: The Trompenaars Group, Database. Amsterdam, 1997.

ways, which would include Aborigines and their 'dream time', is *not* sufficient for wealth creation. Diffusely scoring cultures include Egypt, Saudi-Arabia, Nepal, Oman and Venezuela—none of them wealth creators of note. What really creates wealth is thinking diffusely while *also* identifying important specifics, i.e. knowledge-which-is-also-profitable. To think effectively you must diverge *and* converge.

Cultures who think diffusely and keep their eyes on the bottom line to make sure their educations are affordable create myriad channels through which information spreads. This enables them to develop successful policies of upgrading and intensifying knowledge, the topic to which we now turn.

The strategy of knowledge intensification

Japanese and Chinese cultures have from their very beginnings upheld knowledge, learning and the elevation of the human spirit. In Confucian tradition, the leader is both sage and teacher, a Master of the Infinite Game. In 622 A.D. an examination for all government officials was instituted in the Confucian classics, which lasted until the revolutions of the twentieth century. The right to rule is based on superior knowledge; the right-conduct of the leader includes the duty to impart knowledge and organize learning, and this is still true today.[3]

Confucian tradition *can* go disastrously wrong: Chairman Mao's Hundred Flowers Blooming, his Great Leap Forward, his Cultural Revolution and the little red book. But it can also go spectacularly right, as in Singapore under Lee Kuan Yew, the father of the modern city state. And China is now learning from Singapore the Asian path to capitalist development.

In 1993 the British author interviewed P Y Lai, then managing director of Intel in Penang, Malaysia and now the President of Greater China for Motorola. What strategy would he adopt if hired? He explained to us:

I believe I know what the Chinese government wants from Motorola and what we have to supply if we are to succeed. They want 'high end' products — that is products full of knowledge and complexity — which they can export to earn hard currency. And they want us, through our subcontracting, to train and educate networks of indigenous suppliers. Their government has the power to make us or break us, so our best strategy for survival is to become part of their knowledge infrastructure, to supply the products they speak through and think with and to be their patient mentors. If we can do this, the Chinese will be our friends for ever. We will have supplied the key elements in their development.

While China has barely begun her growth process — her forecast GDP per person for 1997 is only $800 — Japan and the 'little tigers' have been following strategies of *knowledge intensification* since the early 1960s. Even after a quarter of a century, most Western pundits have failed to

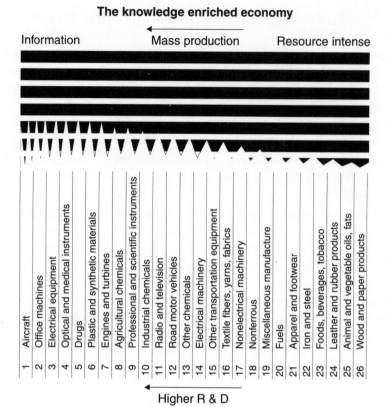

Figure 3.1 The knowledge enriched economy.

awaken to this logic. To the best of our knowledge it was first set out in detail by Professors Bruce Scott and George Lodge.[4]

Scott first rank ordered various global industries according to their 'knowledge intensity'; that is, the amount of scientific knowledge which enters into their products. He defined this as the ratio of Research and Development expenditure to total product costs. This ranking puts aircraft, office machines, electrical equipment, and optical and medical equipment in the first four places, with foods, beverages, tobacco, leather and rubber products, animals and vegetable oils and fats, and wood and paper products in the four lowest places. The full list is given in Figure 3.1.

Knowledge intensity increases from right to left. As we move to the left two other characteristics are notable. There is an increase in the number of *niches*, hence the saw-tooth pattern, and there is an increase in *informational connections between products*, hence the white stripes.

Scott compared the performance of Western economies, the USA, Great Britain, France and Germany with the performance of Japan and four 'tiger' economies: Singapore, Hong Kong, Taiwan and South Korea. He especially examined how each economy had fared in each industry. His conclusions were extremely important. Between 1960 and 1985 Japan, Singapore, Hong Kong and Taiwan had *gained* market share in industries with high knowledge intensity while losing market share in industries with *low* knowledge intensity. In the top twelve categories, for example, the 'little tigers' had made ten gains in market share. In the bottom twelve they had made seven losses and four gains. He concluded that this was the result of an industrial policy, which all five shared, to *systematically upgrade the knowledge content of their industrial portfolios*. The four 'little tigers', especially, were deliberately running down the simple products they made and switching human and capital resources to industries of higher complexity.

In direct contrast, the USA, Britain, France and Germany were either *not* upgrading their knowledge intensities or, in the case of the USA, increasing its share of relatively simple products. Indeed, assistance from the US government goes chiefly to low tech. products, like tobacco price supports. Sophisticated, high-knowledge products in electronics and biotechnology get almost no assistance. Industries in trouble lobby Congress to be placed on the 'injured industries list'. Not surprisingly these tend to be simple products capable of manufacture by lower wage economies abroad. The perverse result is that the US government subsidizes weakness and relative simplicity, using a 'welfare logic', while Pacific Rim governments subsidize learning by the economically sophisticated and strong. A study by David Sainsbury in the late 1980s showed no gains in knowledge intensity by Britain during the previous ten years.[5]

The one major exception to Western refusals to subsidize sophistication is expenditure on defense and space. The historic lead of the USA in aeronautics and electronics would not have been possible without the Pentagon and NASA. Prototype airliners were originally troop carriers. Even the Internet and half a century earlier the Interstate Highway system were defense oriented subsidies.[6] With the end of the Cold War Western governments are running out of excuses to subsidize high tech. The justification for doing this never lay within economics itself but was literally 'out of this world' in the heavens or in saving mankind from communism. In contrast, the accelerated learning programs of tiger economies are the centerpiece of *economic* policies, not backdoor subsidies and lucky spin-offs.

Singapore's successive stages

Let us now trace in more detail the evolution of knowledge-intensifying economic strategies. The clearest and best documented case is of Singapore's Economic Development Board (EDB), whose members were recently interviewed by Ed Schein of MIT and encapsulated in his book *Strategic Pragmatism*, a history of the Board's thought and action.[7] Under various chairmen the EDB's strategy fell into six phases.

1. Curing unemployment through import substitution (1961–1965)
2. Shift to export orientation and internationalization (1965)
3. Shift from labor-intensive industries to capital intensive and higher-tech. industries (1968)
4. Shift from skill-based industries to knowledge-based industries (1970s evolved, 1980s articulated)
5. Regionalization, the growth triangle and development of local industry (1986–)
6. 'Singapore Inc.', 'Singapore Unlimited', 'The Next Lap' and 'The Learning Nation' (1990s–)[8]

The strategy of knowledge intensification began in 1968 with phase 3 and has energized all subsequent phases. In a very real sense this policy was a response to Singapore's particular circumstances. The city state was very short of land. It had a population of three million pressing on its scant resources and meager capital resources. Its major asset was its harbor facilities and their strategic placement close to world shipping lanes.

Not surprisingly the EDB's first move was to put Singaporean citizens to work and employ the conventional wisdom of the time, import substitution. There was serious unemployment, with worse to come when Britain announced that it would abandon its naval base. Shell and BP did move into the vacuum created, but oil storage is not a great employer of labor. The EDB under Hon Sui Sen set up labor-intensive businesses making nails, paint, textiles, footwear and plastic flowers, and set out to convert the harbor to civilian use.[9]

This policy met a serious reverse when Singapore lost its place in the Malaysian Federation in 1965. It was at once clear that the rest of the Federation would not make room for the simple manufacturing in which Singapore was specializing. Every neighboring country would seek to protect its own infant industry, and tariffs would be raised against her. 'We have to do it on our own' became the watchword. To this end Singapore now looked further afield to foreign multinationals (MNCs), especially in the USA.

The EDB began a drive to recruit MNCs to set up facilities in Singapore. Early recruits in the late 1960s included Hewlett-Packard, American Optical, Timex, GTE, Grumman and Lockheed, with Siemens, Olivetti and Philips coming from Europe and Seiko and Sumitomo from Japan. In the space of a few years the new nation moved from unemployment to a labor shortage. Moreover some 50 percent of all Singaporeans now worked for foreign companies. The shortage of work *per se* was no longer the problem. The problem was the *quality* of work demanded by international business.

So there now followed the third phase of economic development under I F Tang (1968–1972) and Chan Chin Bock (1972–1975), who were known as 'The Deal Makers'. It was clear that multinationals wished to locate in Singapore. The EDB would negotiate conditions of entry and try to make room for them in a very crowded island. It became obvious in deciding how to allocate land that not all uses of space were as profitable as others. There emerged increasing preferences for high tech. industries, but this in itself provoked a potential skills famine, with rare skills being bid up. The deals struck by Tang and Chan therefore increasingly stipulated that the companies must agree to train Singaporeans. Joint training institutes were set up with companies from Germany, Holland, Switzerland and Japan. Singaporean workers entered apprenticeship schemes in Germany and Switzerland. A condition for doing business in Singapore was to share your learning with the host country. All new entrants had to agree to help make Singaporeans smarter.

This led naturally to a fourth phase. While MNCs had agreed to train Singaporeans, none could be expected to train them to levels higher than their technologies required. It followed that the skills of Singaporeans and their value added per person could not continue to rise unless industries themselves became more knowledge-intensive.

The only way to do this was to upgrade existing technology and select for entry into Singapore only the most sophisticated and innovative activities of the most sophisticated and innovative companies.

What had been tacitly accomplished in the late 1970s under EDB chairman Ngian Tong Dow (1975–1981) became official policy under his successor P Y Hwang (1982–1985). The switch to knowledge-based strategy was called The Second Industrial Revolution (SIR), a development the first industrialists had failed to grasp and to act upon. When Goh Chok Tong, minister of trade and industry, presented his budget in 1981 he announced that the replacement of labor intensity with knowledge intensity was the challenge of the new decade. Textiles, shoes and furniture would run into import barriers everywhere. Singapore must leap to a higher level, that of a modern industrial economy mastering complex tasks, based upon 'science, technology, skills and knowledge'. There was not room enough for industries that did not upgrade. Prime Minister Lee Kuan Yew threw down the challenge: 'All sectors of the economy have to mechanize, automate, computerize and improve management, or relocate their factories'.[10]

The search was now on for high-wage, high-knowledge industries, including semi-conductors, integrated circuits, computers, speciality chemicals and pharmaceuticals and industrial electronic equipment. Hwang oversaw the founding of the Brown–Boveri Government Training Centre, a joint venture with the Swiss company, later to attract more sponsors and become the Precision Engineering Institute. Also established at this time was the German–Singaporean Institute, which offered training in advanced manufacturing systems and automation, the Japanese–Singaporean Institute for Software Technology and the French–Singaporean Institute to teach electro- technical engineering disciplines. All these finally converged into the Science Park.

Among its functions was an idea borrowed from the Ministry of International Trade and Industry in Japan. Manufacturing robots were innovating so fast that factories feared getting stuck with an expensive system which would soon become obsolete. Under a government sponsored system the very latest robots could be leased and returned as soon as an up-dated technology became available. What the EDB had done was trawl foreign cultures for their most finely honed skills.

This phase of Singapore's growth ended rather abruptly in the 1985 recession in which the economy showed slightly negative growth. Too much reliance was being placed on MNCs, it was said. Singapore was a good host to foreign enterprise but not sufficiently active in its own cause.

In 1986 Philip Yeo took up the Chairmanship of the EDB and there began the phase of regionalization, the growth triangle and the development of local industry as before. This new phase was a further development of earlier policies. What was to become of companies long a part of Singapore, but now performing simple tasks which impoverished the minds of employees? What could be said to MNCs who wanted to come to Singapore but had a mix of activities, some complex, some simple?

The regionalization strategy moved activities which were essential but low value-added out to the growth triangle in the regions around Singapore. This consists of Malaysia and Thailand to the north and the Indonesian islands east, west and south. Activities high in knowledge intensity, senior management, product design, research and development and some marketing were best performed in Singapore, while simpler, more routinized activities were more economically performed in lower-wage, lower-skill locations in the regions.[11]

Under this strategy the knowledge workers of Singapore instruct the manual workers of Riau, Myanman and Ho Chi Minh City. It is a 'value chain' strategy which locates activities wherever costs are lowest yet skills are sufficiently high for work at that level. Bottling plants, warehousing, assembly, mass manufacturing all take place at the requisite skill-level outside Singapore yet coordinated by the 'Intelligent Island', whose deal making now extends to optimal location of a multinational company's functions throughout the region.

The EDB had become a 'business architect' negotiating with MNCs on how a company headquartered in Singapore, or with its regional headquarters there, could best allocate its resources (see Figures 3.2 and 3.3 taken from the EDB's Annual Report). The architect can, as needed, broker relationships, provide or obtain financing, manage the industrial park, find joint venture partners, set up the requisite technology and provide what Lee Kuan Yew called the 'software' or mental programing to industrialize.

All this requires more than civil service integrity and reliability. It requires of EDB employees an entrepreneurial spirit, the creativity and initiative to 'take their place between' (*entrepreneur*) several different ingredients of business success and develop a working synthesis. It is a tribute to Yeo's vision that most executives retired from the EDB

Figure 3.2 Economic Development Board as 'Business Architect'. Illustration from the EDB Yearbook of how clusters are developed. Note the circular iterations. The process never ends.

but still members of the EDB Society now describe themselves as entrepreneurs.

Yet the EDB never forgets its public service ethos. It invests not to make a profit, although it usually does, but to give its corporate partners the confidence to proceed, to share risks and so cement partnerships. The EDB asks to be bought out as soon as success is assured, so it can use the money to launch another partnership.

Another major initiative of this period was to upgrade locally founded business. Here the emphasis was on partnerships with the best foreign companies and on becoming trustworthy, single source suppliers to MNCs. This is one area in which Singapore is not yet as successful as it would wish to be. World class companies of Singaporean origin are still considered to be too few.

The final phase of Singapore's learning journey was celebrated through a succession of slogans and watchwords. It began as Singapore Inc., the recognition that the nation's enhanced knowledge was the prime objective. It mutated to Singapore Unlimited, the idea

Figure 3.3 Economic Development Board as 'Business Architect'. Singapore's EDB sees itself as in the business of enterprise building.

that information is borderless and diffuses the whole region, and by way of The Next Lap, culminated in The Learning Nation.

Among scores of new ventures are the Matsushita-Kotobuki Advanced Robotics Centre which educates all Singapore's manufacturing, Reuters new Asian headquarters, an Educational Theme Park demonstrating 'edutainment' or learning as entertainment, Tang Village—a replica traditional Chinese village, a $65 million Telecommunications R & D Park, and many others.

Singapore has launched the International Hub 2000 program, aimed at turning the nation into the intellectual and strategic headquarters of burgeoning regional economies. The Business Headquarters Program invites MNCs to locate world or regional headquarters in the City State, where information about neighboring economies is at hand and potential partners abound. The most recent watchword is to 'Think Network'.

Realizing that aerospace represents the highest concentration of scientific and engineering intelligence, the EDB and other agencies sponsor Asian Aerospace, a bi-annual conference whose eighth event was held in February 1996 with over one thousand exhibitors. Singapore's $1.5 billion aerospace business is mostly in repair, overhaul and maintenance, but new designs are afoot. By 1999 there are plans to launch communication satellites, using the Great Wall of China Company, China's space agency.

Western misconceptions about the strategy of knowledge intensity

We now need to ask ourselves why this seemingly admirable path to accelerated economic development via learning is so difficult for Western governments and economies to grasp. For the irony is that Singapore would never have made it without Western MNCs as its major source of propulsion. The ingredients are mostly foreign: American, European and more recently Japanese corporations. The success of the nation has been built upon the local successes of foreign companies, who so flourish in this climate. But the success of the *whole* is undoubtedly Singaporean, the management *of* managements is theirs. The conditions for admission into this city include the sharing of company plans with the EDB and other agencies, who then make sure that the skills, the training and the informational support are in place and that partnerships are created.

Now none of this is beyond the comprehension of Western governments and planners, so why have we not accomplished what Singapore has accomplished? Why is so much energy misdirected at trying to explain such successes away, rather than embracing and emulating these? Because, we suggest, Western ways of thought are still in thrall to the Finite Game. We cannot grasp that the State of Singapore has orchestrated these contests and made of their finite competition a larger, more inclusive Infinite Game in which nearly everyone wins and learns.

Consider two major objections to what the Singaporean government, and 'tiger' economy governments in general, have been doing. The first objection is to 'picking winners', to claiming that certain business activities are superior to others. This is said to distort free markets, to infringe consumer sovereignty and to claim an omniscience which no government could possibly achieve. Only finite contests between rival players can reveal which has the superior product.

Any attempt to call the winner before the contest is over, or any attempt to prevent entry into the contest, corrupts the umpire or referee, who is there to guarantee fair play by all contestants. The governments of most tiger economies are, in any case, 'authoritarian'. The powers they have assumed must soon corrupt them.

We should consider this argument carefully since it reveals the depths of our misunderstanding. The first point to note is that the 'picking winners' argument rests entirely upon the concept of a series of Finite Games, with no idea of any infinite connections between these. In this view the government acts as incorruptible umpire and cannot, therefore, favor any contestant's chance above another's.

But the governments of Japan, Singapore, Malaysia, etc. are not so much picking *winners* as picking *teachers*. They are not favoring one company over another in precision engineering, they are favoring precision engineering *per se*. They are saying that these processes will educate the whole economic infrastructure.

Consider the Intel Pentium processor which we watched being made in Penang, Malaysia. It goes into many intelligent products, including the personal computer. Now everyone designing, making, distributing, selling, inserting the product into original equipment, selling-on that equipment, using it and maintaining it *learns from that process*. Everyone whom that product touches learns, not just because it is a 'brain' in its own right, but because it takes high skill and intelligence at every stage to move it from conception to use, even to maintenance and repair. We learn through it, in it and around it, and all the original equipment which the processor animates becomes more intelligent and versatile as a result, an extension of the human nervous system.

What the tiger economies have decided is that $1,000 worth of potato chips and casino chips are *not* worth as much to a culture as $1,000 worth of Pentium chips. All three may fetch exactly the same in the market place—$1,000—but that is merely the outcome of Finite Games. The enhanced intelligence of Pentium chip-making ramifies on all subsequent games. What looks to us in the West like a series of one-off contests is for tiger economies *successive rungs in a knowledge ladder by which they ascend to infinite heights.*[12] Because, of course, the microchips of advanced design make more competitive every product they enter.

It is also wrong to claim that preferring more over less intelligent products distorts the market. On the contrary, the decision to engage consumers at a heightened level of complexity is made *before* the product is offered, or the market for that product is yet formed. In no way are consumers prevented from choosing the products they prefer. It is simply that this choice now occurs among complex alternatives rather than simple ones. Consumers remain sovereigns over a kingdom better informed than it might have been otherwise.

The real problem is a stubborn piece of orthodoxy at the heart of neo-classical economics. According to this dogma all human values are subjective and merely relative, *until* the market prices them. When this happens their price is their objective economic value.

This might indeed be a fundamental principle of Western economics, but it is also fundamentally wrong. *Provided* markets accept both simple and complex products there is greater *potential* value within the complex products, because processes involved in making them and using them educate everyone.[13]

The policy 'make knowledge intensive products and services in Singapore' does *not* tell the supplier what he must make. It only requires that whatever he *chooses* to make should be as intelligent as possible. Is this an infringement upon his freedom? On the contrary, it is long term a guarantor of freedom, since the more complicated production becomes the more human discretion goes into it, and the more futile becomes any centralized efforts to control the economy. Simple technologies can be operated by child labor and/or slave labor, but complex technologies require autonomous, self-organizing superteams. The pursuit of learning may bring more freedom in its wake than beating the drum for human rights. It was always wrong to exploit workers, but as the world complexifies it becomes uneconomic and plain stupid.

So, far from a policy of knowledge intensity distorting free markets, there are reasons to believe that this promotion of more intelligent goods and services *anticipates* the markets and does, with far less pain and dislocation, what free markets would have forced upon the economy a few years later. The reasons are as follows.

Relatively simple jobs can be performed more cheaply by less developed countries with lower wage rates. Indeed, the collapse of jobs in developed economies will start with the simplest ones and climb from there. Nearly all affluent countries now experience this inexorable erosion of simpler tasks. You can either wait for the crisis and de-industrialize, like America's rust-belt and Britain's traditional industries, *or* you can start upgrading skills and complexifying technologies *before* unemployment strikes the economy.

It is the genius of Singapore's regionalization program that it has *handed over* these simpler jobs to Indonesia, Malaysia, China, etc. without waiting for these countries to seize these markets via the Finite Game of low-wage competition. This means that no one need be driven out of business in Singapore or thrown into unemployment. It means that the need to maintain low-wage enclaves, as in South Carolina's textile industry, with all the accompanying racial tension, is avoided. Instead Singaporeans voluntarily move up to 'high end' products and let the simpler jobs go to the countries whose infant industries desperately need them.

What we have here is a new principle of world economic order in which it actually pays rich countries to devolve their medium and low tech. production processes upon poorer neighbors. That Japan and Singapore saw this first is probably a result of being densely populated islands who realized quickly that they could not *afford* to fill up scarce space with simple activities, nor the spaces in the heads of their citizens with simple problems. It would pay to import raw materials and export complex products full of knowledge.

But why does a knowledge intensive strategy lead to increases in value added per person within the tiger economies? Because *complex knowledge is inherently scarce*. There will always be fewer competitors at the leading edge of knowledge because few cultures have the educational institutions and the training facilities to produce complex products. It follows that a knowledge intensive strategy *anticipates* the

Box 3.1   Malaysia's Multimedia Super Corridor (MSC)

Malaysia is challenging Singapore in an attempt to become the hub for Information Technology in SE Asia. Microsoft has moved its Asian HQ to Kuala Lumpur and other MNEs are following. From Kuala Lumpur International Airport through Putrajaya and its adjoining 'IT City' to Kuala Lumpur itself will run a high speed optical fibre network or corridor. It will have a broad-band infrastructure, joining the smart airport with electronic government in Putrajaya. These multimedia cities will be connected by a smart highway, electronically signed, controlled and tolled.

The purpose of the MSC is to act as a global test-bed for a number of 'flagship' applications, including telemedicine, telematically connected to world medical databases; multi-purpose smart cards; a smart school with world data retrieval and exchange; an R&D cluster; a multimedia funds haven; and a Worldwide Manufacturing Web to link operations and transmit accurate images for remote manufacturing. MNEs can test their products within a total infrastructure of complementary products also being tested, so the experimentation in whole systems becomes possible.

By the year 2000 the Prime Minister's office is to become paperless; two million multipurpose smart cards will be distributed; most schools will be joined to the Internet; and the Multimedia University will be linked to five affiliated corporate R&D centers. Two hundred small and medium sized Malaysian companies will be part of this multinational net, leveraging information and skills transfer. The City Flagship Development Zone will be established, together with the study of emerging 'cyberlaws' for the regulation of telephony and intellectual property, while sponsoring its first diffusion.

By 2020 sixty Malaysian 'webshaper' companies will have made of themselves vital nodes in a knowledge net, orchestrating international alliances and joint ventures. IT City will have 80,000 knowledge workers. Sixty countries will recognize the International Cybercourt of Justice in Putrajaya and rely on the MSC for arbitration as East Asian values become a world resource. All this will be orchestrated by Telekom Malaysia, using the lowest tariffs in the region, the most connections, the best support services.

Source: *Making a Malaysian Miracle* by Mohd Taib Hassan, Telekom Malaysia, 1996

higher prices which scarce intelligence commands. If you learn faster than other companies your prices will remain high, provided of course that consumers want your products.

Is this strategy exploitive of poorer countries? It certainly maintains them at a lower level of knowledge intensity and hence value added per person than Singapore itself. So long as they fall in with plans made at the International Hub, they are likely to remain provinces in all senses of the word. Yet they are likely to develop much faster as recipients and extensions of Singaporean expertise than they would have on their own. They are actively assisted, not exploited.

They receive technologies and systems which they would otherwise have to fight Singapore to win, using lower wage rates as their weapon. It is easier, quicker and much less destructive for Singapore to anticipate the long term outcome and vacate the lower rungs of the knowledge ladder voluntarily, moving simpler technologies out into the regions. Nor is there any reason why the 'provinces' should not challenge Singapore if they wish. Malaysia has created the Bayan Lepas Free Trade Zone for multinationals and more recently the Multimedia Supercorridor (see Box 3.1), in order to concentrate foreign intelligence within its own industries. Singapore is being widely imitated. In any network there are many 'brains'. Singapore is just one of the largest and most intelligent.

Summary

We are now in a position to show how the Infinite Games played by the tiger economies outperform the Finite Games of Western corporations. In the case of Singapore the EDB *starts with* finite game players in the shape of Western companies, but negotiates with these terms for entering Singapore which ensure that they complement and balance other players, inform the Singaporean culture and are informed by it.

Let us first consider MNCs in their 'unsocialized' form of finite game players:

One MNC, already an
accomplished predator

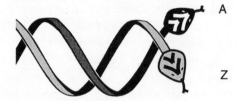

A

Attempts to conquer or acquire
rival companies.

Z

Compare this to MNCs invited by Singapore to negotiate terms of entry into the City State:

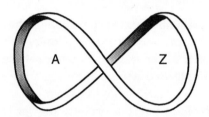

A. Winning MNCs with vital core competences are invited to locate in Singapore provided that...

Z. They train Singaporeans, develop new technologies, cross-fertilize intelligences, so as to remain...

The game is infinite because the knowledge concentrated within Singapore guarantees that the already 'winning' MNCs will soon have very much more intelligence and information *with which* to win still more. Hence the dynamic is self-perpetuating and self-augmenting. The point is *not* that Asian corporations outperform American and European corporations. On present evidence they do not. The point is that MNCs from the US, Europe or Japan *do better in this part of the world than elsewhere*, because they have been invited to form learning partnerships with would-be rivals. Box 3.2 includes just a sample of the 'marriages' brokered by the EDB, many of them cross cultural.

A second major argument in this chapter concerns the interface between 'abundant' exchanges of information and the scarcity of markets, the lush oases trading in the desert. We also saw that to advance knowledge and fill products with information will increase the price they will fetch in the market, since advanced knowledge is scarce.

The conventional Western view represented by Michael Porter is

---

**Box 3.2   Some Recent Singaporean
'Marriages' Brokered by the
Economic Development Board**

TECH SEMICONDUCTOR ($300 million)

Hewlett-Packard, Texas Instruments, Canon and EDB (American Japanese and Singaporean)

Bachtel International and the Sembawang Group (American–Singaporean)

Golden Village Yishun (motion picture multiplex), Golden Harvest Roadshow Corporation (Hong-Kong–Australian–Singaporean)

Second Petrochemical Complex ($3.4 billion), Shell, Sumitomo Chemical, Phillips Petroleum, Singapore Chemicals (British–Dutch–Japanese–American– Singaporean)

Residue Catalytic Cracking ($1.4 billion), BP, Celtex, Singapore Petroleum (British–American–Singaporean)

PW4000 Advanced Turbo-fan Aero-engine Program, Pratt and Whitney, AMS Precision Engineering (American–Singaporean)

HBM Film, Grundy Australia, NDF Japan, Ngee Ann Polytechnic's Film Sound and Video (Australian–Japanese–Singaporean)

1BIT 2000 (Logistics), Scandinavia Warehouses and Jin Xing

(Swedish–Singaporean)

Source: *EDB Yearbooks, 1993–1996*

---

that strategic advantage lies in two principal sources: lower cost production and distribution, or the belief by customers that the product has premium qualities. Both forms of strategic advantage tend to precipitate Finite Games. There is a struggle to reduce wage costs which has managers struggling with employees. There is a struggle to manipulate consumers into believing that the brand has better qualities than other brands.

The absence of such 'games' in tiger economies is notable. Products with only imaginary worth and specious virtues are not pounded into the heads of consumers. 'High commitment purchasing' of products

Corporations fight to achieve lower
costs and superior brand
recognition

A

By forcing wage reductions and
beguiling consumers with
commercial persuasions.

Z

with genuinely superior information-content is the preferred style over low commitment purchasing, of the Battle of the Underarm Deodorants, the Cola Wars and celebrations of the squeezability of toilet tissue we see mercifully little, and what there is is of American origins.

The tiger version of this strategy stresses value added per person by way of increases in knowledge content. The Infinite Game reads as follows:

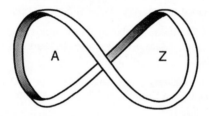

A. The more abundant knowledge is distilled within products, via accelerated learning...

Z. The scarcer these grow and the higher prices these fetch, thereby sponsoring...

The money earned by higher prices is fed back into the values system to sponsor more abundant knowledge. A culture can only afford its museums, universities and training institutes if the learning these impart infuses its products, otherwise the public sector comes under remorseless pressure and a finite contest breaks out between 'philistine business' and 'high culture' living at public expense.

The third major dynamic discussed in this chapter was the voluntary relinquishment, by relatively wealthy cultures like Japan and Singapore, of products at the lower and middle levels of knowledge intensity. These were devolved to regions or imported from outside, while labor was retrained for more complex activities.

Where this is *not* done low-wage countries will eventually capture markets for simple products, wresting these away from richer nations, who on the present evidence penalize the manual working class and poorer section of their own societies. Inequality grows rife. The Finite Games are as follows:

Low-wage economies attack and eventually wrest markets for simple products away from high-wage economies.

A

This is typically met by depressing wages and living standards in developed economies.

Z

We see this happening in Britain and in the USA, where union membership is down and blue-collar earnings are stagnant or declining. Part-time work is casualizing large parts of the workforce.

In contrast, the strategy of relinquishing less complex work and regionalizing it means that economies doing more and less sophisticated work can help each other, the richer pulling up the developing nation behind it, like climbers roped together. The Infinite Game reads as follows:

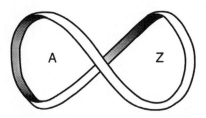

A. The developing economies grow faster by taking over technologies which richer economies have voluntarily...

Z. .. .relinquished, so as to upgrade their skills, raise their wages and so better afford to buy from...

If economic development is really about learning as opposed to destructive encounters between countries and corporations, then it saves time and energy to anticipate the outcome of contests and let lower-skilled and higher-skilled organizations specialize in what they do cheapest and best.

A final word needs to be said about knowledge increase as an Infinite Game and perpetual feast of the mind. *The more you already know the more you want to know.* This is an appetite that feeds on itself. There is every reason to believe that nations once ahead will *stay* ahead and even lengthen their leads because they know what they are looking for. They have discovered how to search, inquire, incorporate and act.

Chapter 4

Beyond the Level Playing Field: Catalysts and Clusters

Democracy and economic growth

. . . take the Philippines. They had a democracy from the word go in 1945. They never got going; it was too chaotic. It became a parlour game—who takes power, then you gets what spoils. Or take India and Ceylon. For the first three elections after independence they went through the mechanics of democracy. But the lack of discipline made growth slow and sluggish.

But once you reach a certain level of industrial progress, you've got an educated work force, an urban population, you have managers and employers. Then you must have participation, because they are educated, rational people. If you carry on with an authoritarian system, you will run into all kinds of logjams. You must devise some representative system.

J. Rohwer (1995) 'A Talk with Lee Kuan Yew', in *Asia Rising*. London: Nicholas Brealey.

A much used phrase by Western managers, politicians, lawyers and journalists is the 'level playing field'. Governments, corporations, sporting bodies are all exhorted to provide a 'level field' on which contestants play on equal terms, with equal opportunities to win, to rise to the top and be immortalized in the Hall of Fame. Democratic elections, free-for-all competition, open markets, trial by jury are all 'level playing fields'. How these contests are *solved* worries Lee Kuan Yew of Singapore, but not the audience of the O J Simpson trial. The prevailing Western ethos is to stage the game and call the victor.

Worries about chaos and intelligent participation worry East Asians but not us!

Financial markets are also 'playing fields'. All publicly quoted companies vie with each other to make returns to shareholders. Those who most succeed get most to invest. Those who disappoint markets have their funds reduced. These rules are, of course, allegedly neutral, value free, meritocratic and governed by timeless economic laws of truth and validity, guaranteed worldwide by American power, which upholds the human rights of all contestants and defines capitalism.

There is a close affinity between the 'economic game' and the 'democratic game'. In the economic game you compete fairly for the dollars of citizens. In the democratic game you compete fairly for their votes. In both cases you stage finite contests of persuasion and the winner is given money and/or power, in many cases greater than his margin of victory.

Now there are some difficulties with this doctrine. It is certainly not as neutral as it pretends. All rules are based on the values of those who legislated them. If finite contests are 'the only game in town' we are obliged to play, or not participate in the economic life of the culture. To equate knockout competition and disproportionate spoils with perfect freedom and meritocracy might be somewhat facile. Is there really no other way?

And then there is the question of size. The Prime Minister of Malaysia recently asked if it were *really* a 'level playing field' to let US banks into Malaysia and Malaysian banks into the US. Was it not Giants versus Midgets?[1]

But all such objections pale before the central fallacy of the Finite Game metaphor: what if various games are *not, in fact, separate episodes of win–lose conflict*? What if games form *clusters*, so that victory in one makes victory in a second game, a third and a fourth much more likely to occur? If these victories help generate each other then what is the secret of their connections? Are there *catalysts*, elements intervening among and between these games, which help to explain how victories themselves cluster?

The argument in this chapter is as follows:

- 'The level playing field' is but one game in a connected cluster of games, wherein each 'win' contributes to victories in related games.

- East Asians work much harder to generate the consensus necessary to clustering. One form of connection among these games is . . .
- 'Catalytic' or 'horizontal' technologies which are used to render games infinite. A vivid illustration of this is . . .
- Creating clusters: the case of Singapore. It is an example convincing us of . . .
- The effectiveness of clustering as opposed to clashing in win–lose finite contests.

The 'level playing field' is but one game in a connected cluster

We saw in Chapter 3 how important learning has become. In this case, might certain games carry lessons which affect the outcomes of many subsequent games? A lesson learned in one game *could* lead to a thousand subsequent victories.

We are back to the vexed problem of defining the right economic unit. Is this unit the person, the team, the department, the corporation, the industry or the nation? Those extolling Finite Games rarely tell us *who* exactly wins.

Consider a case we encountered, that of the after sales service department of a white goods manufacturer.[2] Because it was a profit center it did *not* warn manufacturing of faults discovered in a new washer, or contact sales so the problem could be easily fixed in the pipeline. It waited for the faulty machines to be delivered and then called on each household individually to make 'after sales' repairs. In this way the department justified its existence, profited and had its budget increased. The company, of course, lost heavily in costs and in reputation. Here the Finite Game being played by after sales was severely suboptimal for the larger corporation.

There is a constant confusion as to whom we are playing *with* and whom we are playing *against*. Competitive units keep changing formation and changing sides. In the case above, after sales did not see itself as playing *with* the corporation but as earning 'profit' and more funds for itself against the corporation. The Finite Game reads as follows:

The more faults found in the
manufactured product and the
more customers complain...

A

The stronger is the position of the
after sales department in the
corporation.

Z

An awareness by the department that a larger, Infinite Game was being played would have evoked a different response:

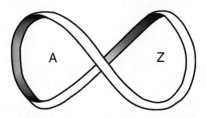

A. Fewer faults in the product and faster advice to manufacturing and sales of any problems...

Z. The cheaper and easier will it be to make repairs so that customers will encounter...

An effective company requires the *joining up* of all games being played by all departments.

But it does not stop there. If departments are better joined, why not companies, technologies and all the games occurring in an industry or nation? Without a much clearer idea of the *unit* which is supposed to survive, evolutionary theories are in deep trouble. Do the *fittest* survive or the *fittingest*? Does the ant, ant colony or colony plus bamboo plants survive when the colony sallies forth to bite the lips of animals browsing on their habitat? In each case we have a progressively larger unit into which smaller units are most 'fittingest'. We are speaking of *co*-evolution, insects and plants in alliance against browsing animals. Nature, too, tends to cluster into an ecosystem of 'hawks' and 'doves', oppositions and alliances. How well you fight depends on how carefully you clustered.[3]

The notion of a 'cluster' was first introduced by Michael Porter.[4] He noted that competitive companies are not distributed across nations in single units, but cluster together in networks. Examples are Danish clusters in high quality furnishings and health products, Swedish clusters in chemicals used to treat paper, which is part of their forest products cluster. Germany has clusters in chemicals, metalworking, transportation and printing. Israel has clusters in agricultural equipment and defense. Japan has strong automobile and electronics clusters, which combine for the purposes of automobile electronics, which constitutes more and more of the value of automobiles. Porter comments:

> Once a cluster forms, the whole group of industries becomes mutually supporting. Benefits flow forward, backward and horizontally. Aggressive rivals in one industry tend to spread to others in the cluster, through the exercise of bargaining power, spin-offs, and relocated diversification by established firms. Entry from other industries within the cluster spurs upgrading by stimulating diversity in R & D approaches and providing a means for introducing new strategies and skills. Information flows freely and innovations diffuse rapidly . . . People and ideas combine in new ways.[5]

Clusters may be precipitated by governments. The Swedish government had a major concern with assisting the physically handicapped. Companies were invited to produce electronic wheelchairs, prosthetic devices and means to gain access to buildings, vehicles etc. Out of this social concern there grew a whole cluster of related companies, which have now achieved a large share of the international market.

Clusters help to explain why films are made in Hollywood, clothes in the garment district of New York, men's suits in Saville Row, flowers in Spenger and Aalsmeer in Holland, and teaching hospitals in London. It is not 'efficient' to have all the suits in one street or so many hospitals in one town, but it is essential for *learning within the cluster*. A total misunderstanding of this process has led to the closure of several of London's famous teaching hospitals by the British Conservative Government in the belief that they should not cluster together!

We see, then, that clusters have evolved historically, especially for industries requiring scarce skills. Route 128 electronic and defense companies circle the schools and universities of the Boston area. Silicon Valley grew up around Stanford University. But clusters can also be deliberately created and this chapter shows that the 'tiger economies' have done just that.

East Asians work much harder to generate the consensus necessary for clustering

Clustering is neither natural nor easy. It is, of course, natural to cluster together for warmth or for reasons of anxiety and insecurity. It is possible to huddle defensively so as to protect inefficiency. Individualistic countries often stigmatize all clustering as motivated by sloth, fear and inertia. 'Corporatism', the practice of economic actors to work for consensus, is currently stigmatized in Anglo-American discourse. And there may be something to this. Finite game players find consensus very difficult and frustrating to achieve. When they *do* combine it is often as allies in a Finite Game against third parties. Hence 'beer and sandwiches at Number 10'—British trades unions meeting with the Prime Minister—was never too popular with those excluded!

We set out to measure the tendency for national cultures to struggle for consensus versus their tendency to settle conflicts by voting down the minority and/or compromising. The results are set out in Table 4.1.

The division between East Asians and the rest is quite sharp and the range is wide, from Korea, 89.0 percent of whose managers seek consensus, to Canada, where only 31.0 percent do. East Asian countries occupy ten of the top thirteen places and none of the bottom thirteen.

Consensus building is not *by itself* a virtue, and as a value may be

Table 4.1   Negotiated consensus versus winning through voting or compromise

Negotiated consensus preferred %

Korea	89.66	Italy	55.41
Hong Kong	85.19	Australia	54.19
Philippines	80.46	Spain	52.94
Singapore	78.20	Germany	50.85
Japan	77.67	Belgium	50.75
China	72.17	Switzerland	50.24
Brazil	71.37	Norway	50.00
Taiwan	70.96	United Kingdom	48.99
France	70.71	USA	48.83
New Zealand	70.00	Ireland	46.28
Malaysia	68.49	Sweden	40.66
Thailand	68.42	Netherlands	39.28
Indonesia	58.21	Canada	31.67

Source: The Trompenaars Group, Database. Amsterdam, 1997.

extolled but not achieved. Among countries valuing consensus but not growing well economically are Kenya, Pakistan and Egypt. And we must not forget that the more you value consensus the greater the pressures to reject those who oppose you. Consensus *between* those of opposite views is the real prize. Among nations not making it easy for opposition politicians is Singapore. Consensus-oriented cultures tend to feel that people who do not even *try* to create consensus are placing themselves outside that culture. To 'oppose' for the sake of opposition is to place your humanity and civility in question. Westerners are quick to condemn this tendency without seeing the opposite weakness in ourselves. If Singapore goes too far in building a participative consensus, which excludes those who declare an opposition to that process, then we surely go too far in staging colorful contests from which intelligent, participative consensus-building is entirely absent. Running negative advertisements on TV, speculating on particular features of the President's male member, putting 'American racism' on trial instead of O J Simpson, is to invite the chaos, the parlor games and slow growth which Lee Kuan Yew deplored in the quotation opening this chapter.

Singapore is both less democratic and more democratic than its Anglo-American critics, depending on how democracy is defined. Singapore is less democratic in its toleration of outright opposition and media attacks on its leaders, but it is more democratic in its struggles to create negotiated consensus and intelligent participation among its citizens and employees. And there is no doubt that negotiated consensus does more for economic growth than do rhetorical battles. Especially crucial is the patient joining together of games to form an Infinite Game, and this requires the vital catalyst of horizontal technologies.

'Catalytic' and 'horizontal' technologies are used to render games infinite

The first 'tiger' economy was Japan, with 7–10 percent growth rates in the 1960s and 1970s. We showed in Chapter 3 that the technologies targeted were high in knowledge-intensity, and that in general high information products have more connections to each other than simpler products. However, this is a tendency only, and simply pursuing complexity can tie you in unnecessary knots. Some technologies—for example, unscrambling the voice of the pilot from surrounding cockpit noise—are exceedingly complex but have no foreseeable connection to the civilian economy and do not catalyze other technologies. The Japanese were not pursuing complexity alone but 'catalyst' or 'horizontal' technologies, sometimes called meta-technologies, i.e. technologies *about* technology. We will now look at some of the technologies targeted by 'Japan Inc.' and ask ourselves why were these selected? We shall argue that in every case these were crucial to cluster formation.[6]

Targeting steel

Japan's era of fast development began with steel. The calculation is obvious. Make the best steel, and all steel-using products benefit. Move up into speciality steels to catch the higher value added. Much steel production in this part of the world has since moved to South Korea, whose engineering services are bundled with its lower steel prices, to capture knowledgeable businesses *around* steel.

Targeting numerically controlled machine tools

A second major focus of Japanese cluster development was numerically controlled machine tools. We have to understand what these do within an industrial infrastructure to appreciate why they were targeted. Machine tools are the tools-which-make-the-tools in any factory. Factories are specially tooled up for particular production runs. The quality and precision of manufacturing processes therefore depend on the quality of machine tools. Numerically controlled machine tools represent a vital synthesis between electronics and tool creation, what the Japanese call 'mechatronics'. The ability to alter *quickly* the dimensions to be cut, bored or drilled means that set-up times, the time taken to get ready for a production run, are greatly reduced. You have only to tap into the keyboard the dimension of the tool you wish to create.

As products grow more complex and more customized, production runs grow shorter and tool changes more frequent. Hence numerically controlled machine tools are very much the key to modern, short-run, flexible, customized manufacturing. The seizure of large parts of the machine tool market by Japan in the 1980s showed their fierce determination to develop hundreds of clusters between the infrastructure of various factories and tool-making technologies. If your machine tools are the best, your factories will necessarily benefit.[7]

A third technology that joins game to game in infinite clusters is industrial and specialized robots and automated production processes generally. Japan enjoys a 46 percent world market share of industrial robots, four times as many as the USA. The decision to target robots follows a communal logic similar to that of numerically controlled machine tools. Robots transform the manufacturing processes of any industry installing them. The Japanese government buys up robots and leases them to various industries, so that the very latest will be used and the obsolescent traded in for the new. Instead of factories run by blue collar 'hands', factories are run by knowledge workers capable of programing and maintaining intelligent machines through which they think and plan. Table 4.2 shows that globally, Japan and Singapore have made the widest use of robots.

Robots and automated processes cluster with any industry needing volume production. They are the machines which make the machines. Go to virtually any state-of-the-art microprocessor factory and read off the Japanese names on the automated machines processing the chips.

Table 4.2 Use of industrial and specialized robots by country

Industrial robots per 100,000 population		Specialized robots per 10,000 manufacturing workers	
Japan	301.2	Japan	277.9
Singapore	136.4	Sweden	83.0
Germany	59.9	Singapore	64.0
Sweden	62.5	Italy	63.7
Switzerland	42.5	Germany	62.2
Italy	38.3	Finland	38.3
Austria	27.7	Switzerland	33.7
Russia	27.2	France	29.6
Czech Republic	25.9	USA	29.3
Finland	25.4	Norway	20.6
France	22.4	Austria	19.5
USA	20.8	Korea	18.6
Belgium	19.6	Australia	18.2
Korea	16.0	Spain	17.8
UK	15.7	Belgium	17.5
Taiwan	15.5	The Netherlands	17.5
Spain	11.5	UK	16.1
Australia	11.3	Denmark	13.7
The Netherlands	9.4	Czech Republic	13.5

Source: *World Competitiveness Report.* Lausanne: IMD, 1996.

Does robotization destroy jobs? Yes, among those who resist it! Among early adopters it creates an aristocracy of knowledge, workers using trigonometry to guide the robots, while consigning to history a large part of the 'low wage' advantage. Robots are not paid.

Targeting 'mechatronics' and microchips

At an even more pervasive level Japan has long since targeted an area it calls 'mechatronics'. So pronounced is this emphasis that there are over 1000 mechatronic institutes in Japan where electrical and mechanical engineers combine their expertise. The calculation is that all production machinery, with the exception of the most simple, is improved in its operations by a variety of electronic controls and monitors.[8]

Take, for example, a machine producing thin-film for dialysis solution. The thickness of the film is finely calibrated and the production machine automatically calibrates and rejects film falling outside exact tolerances, recycling the defective film back into the extrusion process. If the film has to meet ten tests of quality, all these can be electronically tested. Wear and tear on machinery, the need for maintenance, lubrication, replacement parts, all can be read out electronically. The sheer numbers of electronic–mechanical improvements are in thousands each year.

Apart from production machinery original equipment is now seeded with electronic forms of intelligence. In the modern automobile, power steering, power braking, anti-skid devices, emission controls, fuel injection, temperature control, automatic locking, airbags, the entire dashboard and the car computer, radio and stereo systems are all electronic.

No wonder that the Japanese call microchips 'the rice of industry' keeping engines of every kind nourished, vital and intelligent. Microchips make a thousand products more intelligent every month, from devices which open and close garage doors, to the TV remote, to controls which turn up or turn down illumination depending on the natural light entering the room, to life-saving heart monitors which automatically summon aid.

Arguably we are not selling stand-alone products any more so much as driving systems, life-monitoring systems, illumination systems, home entertainment systems, office systems, all capable of being triggered by communication systems, so that you could turn on your home heating system via your mobile phone on your journey home from work. You create systems out of clustered units each providing the elements necessary to the system as a whole.

Targeting metal ceramics

Consider a fifth area targeted by the Japanese, metal ceramics. These are metal, silicate, clay and bauxite compounds which are fired at very high temperatures, 649–1649°C, to make them durable and heat and stress resistant. As with certain metal alloys the combined strength of these ingredients, fused at high temperatures, is far greater than the sum of their strengths. The nose cones of space rockets, the linings of jet engines, and electronic circuits all require ceramics.

What advances in metal ceramics could entail, is nothing less than the obsolescence of every engine made from conventional materials. Much improved heat conservation, for example, makes engines more efficient and fuel conserving. The 300 mpg auto engine could be a reality with massive implications for preserving the environment and saving energy costs. It is by no means certain that this strategy will pay off for the Japanese. More important for our purposes is its underlying rationale.

The purpose is not to win one Finite Game for the materials market, but to win *every Finite Game in which the quality and cost of engine performance is a decisive issue*. In other words, the purpose is to form these games into one Infinite Game. Catalyzed by superior ceramics as the key ingredient of that cluster, you go straight for technologies which *cut horizontally across other technologies*, so as to help you win an infinite number of additional games.

Targeting photovoltaic cells

The purpose of clustering is not simply to array many business units around one catalyst technology likely to transform the fortunes of all, but to include in this cluster other major problems facing a nation's economy. Japan, for example, has a serious dearth of indigenous energy. It has to import nearly all its energy over great distances, at considerable expense, from parts of the world which are turbulent. Hence a fuel-conserving ceramic engine would help solve *this* problem as well. But a technology which might in the long run make fossil fuel imports a thing of the past is the development of photovoltaic cells, which absorb and store sunlight. After the second oil-crisis of the 1970s, both the US Office of Management and Budget (OMB) and

Japan's Ministry of International Trade and Industry (MITI) decided that solar energy should be given priority. It is instructive to note which of the two persevered and which dropped out.

For nearly twenty years previous to these efforts, the costs of solar energy had been chasing the costs of non-renewable energy sources, and had closed the gap considerably. The two price hikes of the seventies had caused many to believe that the graphs could cross in a matter of years. MITIs 'Project Sunshine' clustered solar power with Japan's huge consumer electronics business. Calculators, watches, radios and audio-cassettes could be recharged using solar cells. By the early eighties 30 million cells a year were being sold. Today this has passed 100 million.[9]

America's solar industry had fewer immediate applications and when President Reagan replaced Carter, and the price of oil was again declining the US government pulled out of solar energy. Casper Weinberger denounced all attempts to 'pick winners', solar energy should make it on its own or not at all. The effect was devastating. While the USA had a 60 percent world market share of solar cells as late as 1983 to Japan's 23 percent, this shifted massively in the next three years with America's change of policy. By 1986 the US share had fallen to less than half, 27 percent, whereas Japan's share had risen to 49 percent. US tax incentives for installing solar panels were withdrawn. Even the panels placed on the roof of the White House by President Carter were torn down by his successor. Solar energy versus conventional energy was an ideological issue, a war of words between them, a Finite Game which demanded a loser, so solar power lost.[10]

In the meantime Sanyo, Fuji, Mitsubishi and Kyocern were forging ahead. The top prize was not rechargeable calculators, but year-round temperature controlled greenhouses. In the early 1990s a transparent solar cell was developed which would admit sunlight *and* store it for night-time emission. The prospect of solar heated homes and offices was not far away, with solar powered transport in the wings.

The sun has special significance for the Japanese. *Ameratsu*, the Sun God, is the spiritual father of the Japanese race, the first among equals in the Shinto pantheon. He is also the progenitor of the Japanese imperial dynasty. The land of the rising sun may be first to trap its power.

Clusters are, in the end, not just clusters of industrial units, but clusters of ideas which reinforce each other and radiate a larger meaning. Clean, renewable energy promises a return to the beauty and serenity of the Tokugawa era and the Great Peace of three hundred years. Visions are realizable through the clustering of ideas.

Creating clusters: the case of Singapore

Always quick learners, the Singaporeans and Malaysians read Michael Porter's description of clustering, hired him to consult with them and set about the deliberate policy of creating clusters. One consequence is Singapore's $1 Billion Cluster Development Fund and Malaysia's Multimedia corridor. As we will see, this is not the only example of ideas articulated in the West, yet run with and enthusiastically implemented in East Asia.

There is a cultural propensity for Pacific Rim economies to grasp and operationalize selectively *those Western concepts consistent with their own philosophies*. Clustering industries is in every way consistent with the logics of community, the patterns of complementarity and esthetics of ebb and flow we saw in Chapter 2, as close scrutiny of Singaporean and Malaysian initiatives reveals.

The Economic Development Board (EDB) has identified at least fourteen 'world class industry and services clusters' which radiate from Singapore's international hub, a cluster *of* clusters. Official policy, as laid out in the EDB's 1984 Yearbook, states:

> The EDB will strengthen Singapore's total business capability and product management through a cluster development approach— Singapore will work with companies to identify and build up core capabilities needed to meet the challenges of the global market place.[11]

It is possible, claims the Yearbook, to ensure that 'gaps in existing industry clusters are identified'. Companies are then encouraged to develop their activities to fill these gaps, or where none is willing, a world search locates the best unit and it is invited to move or extend to Singapore. Clusters take the form of industrial parks, business incubators, or simply business districts in which related businesses are co-located for easy access and face to face meetings.

It is *not* the EDB's policy to promote forced marriages. The policy is to pool investments, with the EDB as one partner of several, to effect mutual introductions, to offer shared training and research facilities—not always taken up—and to generate cross-contacts through common Singaporean suppliers. It is believed that creative connections within the cluster will arise spontaneously as a consequence of intellectual and geographical proximity. While some of these are formalized into partnerships and value chains, many are the stuff of restaurants and coffee bars, as when people ask each other, 'So what are *you* doing?' Clusters are like live electric wires tossed into a heap and giving off flashes of electricity as they co-mingle.

Western approaches to creativity tend to focus upon the heads of lone geniuses in which divine sparks fly. Asian approaches to creativity steer disciplines and professions into conjunction and cross-fertilization, wherein ideas are likely to fuse and hybridize. It is a similar pattern but at the social level.[12]

The EDB has now identified fourteen clusters which will play a major part in its future, including:

- Aerospace
- Petroleum and petrochemicals
- Speciality chemicals and pharmaceuticals
- Electronic components and systems
- Precision engineering
- Heavy engineering
- Marine engineering
- Light industries
- Construction
- Commodity trading
- Shipping
- Tourism
- Insurance
- Finance and information technology[13]

However, development of these clusters will be phased with the immediate emphasis on aerospace, chemicals, electronics and precision engineering. Since we dealt briefly with aerospace in Chapter 3, we will now look at clusters in the last three of these categories. All three of these are key elements of focus as parts of manufacturing 2000. The plan is to keep manufacturing at above 20 percent of Singapore's employment and 25 percent of her GDP. Manufacturing has realized massive increases in productivity historically, and all fast-growing economies retain strong manu-facturing presence. Hence Singapore is determined not to suffer the manufacturing decline of several developed economies in the West.

Chemicals are now worth in excess of $20 billion to the Singaporean economy. A second $3.4 billion petrochemical complex has been built with Shell Sumitomo, Phillips and the EDB as partners. Mobil recently opened a $1.15 billion aromatics complex; Atochem has built a polystyrene plant. Dupont has added a nylon compounding facility, and GE Plastics an engineering plastics project; and the Singaporean Aromatics Company, in a joint venture between Exxon, Amoco and China American Petrochemical, has built a new aromatics complex. Aromatics are chemical compounds which are typical products of clustered industries, able to pool resources and share processes.[14]

Electronics is probably *the* mainstay of Singapore's rapid development, accounting for 46 percent of manufacturing output and 41 percent of value-added. Indeed, current criticism claims that Singapore is *too* reliant on electronics, now in a world recession. It reads like a Who's Who of world electronics: Hitachi, Compaq, Sony, Apple, Motorola, Hewlett Packard, Texas Instruments, JVC Electronics, Murata, Matsuchitu Electronics, SGS-Thomson, Siemens, Western Digital, Kotobuki, and so on. But for clustering to take place, as many 'front end' businesses—that is, originators of new products—as possible are essential. 'Back end' businesses do the final assembly and testing of products created elsewhere.

The EDB has exercised all its considerable influence to ensure that this cluster innovates from the front end. Brooktree Corporation does much of its chip design in Singapore. Western Digital has built a $3.6 million design center for disk drive components and engineering software. Murata, the Japanese ceramic chip maker, will maintain a bridge to the metal ceramics sector by making sure its chips can function at very high temperatures. Siemens has opened up a design center for integrated circuits, Sony Precision Engineering center is pioneering in magnetic heads for video recorders. Apple has located research and development and design functions in Singapore. It is at least possible that any of the new developments described here could ramify through the entire cluster, raising all boats like an incoming tide.

The third cluster now in priority phase is precision engineering. This is very close to what we described as the targeting of numerically controlled machine tools, plus robotization and automated processes by Japan's MITI. Precision engineering refers to much the same set of tools which very precisely make other tools or products. This is a relatively new field for Singapore, which at around $750 million is small compared with the two clusters described earlier, yet it remains extremely important and like a small amount of catalyst can make a big amount of difference.

Prominent in this cluster is Yamaki Mazake, one of Japan's larger machine tool makers and perhaps its most advanced. A $47 million facility in Singapore makes the very latest combinations of computer integrated manufacturing with flexible manufacturing systems. A second Japanese tool maker, Makino, has opened a $33 million plant for the computer aided designing of precision tools and parts. It has completed a new-generation CNC machining center, ranked in the world's top 5 percent. Molex, the tool design, molding and stamping company, has founded an Automation Design and Development Group. One of the largest connector manufacturers in the world, Molex, and the other companies sited here have the capacity first to transform, automate and modernize the entire Singapore industrial base and then to keep it up to date.

Murato Machinery specializes in the latest textile machinery, which Singapore devolves upon its regions. Seiko Instruments, a branch of the Japanese watchmaker Minebea and WMF are other units in this newly forming cluster. Robotization is supplied by Kikkomen among others.

Precision engineering is not simply a cluster in its own right, it is a crucial ingredient in the modernization of *all* complex manufacturing, and clusters *with* industry after industry. Giant robots, for example, make Sony Display Devices, the picture tubes on TVs and monitors generally. SDD is itself a core competence clustering with all products using tubes and screens.[15]

Although the three clusters described, plus the aeronautics cluster, currently have priority, clusters in ship-building and heavy engineering, in pharmaceutical and speciality chemicals, in finance and information technologies and in the recent multimedia park cannot be ignored. Singapore is especially keen to be culturally influential and to make Chinese language films and programs for the one and a half billion Chinese. The world search is on for producers and directors of genuine caliber. An Asian Hollywood is in the making—perhaps one with very different values.

There is a clear contrast between Western and 'tiger' approaches to government intervention. In Western economies, where state initiatives are permitted at all, these are all product or project specific. The Tennessee Valley Authority, Operation Manhattan, the Lunar Landing project, *Concorde, Ariane,* Minitel in France and Star Wars were all specific objectives. They are high risk in the sense that they visibly succeed or fail. All efforts converge on a single aim. You win or you lose.

But the interventions by tiger economies are quite different. Initiatives are aimed at improving 'seminal' technologies, in which a great many businesses need to be successful. The metaphors are biological, 'rice of industry', 'blood of business', 'food chain', 'seed corn', 'technology trees'. Where the tiger economies *did* plump for specific objectives, HDTV and Fifth Generation Computer in Japan, they largely failed. In 'seminal' interventions, clusters beget clusters: machine tools, robots and semi-conductors procreate successive generations of new products. Products have knowledge 'genes' which are passed on from one generation to the next. Seminal products are *so* much more important than products in general that these cannot be allowed to fail and often reap meager profits, with the result that Western corporations voluntarily withdraw! We thereby surrender the secrets of a thousand victories.

The decision to target micro-brains and product-forming products etc. is not genuinely risky so much as self-evidently effective. Even slight improvements in every tool or chip would pay back a thousand times in all the products to which these had contributed. We are reminded of the bumper sticker displayed by Canadian teachers, 'If you think education is expensive, try ignorance'. This could equally well read 'If you think improving the intelligence of products is expensive, try *not* improving them'. America's huge contemporary success is the Internet, an Infinite Game which could enrich all players, joining clusters to clusters. Yet the irony is this. It was *intended* to be a specific defense project, enabling security agencies to stay in touch during national emergencies. It became a seminal, horizontal technology by accident!

The effectiveness of clustering as compared to clashing

Why are corporations in the West slower to realize the accelerated learning inherent in clustering? Because they are more concerned to clash than to cluster, more interested in eliminating one another from the Finite Game than joining each other in an Infinite Game. We can see this more clearly in the following settings:

- Putting out bids for competitive tendering.
- Meeting the specifications at the lowest cost.
- Clawing back monies from distributors, sub-contractors etc.
- Chaos pricing.

The routine procedure in Western economies is to put out bids for competitive tendering. You invite would-be participants to compete in a Finite Game of bidding and you go with the winner. This is so obviously 'fair' that we make it legally compulsory, to do anything less is 'corrupt'.

But there are several problems here. The first is that with say—five players, the efforts of four are wasted. They cannot count on steady work in such environments. Long losing runs are occasionally inevitable. Also fees charged must include the costs of unsuccessful bids. Another problem is the treatment of your current sub-contractors. Is their past service to your company to count for nothing, or should it be allowed to bias the outcome of a supposedly fair contest? The 'level playing field' is supposed to know no favorites and feel no obligations to the past.

And what of the lessons you have learned and the ideas you have shared with current suppliers and contractors? Are these to be revealed to all new entrants? Are these to be taken from one faithful contractor and shared with all contestants? Clusters are less likely to form if you run suppliers and sub-contractors *against* each other, and if you break past confidences by 'updating' information. They will not trust your on-again, off-again patronage.

An important part of the process of competitive bidding and finite game playing is to specify *precisely* the standards to be attained, so as to be able to award the contract to the cheapest bid. As in football, everyone will then 'know the score'. Decisions to declare a winner can be justified by the numbers. Voters, shareholders, accountants and colleagues cannot criticize so objective a decision.

But there are problems here too. Competitive ideas *not* anticipated in the specifications and not affecting costs get ignored. Improvements which go beyond what the specifications envisaged may not be implemented. The object is to win the game, not to improve the plays.

It may take weeks or years to complete the contract. During this time new ideas may arise, new processes can become available. Yet you are frozen in time by the specifications in the original contract. Try anything fancy and you could be sued.

The 'ideal' situation for finite game playing assumes identical work for varying costs, so that the lowest bid wins, while compliance with the specifications is enforced by law. But in modern conditions of clustered complexities this simple situation is rare. In practice, quality is the most important criterion, setting new standards for the industry. The reason quality is so crucial is that defective components are paid for many times: in being unfit for use, in necessitating disassembly, diagnosis, replacement and rework. If you have a thousand components each with a 1 percent defect rate you cannot rely on assembled equipment working. Hence quality is king and constant improvement vital. All bids are *not* qualitatively the same, and the lowest bidder may well have cut corners to end a losing streak of bids.

The reason many Western corporations have several alternative suppliers is that they dare not trust a single-source supplier. With just one source you become vulnerable to opportunistic behavior. 'Pay me more or you get nothing!' If your supplier finds another customer he may threaten to switch or simply dump you. Finite game players jostle for advantage.

If you have taken the precaution to have one or more alternative suppliers you can punish opportunistic behaviors, while spreading the risks of opportunism so that you are not completely at the mercy of one player. Many large American corporations behave like referees in a game of soccer, handing out 'cards' on which the relative failings of players are described: 'you had *this* percentage defects in your last batch, you were so many minutes late, with so much rework needed'.[16] The palpable threat is that those with the poorer records will be expelled from the game in the next round. This threat keeps everyone on their toes and keeps the customer in control.

But this is much less effective than developing a learning relationship with one, committed supplier, whom you trust and who trusts you. One reason the tiger economies cluster more readily is their cultural predisposition to form *quanxi* relationships of trust with chosen suppliers, who can share visions, aspirations and secrets, who can co-experiment and co-research. For the *real* competitive advantage lies with those who form the most effective supply chains. This

Table 4.3 How US and Japanese automobile MNEs relate to their parts suppliers

US companies	Japanese companies
Several alternative suppliers.	Preference for sole suppliers.
Suppliers independent of their clients.	Suppliers symbiotic with their clients.
Engineering and design capability is largely with MNE.	Engineering and design capabilities exchanged between supplier and MNE.
Price quotation is major reason for frequent re-selection of suppliers.	Equipment capability and compatibility plus shared learnings are reasons for supplier retention.
Them versus Us.	
Market needs' assessment.	R&D.
Quality control exercised after delivery.	Quality 'built into' on-going relationship.
Low user–producer interface.	High user–producer interface.
Specifications spelt out in advance.	Improvements negotiated as these arise.

Source: D. L. Blenkhorn and H. Noori (1990) 'What it Takes to Supply Japanese OEMs', *Industrial Marketing Management*, 19 February.

requires creative inputs from both parties at both ends and fine degrees of *wa* or harmony via mutual accommodation.[17]

A major recent study contrasted the relationships of Japanese and US multinationals in the automobile industries with their respective parts suppliers. The comparison is set out in Table 4.3.

It is important to see that among US multinationals supplier innovation can threaten relationships. If the supplier develops a superior way of working he may *not* tell his customer but try to make more profit for himself while delivering to the old standards. New ideas or opportunity may not be shared if there are simmering disputes over the relative margins made by suppliers and customers. Perhaps the supplier finds a less costly source, but instead of passing on a portion of these savings to his client, pockets the difference himself.

When the MNE suspects that this is happening he may use his clout to strike back, demanding lower prices if he is not to switch suppliers. Clawing back money from distributors, subcontractors and/or suppliers is a well-known Finite Game, as is paying small creditors late and the floating on their money. You must cheat or be cheated, grab the lion's share or be sucked dry. But of course you never really *know* whether you are 'starving out' the organizations that serve you, or curbing their 'greed', as in all such secret wars, truth is the first casualty. In the game of bluff and counter bluff each threatens the relationship. Even where you keep your subcontractors their trust is often gone.

The general practice in the Japanese auto industry is to take the rivalry out of the relationship by agreeing the subcontractor's or supplier's profit margin *in advance*. He will make 8.2 percent, period. Both parties are then free to make *their relationship* more and more valuable and less and less costly. They now have joint ownership and joint interest in the improvement process.[18]

The final stratagem which substitutes clashing for clustering is

Box 4.1   Confusion Marketing

Many economic orthodoxies, like price competition, are easily circumvented. As with several 'laws' of economics, they stop working when you are aware of them and devise a way of defeating them. A way to stop consumers choosing the cheapest product is to confuse comparison, 7¾ oz for $1.25 or 6¼ oz for 99 cents. 'Confusion marketing' comes hot from the USA to Britain.

When customers called one of the many private companies into which British Rail has now been split, 80 percent of them were offered more expensive routes than the cheapest, with sellers pushing their own companies. British Telecom quotes three different rates for calling New York, each of which are subject to various forms of discount (i.e. 'friends and family'). The operator can no longer tell you which call is cheapest without questioning you extensively, for which you are charged.

Supermarket 'loyalty discounts' reduce purchases by varying percentages depending on the size of your purchase. Mortgage companies offer seven different plans for first-time buyers. Mobile phones are priced from $10 to $100 but you have to buy a contract with such tempting offers as 'one free call in three, with 15 minutes a week free till December 15th'.Work *that* one out! As the deputy editor of *Marketing Week* put it, 'The trick today is to offer so much choice that people just give up and go with names they recognise' (which is where advertising comes in). All that ferocious energy poured into Finite Games with people you are supposed to be helping...

Source: '"Chaos pricing" baffles customers out of bargains', *The Sunday Times*, January 26, 1997.

'chaos pricing' or 'confusion marketing' in which the customer is deliberately confused (see Box 4.1).

Summary

The belief that capitalism, democracy and the court are some kind of competitive arena or level playing field leads to win–lose conflict with more heat than light, more public posturing than consensual solutions. A greater emphasis on intelligent participation through consensus and problem-solving may be as important to democracy, and is clearly more vital to fast economic growth. The nations of East Asia value consensus building more than the public display of opposed opinions, sometimes to the detriment of the latter. Anglo-American democracy and industry have the opposite tendency, a tendency to split into rhetorical factions and vilify opponents.

A consensus orientation is vital to the building of clusters, in which victory in one game contributes to victories in clusters of games or one Infinite Game. These are typically joined by horizontal technologies which act as catalysts. Targeting a technology common to a cluster develops the entire cluster. Clustering also greatly increases the chance of fortuitous and creative connections.

There are at least two issues here. First, what *size* is the optimal competitive unit? With whom must we fit to be fittest? Second, is there a serious miscalculation in valuing all technologies according to the immediate profits of the contest to capture them? Might they not have subsequent uses? The finite, short term game reads as follows:

Economic growth requires a constant struggle between persons, profit centers and companies. This weeds out the weakest...

... And increases the power and influence of those strongest and fittest to survive who are naturally selected...

According to this view it is desirable for American MNEs in the automobile industry to dominate their suppliers and discipline their output. Like Tarzan, they are 'kings of the jungle' ruling over lesser creatures.

The view of the Infinite Game is very different. Here the cluster or eco-system of players develop around a catalytic technology.

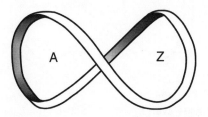

A. Catalytic technologies, e.g. microchips, robots, metal ceramics, are targeted for superlative performance, thereby enhancing...

Z. Competencies which cluster around these whose combination creates a 'survival of the fittingest' and whose success sponsors more...

A second issue arises when Western companies engage in win–lose battles with tiger economies over technologies which tigers see as having infinite ramifications. Western economies see this as just one more battle to win if the price is right, or surrender if the price is poor. It is not difficult to take the profits *out* of any battle for a seminal technology. You have only to cut your margins wafer thin. It is then that Western companies simply throw in the sponge (?towel), *not* seeing that this particular technology is the key to a thousand other battles. The Finite Game works out as follows:

When tiger economies want a technology badly enough to take most of the profit out of the battle...

Then Western companies switch their attentions to markets in which they can still win big...

Given this finite definition, the tiger economies have lost by pursuing crumbs, while profit-maximizing Western companies believe they have been smart to go for the lower hanging fruit. But tiger economies are thinking in a quite different way.

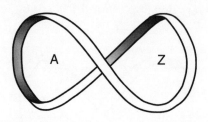

A. Capturing markets for seminal and catalytic technologies even at no profits, helps to catalyze...

Z. One or more clusters, whose several members mutually enhance their learning and assist in...

The weakness of many Western strategies stems from a fatal miscalculation. We ask 'Is *this* game profitable?' But games are not isolated episodes. They are grand rehearsals for a hundred other games in which the procreative potentials of seminal technologies generate economic development. Like the cynic described by Oscar Wilde, we know the price of everything but the value of nothing.

Chapter 5

Beyond Competitiveness: Competing Cooperatively to Learn

The Asian perspective is also manifested in the work ethic. The factory and the office is an extension of the family: the employee is a loyal and valued member of the company. Labour–management relations are not class struggles with workers pitted against capitalists. Executives and workers need each other: both can prosper through co-operation. Just as a son or daughter realises when they have to forgo a personal pleasure or goal for the good of the family, a company's staff, from the boardroom to the assembly line, know that compromise accomplishes more than confrontation. The sense of common welfare also connects citizens to the nation and has fuelled East Asia's economic growth.
Mahathir Mohamad and Shintaro Ishihara, *The Voice of Asia.*

Competitiveness varies in its significance, depending on whether it is the individual who competes or the group. Where groups compete there must have been an agreement among individuals to cooperate to that end. Competing and cooperating combine.

From the beginning of industrialization the competitive ethos used by the West to explain and justify its success has posed a dilemma for East Asia and its tiger economies. These nations and other emerging economies of the region are overwhelmingly communitarian and cooperative in their cultural values. In fact, until quite recently Western scholars were pointing to Confucianism and Taoism as ethics *preventing* economic development in this part of the world.[1] It was said that East Asia blocked its bourgeois revolutions and was too feudal and authoritarian to permit the emergence of an assertive middle class.

Certainly Maoism in China defined the peasantry as the proletariat, and bourgeois aspirations as the enemy of revolution, celebrating those who had *lost* Finite Games, while excoriating the winners as selfish and decadent. So long as becoming wealthy involved violating deeply held beliefs in the cooperative nature of man, much of East Asia resigned itself to a virtuous poverty and even regarded intellectuals with suspicion.

This issue is not simply moral but practical. Shared systems of belief hold nations together. If the only alternative to underdevelopment is a descent into chaos and disorder, the former is preferable. Cultures develop economically, or fail to develop, on the foundations of their own ethics. Invitations to 'become like America' sound to many like the blandishments of The Great Satan. To this day, large parts of the Muslim world reject what they see as the unacceptable face of capitalism. Ezra Vogel has distinguished early capitalism (18th–19th centuries) from late capitalism (late 19th and early 20th centuries) from late-late capitalism (mid to late 20th century). East Asian economies generally represent late-late capitalism.

It is simply not possible to bootleg American cultural values and impose these on the Chinese. We have met many Chinese who regret the violence and the repression occurring in Tiannamen Square. But we have met far fewer who believe that the demonstrators' demands were culturally viable or could have been accepted. To erect a statue of liberty in a totally different culture has explosive consequences.[2]

East Asians *are* now learning to compete, often with an enthusiasm and effectiveness that leaves us gasping. But they have *not*, as we shall show, surrendered their cultural preferences for cooperation and community. Instead they have discovered a mode of competing that *improves* their communities. This combination, which we call 'coopetition', or cooperative competition, may prove far more powerful than the 'pure competition' advocated by Britain, North America and the OECD. We shall be teasing out this important distinction in the course of this chapter.

The argument in this chapter is as follows:

- Cooperative competing or 'coopetition' is an Infinite Game; pure competition is a Finite Game.
- East Asian cultures compete hard while remaining com-munitarian not individualist. They are competing in order to cooperate better and to share information about what proved best.
- Pure competitiveness or finite game playing engages the Knowledge Society with ever decreasing effectiveness. It is blind

to 'complementors' in the economy. It reduces diversity and complexity and traumatizes too many losers. In contrast . . .

- The Japanese model and the economies deliberately emulating it contain many examples of cooperative competing. It is notable, for example, how many domestic players there are in key industries. These deliberately keep each other 'in play' so as to learn from each other.
- Recent investigations of the culture of Singapore's EDB shows similar patterns.
- Several outstanding MNEs with East Asian experience now practice 'coopetition'.

Cooperative competing or 'coopetition' is an Infinite Game, pure competition is a Finite Game

The conventional wisdom holds that there is no limit to competitiveness. The harder you play, the better you will do, and sweep all doubters, all 'handkerchief holders', all limp-wristed lefties from the field of play. Since driving all incompetents from the competitive arena is of inestimable benefit to customers and spectators, these should be enjoying themselves, cheering the excitement of the contests and sighing with satisfaction that from here on they will be served only by the best.

The Cold War was fought between those who idealized competing and those who idealized cooperating, and we all know who won! The greatest Finite Game of all has ended with the death of socialism, the collapse of the cooperators and all those without the realism and intestinal fortitude to proclaim 'Greed is good!' Let the lean and mean inherit the earth.

The Finite Game reads as follows:

Those loitering in the cosy familiarity of *cooperative* enduring relationships...

Are *competitively* assailed by the lean and mean who soon eliminate...

A

Z

All of which *sounds* marvellously logical and persuasive, yet fails to explain why East Asian economies are so rapidly overhauling the advocates of this 'tough talk'. The values expressed in the quotation at the opening of this chapter are all about the enduring relationships supposed to be in headlong retreat!

The logic of cooperative competing, in contrast, uses competition to discover which of several solutions, processes or products are best and then shares these among all players, so that play improves overall and the game itself evolves. The Way of Mechatronics gets better and better, as plays compete with each other, *so as* to enhance the harmony and cooperativeness of society. Under this logic competing is both play and learning. By comparing many rival efforts and ideas you differentiate the very best. By swiftly disseminating best practices you incorporate this vital knowledge, so that all players benefit. We are speaking, then, not simply about *competing* to better *cooperate*, but about *differentiating* ideas the better to *integrate* these into mental maps of even greater complexity. The Infinite Game so formed reads as follows:

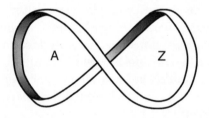

A. We *compete* even harder so as to *differentiate* among rival ideas, practices and processes...

Z. Those which are the best, which we *cooperatively integrate* into industries so that...

Close enduring, intimate, relationships best convey subtle, complex information.

East Asian cultures compete hard while remaining communitarian rather than individualist

In order to test the individualism and communitarianism of a culture, we use our dilemma methodology that forces managers to choose between two values representing this polarity. The three dilemmas were as follows:

Question 1 asked whether the quality of life is improved by gaining 'as much freedom as possible and the maximum opportunity to develop oneself' or by 'continuously taking care of one's fellow man even when it obstructs individual freedom and development'.

The results are dramatically skewed. Ten East Asian cultures are in the top twelve. None are in the bottom twelve.

Question 2 asked which kind of job was found most frequently in your organization: 'the kind in which everybody works together and where you do not get individual credit', or 'where everybody works individually and individual credit is received'.

Those opting for the first communal type of work are set out in Table 5.1, Question 2. Again East Asian nations occupy the first four places and ten of the top fourteen. The USA, UK, Canada and Australia, English speaking individualist cultures, are consistently on or below the 17th place.

Question 3 is perhaps the most interesting since it contrasts working 'as an individual, on one's own . . . pretty much his own boss, taking care of himself . . . he does not expect others to look out for him' with being 'in a group where everybody works together. Everybody has something to say in decisions that are made, and everyone can count on one another.' In this question, ultra-individuality is compared with

Table 5.1 Scores on communitarianism

Question 1: *'Continuously taking care of one's fellow man even when it obstructs freedom'*
% agreeing:

1	Japan	61.32	14	Italy	49.18
2	Hong Kong	60.71	15	Germany	46.73
3	Thailand	60.49	16	Norway	45.36
4	Philippines	60.44	17	Belgium	43.15
5	Brazil	59.49	18	Sweden	40.20
6	China	58.93	19	Australia	38.66
7	France	58.89	20	UK	38.33
8	Taiwan	58.80	21	Spain	37.02
9	Singapore	57.67	22	The Netherlands	35.19
10	Korea	56.07	23	Switzerland	33.70
11	Malaysia	55.48	24	USA	30.49
12	Indonesia	53.31	25	New Zealand	30.23
13	Ireland	49.31	26	Canada	29.80

Table 5.1 Continued

Question 2: *'Everyone works together and where you do not get individual credit'*
% agreeing:

1	*Hong Kong*	66.17	14	*Korea*	39.88
2	*Indonesia*	61.98	15	Germany	37.73
3	*Philippines*	60.44	16	Sweden	34.42
4	*Japan*	56.04	17	Australia	33.88
5	Brazil	50.18	18	Switzerland	33.46
6	France	50.04	19	Ireland	31.16
7	*Singapore*	44.39	20	UK	30.64
8	*Malaysia*	44.12	21	The Netherlands	30.33
9	*China*	43.15	22	USA	27.48
10	New Zealand	42.53	23	Norway	26.80
11	*Taiwan*	42.51	24	Spain	26.18
12	*Thailand*	41.98	25	Belgium	25.97
13	Canada	41.73	26	Italy	23.88

Question 3: *'Everybody has something to say and can count on everyone else'*
% agreeing:

1	*Malaysia*	87.05	14	*China*	71.43
2	*Thailand*	82.72	15	*Taiwan*	71.31
3	*Hong Kong*	82.14	16	New Zealand	71.26
4	France	81.62	17	Switzerland	70.30
5	*Italy*	81.56	18	Germany	70.22
6	*Korea*	81.50	19	UK	67.37
7	Ireland	81.29	20	Australia	66.49
8	*Japan*	80.88	21	Belgium	66.21
9	*Philippines*	79.12	22	The Netherlands	64.14
10	Spain	76.19	23	Sweden	62.31
11	*Indonesia*	75.93	24	Canada	58.23
12	Brazil	73.37	25	USA	56.09
13	*Singapore*	74.83	26	Norway	54.64

Source: The Trompenaars Group, Database. Amsterdam, 1997.

the *reconciliation* of the individual and the group, since 'everybody has something to say' in this group.

Not surprisingly the overall acceptance is very high, ranging from 87.05 in Hong Kong to 54.64 in Norway, yet once again East Asia occupies ten of the top fifteen places, suggesting not simply that they aim to serve the community, but that the individual gets to participate in that community and find fulfillment therein.

'Pure' competition or finite game playing engages the Knowledge Economy with ever-decreasing effectiveness

Nothing is more fundamental to the Finite Game than the competition. As the American football coach put it, 'Winning is not the main thing, it is the *only* thing'. The harder you play the more probable is victory. You cannot be 'too competitive' provided you stay with the rules of the game, eschew dirty tricks and are 'sporting'. Anything not expressly forbidden is permissible, and will surely be done to you if you do not do it first. Nor should you ever ease pressure on your competitor to spare him/her pain or trauma, or let sympathy intrude. To let this happen is to perform less than your very best and that is not permissible. Your customers, your co-workers, your nation and the whole world economy require you to excel. In that determination there should be no compromises.

For it is, of course, in the interests of the larger society that winners take from losers, the resources they are managing with less success. It is wasteful and harmful to leave these in less competent hands a moment longer than necessary. Not only must this reallocation proceed, it must do so *fast*. Economies or organizations who reallocate resources slowly will lose out to those who reallocate them fast and are in better fighting trim, with the best weapons in the best hands. You cannot be kind to competitors without being unkind to customers. It is a tough world in which incompetents should be hustled off the field of play in short order.

Despite our broad acceptance of this view, it is seriously outmoded and will doom Western economies to continued underperformance if we persist in it. It sees no further than the finite-game-with-booty.

Before we describe in detail how cooperative competing is managed and becomes mutually generative, let us consider some 'objections to pure competition'. Unless we can show that pure competitiveness is a poor strategy, there is no motive to look beyond. So what problems arise?

- Failure to appreciate 'complementors'
- A reduction in diversity and complexity
- Trauma affects subsequent competing and learning
- Losers multiply and compete at losing

The problem with 'promiscuous' competitiveness is that the whole world is seen as competing with you when in fact scores, perhaps hundreds, of business activities do not compete with yours so much as *complement* yours.[3] This failure to see complementarities vastly diminishes your strategic intelligence. Suppose you owned a men's shirt-shop at the corner of an intersection in the financial district of a city. Complementors include virtually all the businesses with executive offices in that district which bring men to commute back and forth. Public transport complements you, three tailors' shops, two tie shops, a dress-hire shop, a gourmet restaurant, and a famous department store which has customers streaming past your window. A conference center on the next block complements you. The laundry down the street sends you customers when all stains prove impossible to remove. Finally the jewellery shop next door has a line in cuff links, shirt studs and tie pins which makes customers think of shirt fronts.

But surely *other* shirt shops are your direct competitors? Up to a point, they are. But this is not always so and not entirely true. What if people come *to* this area for men's tailoring and fashions? In this case you are part of the cluster we described in the last chapter. You *might* do better far away from other dress shops or much worse. It is hard to be sure. Tourists especially, head for parts of the town, like Jermyn Street in London, where shirt shops cluster.

Complementors are hugely more numerous as we move into information and information technology. And we are usually wrong in believing that various media compete rather than complement each other. How often have you heard about books and reading being killed by videos, TV and computer games? Yet books steadily multiply, including books *on* these topics. Who can have missed the 'paperless office', yet offices today have more computer memory, more software *and* more paper! Hollywood was in a panic about videos replacing movies and so priced videos sky high. It now turns out that the two complement each other. By lowering the price of videos, audiences buy mementoes of their favorite movies. Today Hollywood makes more than it ever did and over twice as much from videos as from showings in movie houses.

Or consider the personal computer. It is complemented by the latest developments in microprocessors, by modems, printers and other peripherals, by desktop publishing, software, computer games, telephone lines, multichannel optic fiber cables, video-conferencing, numbers of additional users, including banks and shops, electricity supplies, repair and maintenance facilities, e-mail, stored information of all kinds, the Internet and education in computer literacy generally. This list could be extended infinitely.[4]

Indeed, the world of information constantly strives to turn competing facts into complementary information. It generally pays you better to create new markets than fight Finite Games over small segments of the *existing* market. The idea that business is largely about competition and only occasionally about complementarity grows less true by the day. Areas of complementarity are increasing exponentially.

Thinking about competition and Finite Games shrinks our colorful and complex world and reduces its diversity. The problem with out-and-out competitiveness is that we *must* want the same outcome, along the same simple dimension, as must the audience and commentators. One business can only 'beat' another if both seek to maximize the same 'score'. Divine discontent gnaws at executives with a 'lousy' $300,000 a year if known rivals earn marginally more. No amount of money will ever satisfy this relative craving for supremacy. His world is not just mentally impoverished but unappeasably hungry for status that is ever threatened. Even should he surpass all known rivals, he will fear being caught up, being only two not three points ahead, becoming older, having eventually to retire. He is as lonely as *The Hustler* in the pool room.

For it is surely no coincidence that the language of the locker-room rings with manly expletives and severely limited vocabularies, barely intelligible to those not fans of the particular sport. What makes life diverse, esthetic, complex, expansive and subtle is that we do NOT have to play the same game and live at loggerheads with rivals. For while it is true that most products become commodities eventually, with little to take note of save price and profit, most newer products are subtle, imaginative and surprise-full. Finite game players have this curious affinity for the butt-end of capitalism, where the contests are closed and clearly defined. Life on the leading edge of product development sees infinite possibilities, not pinball games for point scorers.

The third objection to Finite Games is the trauma these often occasion. While it is important that people succeed or fail and have that difference register, it is not in anyone's interest to make that failure traumatic. There are two dangerous consequences of trauma. Persons stop trying and stop learning from previous attempts. Arguably we *only* learn from negative feedback. So long as we win we persist in our presumptions. Only when some person or some event says 'no' to us, do we reconsider. It follows that learning requires negation which is *non*-traumatic. It requires that we 'lose' but in ways that give us time and enough confidence to learn. Finite games are too final, too cruel, too wasteful of talent and hope. The sixty girls summoned to the audition for the motion picture, or 'the meat market', and the fifty-nine whose hopes are dashed do not learn from such experiences.

The final problem with the pure competitiveness of Finite Games is that losers multiply until they form an underclass or dependency culture, a permanent drag on the economy, a charge on the public purse, and are objects of detestation by the working majority. Members of this underclass actually compete *at losing*. The more abject they become, the more needy, hopeless and helpless, the more they qualify for assistance. There arises a kind of organized satire upon the dominant society of competitors, a rivalry to exact unearned benefits. The underclass cannot win our games but they can invent their own: drugs, prostitution, loan-sharking, racketeering, forgery, protection. Illegality mocks legality by copying its finite forms. We get the criminals we deserve.[5]

Consider a process in evolutionary biology which is somewhat analogous to the difference between traumatic competing and non-traumatic 'coopetition'. Stags butt heads in ritual conflict over mates. Implicit in this process is the Infinite Game of evolution, since only the stronger stags pass on their genes for the benefit of the whole species. There are a series of staged contests, Finite Games, following which the best available information is passed onto the next generation, in ways which make the results of those games infinite.

But suppose these games involved trauma. Suppose there are ten stags with strengths from 1 to 10. If contests were traumatic, stag number 2 could *wound* stag number 1 in the process of fighting, so that stag number 6 could defeat number 1 in a subsequent bout. Now the whole logic of passing on the genetic secrets of strength is lost. The species could grow weaker instead of stronger. 'Coopetition' requires *non*-traumatic contests, or the cooperative phase of passing on information does not work properly.

It is the same with business. We need ways of competing that do not impede the readiness to learn. We need to impart a sense of adventure and discovery, not of pain and punishment, the gusto of friendly competing but not the grief of destructive conflict. For above both processes of competing and cooperating stands the process of accelerated learning and knowledge acquisition described in Chapter 3. It is knowledge which upgrades all players and all play. Now this simply cannot happen if the combatants are reeling from rancor and resentment, if their judgements are distorted by old rivalries, and if the shame of losing has worn them down. If all we see are finite plays then losing may become irreparable. The person thrown out of work in middle age never recovers. Lives are wasted in defeat. Competing is only *half* the necessary process. Learning and incorporating the reasons why contests were won or lost is the second half. We now turn to examples of this process.

The Japanese model, and economies that deliberately emulate it, contain many examples of cooperative competing

The pathfinder of cooperative competing was undoubtedly Japan. It was the first East Asian economy to lift off and did so spectacularly. Korea has extensive knowledge of Japan. Taiwan and Singapore had been occupied. Despite the sufferings of occupied nations, the displacement of Western powers by Japan gives more than a smidgen of satisfaction. 'The Singapore Experience' lovingly details the surrender of the British force to Japan, in a complete waxwork representation of the ceremony.

But in any case, competing in order to cooperate better in the future had been a feature of Chinese civilization for nearly twenty centuries, and has been adopted by the Japanese. It applied originally not to merchants but to the Imperial Civil Service which was selected by examination based on Confucian and Mencian texts. In Japan, Taiwan, Singapore, Korea and Hong Kong the tradition continues. Hong Kong and Singapore also perpetuated the British tradition of 'picked, clever young men' and increasingly women, often educated abroad to give them international exposure. Singapore even extends competitive selection to politicians. The ruling Peoples' Action Party has their legislators take exams![6]

Yet the Civil Service is more ambitiously conceived of in many East Asian economies. Instead of simply administrating what politicians have decided, civil servants decide *and* administer in the Confucian tradition of sage leadership and mentoring the nation. Nations resemble corporations, hence 'Japan Inc.' and 'Singapore Unlimited', and have civil servants at the helm. While politicians fall from grace, as in the Japanese 'Recruit Scandal' and the murder trials of Korean presidents, continuity is maintained more through the permanent Civil Service than through elected officials.

But apart from the jobs to which people go, the whole system is geared to allow individuals to *compete when young so as to cooperate in the most suitable positions when adult*. The initial competition is *for* better cooperation. Unlike systems in North America and Great Britain where you exit educational institutions with an individual rank order, East Asian examinations are for *entry* into elite institutions. Once included in the group, attempts to distinguish oneself from colleagues cease. You are a *Todai* graduate, your destiny is to add luster to your group. It is the same in parts of Europe. You do not ask the graduate of the *Grand Ecole* how they ranked. It is enough that they were admitted and graduated.

The important issue is less whether competing or cooperating is preferred than whether they are *connected*. John F Kennedy's famous inaugural address, 'Think not what your country can do for you, but what you can do for your country . . .', is inspiring and marks the apex of America's world power. Nixon's reply a few years later was more weary and cynical: 'Think not what your country can do for you, but what you can do for yourself'. Self and community were here disconnected.

The vitality of connecting self to society is that each one of us dies but the society, the school, the corporation, its products and processes continue, as do our genes and the 'genes of knowledge' we are able to pass on. Without the wider community the individual has nothing to live *for*. We fail to transcend ourselves.

One measure of the concern of individuals for their wider society is the rate of savings, much of which ends up as investment in people, plant and equipment. In contrast, debt is an attempt to get the community to do more for you. Table 5.2 shows that the countries of East Asia occupy the first eight places in the savings league, with Taiwan as number 13. The UK is 43rd and the USA 41st. The fashionable explanation that East Asians save because they have no welfare provision is only true in a few instances, and high savings rates persist *after* welfare provision. Japan, for example, with a population less than half that of the USA—125 million versus 264 million—saves 10 percent more overall *and* has better welfare provision with more money reaching its poorest 20 percent.

Table 5.2   Investing in the community: gross domestic savings as a percentage of GDP

1	*Singapore*	48.00	24	Brazil	20.50
2	*China*	40.50	25	Germany	19.60
3	*Indonesia*	38.70	26	Ireland	19.30
4	*Thailand*	32.20	27	Spain	18.70
5	*Malaysia*	35.60	28	France	18.10
6	*Korea*	35.10	29	Hungary	18.00
7	*Hong Kong*	33.00		Italy	18.00
8	*Japan*	32.50	31	Argentina	17.70
9	Russia	31.50	32	Denmark	17.20
10	Switzerland	29.60	33	South Africa	17.17
11	Chile	28.75	34	Iceland	16.90
12	Czech Republic	28.71	35	Australia	16.70
13	*Taiwan*	26.00	36	Mexico	15.80
14	Austria	24.20	37	Greece	15.50
15	Portugal	23.70	38	*Philippines*	15.40
16	The Netherlands	23.30	39	Columbia	15.33
17	Poland	23.00	40	USA	14.90
18	India	22.10	41	Canada	13.30
19	Norway	21.90	42	Finland	13.00
20	Belgium	21.60	43	UK	12.70
21	Israel	21.00	44	Sweden	12.30
	New Zealand	21.00	45	Venezuela	10.80
23	Turkey	20.60			

Source: *World Competitiveness Report*. Lausanne, 1996.

That said, savings are sometimes obligatory as Singapore's Central Provident Fund, which withholds money from employees and employers. The money is kept in the name of the employee who can draw upon it to secure mortgages, including down payments, medical, retirement and other welfare needs. A paradoxical result of this public provision is that 80 percent of housing is privately owned.

There is a second important respect in which competing serves a central cooperative core. East Asian corporations tend to be M-form (multidivisional), while many Western companies have preserved an H-form (holding company) structure. William Ouchi, the Japanese-American academic, has argued that M-forms outperform H-forms even within the USA where both types co-exist.[7]

The H-form is the traditional conglomerate, with a financial holding company which acquires a portfolio of companies in different industries and manages them through an 'internal market' with most investment funds going to those with the highest returns. This is, of course, a Finite Game, with every business unit competing with every other for scarce funds. It is 'pure competitiveness' in which all aim to return higher profits to the parent company and be rewarded in self-interested opportunities to expand. The system operates by a logic of money, but knows not and pays no heed to the various technologies of its units. While there may be cooperative behavior *within* units, there is none *between* them. All sink or swim by the value of their separate performances.

In the great ages of agglomeration in the seventies and eighties, it was sometimes joked that 'Consolidated Everything' would one day own all viable businesses. The H-form misses out on the opportunity to cluster and cross-fertilize technologies as described in Chapter 4. Its leaders are largely accountants and lawyers with scant knowledge of the scattered technologies within the portfolio, but astute about what all those businesses share—money. Typically therefore, the businesses are low in knowledge intensity, something that can be managed at a distance without involvement.

In contrast, the M-form corporation groups all its divisions around *one central core of developing technology* which all cooperate to enhance. The divisions compete in selling the different applications of these technologies, e.g. watches, calculators, organizers. It follows that decentralized competing is the derivative of centralized cooperation and feeds back profits to sustain the process. Examples of M-forms include Sony, Toshiba, Acer, Samsung and Mitsubishi in East Asia, and Hewlett Packard, Intel, TRW, Texas Instruments, Siemens, Glaxo and Thomson among Western companies.

The M-form is able to cluster itself strategically and is high in knowledge intensity to the point of being world-class. To the best of our knowledge, the Economic Development Board of Singapore admits foreign M-forms to the City State exclusively. The leaders of M-forms are typically scientists, engineers and inventors, who share a knowledge of the corporation's core competence. Its logic is less of money than of science and technology. This development of core competence is an Infinite Game.

While the H-form has the virtue of *allocative efficiency*, to use Ronald Dore's term, the M-form operates by *concentrating effectiveness*.[8] It is usually characterized by what Ouchi calls a *clan culture* of enthusiasts for the potentials of their technology, be it micro-electronics, photovoltaics or metal ceramics. In contrast, the H-form has a *market culture*, very flexible and very fast in its optimal allocations, but also superficial, abstract and overly quantitative. It cannot grasp the density of interconnections, cannot see the new emerging.

East Asian economies are also more adept at keeping many contestants in play. If you want the very best plays to be discovered by competition and then shared through cooperation, it is important to have many—not few—contestants coming up with a wide diversity of plays. Michael Porter recently drew attention to the large number of Japanese companies competing for domestic markets.[9] There are an astonishing 14 copier companies, 16 personal computer companies, 15 TV set makers, 9 automobile and truck companies, and 112 machine tool companies—all for a market of 125 million. China has one thousand pharmaceutical companies. Seventy paging companies have been established since Motorola's arrival in 1990.

Why is there so much wider participation in these key industries than in Europe or North America? Akio Morita of Sony gave us a clue when he remarked on an important proviso among Japanese competitors, 'never break another man's rice bowl'.[10] If you have a worthy competitor who is on the ropes, you do not close in for the knockout blow, but give him time to recover. Why? Because eliminating contestants from the game reduces its quality, because the contestant who lost today may win tomorrow, because the *purpose of competing is to improve the cooperation which follows*. Since competing is the *means* to cooperating more effectively, not an end in itself, it makes no sense to exclude players whom you seek to educate and who could educate you.

None of this, however, detracts from the fierceness of the competition or the challenge of staying in there. It merely points to the fact that the system wants you *in* the play not out of it. East Asian exporters are so powerful because they have run the gauntlet of domestic competition. The paradox is that it takes tacit agreement and cooperation to keep so many contestants in the game. Without this, there is the drift to oligopoly and monopoly we see in the West, where competition leads to a position so dominant you can stop competing!

The system in East Asia has several ways of arranging for contestants to survive and go on battling. With high degrees of cross-shareholding, your customers, suppliers, sub-contractors, bankers and partners *also* hold shares in your company and do not wish you to collapse. The collapse of most or all Japanese banks was confidently predicted by Western observers from 1994 onwards, but still they survive, with bad debts that would doom them in the West. But if customers go on buying, bankers lending and suppliers supplying, most companies can be saved, while the pressures to improve from people who buy your product remains very strong.

The amazing resilience of East Asian corporations has other sources. If a corporation gets into trouble, at least in Japan, senior managers cut their own salaries first. The point is not that much money is saved in the process, since top managers are too few. The point is that every employee knows whose salary will be cut *next*, and in the grace period, they come up with many suggested cost savings that can rescue the company.

Another 'shock-absorber' of this kind is the annual bonus system. If nearly 30–40 percent of annual pay is in the form of a bonus, a tribute to good fortune and prosperity, then cuts of that amount can be made in wage costs, *while laying off no one*. The cooperative unit is preserved at all costs.

A good way of finding out whether a culture is really more cooperative or more competitive is to see how it behaves in a crisis when thrown back on basic values. While the Japanese have elaborate contingency plans to save the cooperative group of employees, the first act of a British or American corporation in trouble is to shed labor. You declare manual workers redundant by the thousands, although they are the least responsible for the crisis, while those who order this chopping are the more responsible. You claw back money from distributors, slow up payments to subcontractors and generally play finite competitive games with anyone in a weaker position than yourself. All of which sends a clear message that we are fundamentally in competition with each other, individual versus individual, the action group planning lay-offs against the rest, company lawyers versus those declared redundant. The much vaunted learning networks we speak about are constituted of fair-weather friends, who will turn on each other in the next recession. The dream of an Infinite Game shatters into finite pieces at the first sign of trouble as we look for people to eject from the game to save ourselves.

Two final examples of how corporations use competing to sustain and finance cooperating comes from the shared R&D facilities in Japan, Korea, Singapore and Taiwan in which companies join forces, only to start competing with each other when the research is over and the race-to-market has begun. Corporations in this part of the world seem to be able to switch between alternate cooperative and competitive modes. We also see this in whole-industry briefings of government officials. The Japanese shipping industry, for example, is capable of a coherent presentation to government on The Future of Japanese Shipping and then returning the next week to competitive activity among presenters.

Recent investigations of the culture of Singapore's EDB show similar patterns

One of the major characteristics of the culture of the Economic Development Board of Singapore is what Ed Schein calls 'individualistic groupism'. He observes:

> One of the most striking characteristics of how the EDB works is the seeming comfort of its employees with their challenging individual assignments and their equal comfort and dedication to the work of the team, the EDB and to Singapore, the nation state. One sees here a cultural legacy from Confucian principles of concern for family combined with a Western concept of individual achievement, leading to an assumption that may be paradoxical in the West, but is clearly workable in Singapore.[11]

For EDB members the prime task of the individual leader is to build a team around himself or herself, and the ultimate mission of the team is to help build the Singaporean nation. Every individual is supposed to generate important information *and then share it*. 'Everything in the EDB has to be coordinated.' The weekly newsletter is called Network. The relationship between individualism and the group represents 'a balancing act', according to Schein. The individual must have . . .

> . . . the ability to think clearly, articulate clearly, write clearly and be able to convince others to 'join one's team' in support of a project.[12]

There are other paradoxes related to cooperative competing which the EDB culture also enshrines. Two of note are *cosmopolitan technocracy* and the HAIR evaluation borrowed from Shell International. Cosmopolitan technocracy demands two contrasting abilities—high levels of technological or scientific training by the individual

Box 5.1   The EDB and Infinite Game

Ed Schein sees the EDB's culture as reconciling opposite and paradoxical characteristics. These include Individualistic Groupism, Cosmopolitan Technocracy, Boundaryless Organizations, Non-hierarchic Hierarchy, Partnerships with MNEs (or clients). Below we take some liberties with his formulations. All the inspiration is the EDB's and his. All the errors are ours!

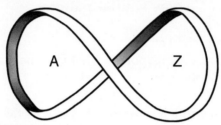

Individual Groupism

A. Each individual takes the responsibility for the assignment of helping...

Z. His group, client, the EDB and the state of Singapore in which...

Cosmopolitan Technocracy

A. The highest levels of scientific and technical training...

Z. Combine with a cosmopolitan capacity to cross borders and recognize...

Boundaryless Organization (modulated openness)

A. The individual confidentiality of every client is maintained, while...

Z. The ramifications for Singapore and world-class business diffuse, yet...

Non-hierarchic Hierarchy

A. The courage to make individually courageous decisions which nonetheless...

Z. Defer to the guidance, the spirit and experience of leaders, served by...

Partnership with MNEs (clients)

A. Respects the autonomy of clients' corporations and their right to make profits...

Z. While harnessing such activities to the long-term benefit of a Singapore which...

Source: *Strategic Pragmatism*, Edgar H. Schein, Cambridge MA: MIT Press, 1996.

protagonist, combined with a cosmopolitan capacity to cross borders, be inter-personally effective and inter-culturally competent. The EDB personnel are largely trained abroad on condition that they return home to develop Singapore. Indeed, their scholarship stipends are repayable immediately unless this promise is kept.

A second form of evaluating personnel for recruitment and promotion has been borrowed from Shell's personnel department. HAIR stands for Helicopter–Analysis, Imagination–Realism. As we might expect, the two pairs are paradoxes or dilemmas. 'Helicopter' means that the recruit must see 'the big picture' of the whole state, as if from a helicopter. Analysis means he must also be able to see things small, at the level of individuals, details, fine distinctions. Imagination involves the power to visualize what has never been, but could come to pass. Realism disciplines imagination, confines it to the attainable, ensures its usefulness. Box 5.1 shows how all these EDB values relate to the Infinite Game.

A team headed by Khoo Seok Lin came up with the diagram illustrated in Figure 5.1, which in turn was influenced by the Systems' Dynamics Group at MIT, especially Peter Senge's *The Fifth Discipline*.[13]

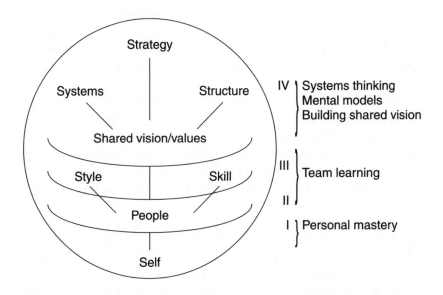

Figure 5.1 EDB model for planned organizational development and learning program.

It is no coincidence that the self is at the bottom of an inclusive circle, that personal mastery includes the 'game' of team learning and the inclusion of as many players as can contribute. Strategy emerges at the top by way of shared mental models and systems thinking inclusive of multiple inputs. You will not be invited to join the EDB unless you have a history of having competed successfully with school fellows, but once there, those abilities are dedicated to the 'learning nation'. Culture, observes Schein, 'is a system of interrelated parts, not isolated elements. It is Singapore's ability to put all the pieces together that helps explain the success of their economic development effort thus far.'

Several outstanding MNEs with East Asian experience now practice 'coopetition'

Cooperative competition is *not* confined to East Asia. Multi-national enterprises have for years put their business units into competition *without* necessarily eliminating those who fail, but rather providing them with opportunities to learn from the best performers. When Apple, for example, discovered that Singapore assemblers were assembling Apple computers with fewer errors and in less time than any other assembly plant in the world, it turned the assembly team into international consultants and had them instruct assembly plants all over the globe to bring them up to Singaporean standards.

MNEs have the great advantage of being able to compare the cost and quality of key operations in up to a dozen different global sites. One of the major reasons for the success of Asian tiger economies is that they have more complex work shifted to them via multinationals' world networks. Motorola, Penang, for example, had fifteen American patents applied for in its Bayan Lepas facility in a successful bid to attract more R&D work to Malaysia.[14]

But it is Motorola's Total Customer Satisfaction Team Competition that perhaps exemplifies best of all how competing and cooperating can be phased over time and fine-tuned. Up to six hundred TCS teams worldwide compete annually for prizes and recognition. All entrants must have a team which came up with a solution that 'totally satisfied' an identified customer. Teams compete in presenting this solution, in showing how much cost it saved, and/or how much added value it delivered to customers and the corporation, and in showing how broadly this solution can be generalized to educate other parts of the company.[15]

Teams compete locally, nationally, regionally and among regions, and eventually the best make their way to the finals at the Paul Galvin Center in Shaumberg, Illinois, Motorola's headquarters. There they present a brief entertainment, symbolizing the culture of their country, e.g. a group of Temple dancers from Thailand, and then present their solution to a packed house in the Galvin Theater. All finalists' solutions end as reports and are shared by all contestants and with all members of the audience. All contain important lessons for the company as a whole. Winners in several categories are chosen amid general celebration and hoopla.

Not only has Motorola's Penang facility been prominent among winners of the TCS competition since 1991, but Malayasia has itself initiated a parallel competition for corporations in that country. Equivalents of TCS contests take place at provincial and national levels within Malaysia, so that the entrants from Penang compete twice in Motorola and Malaysian heats. Prominent members of the Malaysian government officiate, emphasizing the importance of TCS to the nation.

For greatest effectiveness, cooperative competition needs to be phased over time. First the satisfaction of customers in a cooperative phase, then a competition among all satisfying teams, then cooperation again around the solutions they discovered. Competing and cooperating do not clash because they are *wave-forms*: the fiercer the competition, the greater customer satisfaction deliverable by that team and by all teams learning from that success; the amplitude of the first increases the amplitude of the second.

Summary

We saw that East Asia was more communitarian than individualistic, more cooperative than competitive, but that this is *not* sufficient to guarantee accelerated economic growth. Valuing cooperation is no panacea by itself. Many stagnant economies are communitarian. Indeed, communitarianism correlates with late development in Europe—Germany and France were later and more communitarian than Britain and America—and with the late-late development of East Asia.

What typically goes wrong with a cooperative, communitarian ethic is that it opposes ideologically the ethic of competition, and Cooperation versus Competition gets caught up in a Finite Game. We can describe the Finite Game within communist Europe in the following terms:

The competitive ethic of the embryonic bourgeoisie was vilified and oppressed by...

A

The cooperative ethic of an idealized proletariat whose 'temporary' dictatorship lingered and continued to crush...

Z

These nations could not prosper economically because the competitive process by which the best economic solutions are selected had been crushed.

But no sooner did China allow competitiveness a place in the communist pantheon than a 10.0 percent growth rate per annum took off spectacularly—40 percent in Quangdung province. Western economists now faced the rather embarrassing fact that the highest growth rates ever recorded over a decade or more in economic history were occurring in a still communist state!

This new dynamic competitiveness harnessed to cooperation with the purpose of improving it reads as follows:

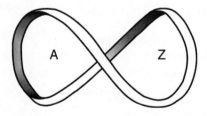

A. No sooner did competitiveness become a way of improving, monitoring and setting higher...

Z. Standards for a cooperative Chinese economic system than growth took off spectacularly...

Even a communist nation with an extremely shadowy concept of private property can grow apace where competitiveness is allowed to inform cooperation.

The second major issue in this chapter was around Traumatic versus Non-traumatic Playing. We saw that Finite Games often traumatized the players, and not just the losers. You could be scarred emotionally and physically by winning if the struggle was ruthless enough. The ensuing Finite Game reads as follows:

Where losing or even winning contestants are mentally or physically scarred in the course of the game...

The less able may rise to win subsequent bouts, and the logic of better plays predominating is lost.

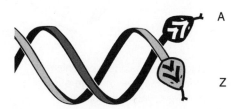

Improved forms of playing and ethically acceptable players can only rise in influence in a non-traumatic Infinite Game, so:

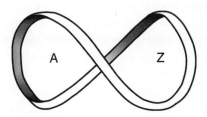

A. Competitions which are friendly and non-traumatic allow winners and losers alike...

Z.... To learn from better plays and share these cooperatively, so as to sponsor...

The third issue was whether we see the world of commerce as consisting of 'complementors' or 'competitors'. To see it as consisting entirely or mostly of competitors dooms us to finite game playing, as follows:

If the business world consists largely of competitors and rivals, then...

We must try to fight, eliminate, subordinate and control other players.

But if we recognize complementors as well as competitors, those who help us create markets as well as those who fight us for existing markets, a whole new (Infinite) game arises:

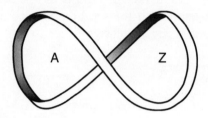

A. Include those businesses which complement and network with our own and we create new markets and...

Z. Grow stronger in our position to compete for and win markets already in existence, giving us the means to...

We also saw that the Achilles Heel of finite competitive games is that these eliminate losers and so there are, in the end, fewer competitors and lazier, more monopolistic protagonists who do not have to compete to stay strong. By acquiring competitors, corporations erode competition itself, like a predator so bloated it loses its agility. The problem looks like this:

The more competitors eliminated from the field of play the more the company that eventually dominates...

Uses monopoly or oligopoly powers to retain its position and stunts its own intelligence...

The Infinite Game in contrast does everything it can to preserve contestants and keep them playing energetically . . .

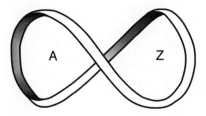

A.... To keep many fierce competitors contributing and the domestic market abuzz with new ideas...

Z.... Tacit cooperation is needed to maintain the numbers playing and not eliminate these, so...

Finally we saw coopetition alive and well in the operation of some outstanding MNEs. Motorola was an example of alternate *phasing* of cooperating followed by competing, followed by cooperating again, and so on indefinitely. The TCS competition operated as follows:

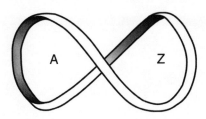

A. Teams vie with each other to compete in satisfactions already delivered to customers...

Z. Thereby informing all teams of the variety and quality of solutions, so that...

Chapter 6

Beyond Reasoning: Cycles of Eternal Return and Continuous Improvement

Great victories scored in the past on behalf of workers or on behalf of the peoples of Singapore over old enemies, are no longer of any value now, other than the experience we gained from them. For we face new challenges. Change is the very essence of life. The moment we cease to change, to be able to adapt, to adjust, to respond effectively to new situations, then we have begun to die. I should be loathe to believe that the National Trades Union Council is one of those . . .

Lee Kuan Yew (1967) Speech to the NUTC.

Almost nothing is as precious to the Western Enlightenment as our reasoning powers. We either deduce events correctly from workable theories or retreat to the Dark Ages. Moreover, the hallmark of Economic Man is that he 'reckons the consequences' of choices, so much to feed his family, so much to save, so much to invest in producing more. Unless he finely calculates the utility of alternatives, most of his economic assumptions fail.[1]

Reason is typically contrasted with instinct, imagination, faith and desire—all of them intellectually untrustworthy. We are exhorted to look to our reason and eschew emotion. David Hume warned us that reason can be a slave of the passions. We may have secret, illicit attractions to the theory we propose, arrange for its confirmation and evade its disconfirmation. Over the centuries superstitions, terror and unfalsfiable beliefs have been gradually forced to give ground to reason. Now is not the time to forgo a faith in reason. The battles have been hard won.

So why is it that we appear to have entered what Charles Handy

calls *The Age of Unreason?*[2] The principal villain of Peters and
Waterman's *In Search of Excellence* was 'The Rational Model'.[3] Just
when everyone appears to have agreed that accelerated learning is
what all leading corporations must do to survive, are we supposed to
sacrifice our reason? It strains credulity. Or is it, perhaps, that a
different reasoning process is now called for? Handy entitled his later
book *The Age of Paradox.*[4] Perhaps reason is less wrong than
incomplete. We need not discard it but qualify and enlarge it.

The argument in this chapter is as follows:

- Reason in the context of the Enlightenment is based on the value
  of inner-direction in which logical thinking or scientific
  calculation *precedes* taking action.
- East Asia is more attuned to outer-direction wherein a
  precipitating act requires reflection and response which *follow*
  that act.
- Where these two processes combine they constitute continuous
  improvement through circular reasoning, which is a logic of
  discovery. Hence . . .
- Thinking in circles, not lines, is a major competitive advantage at
  which tiger economies excel.

Reason in the context of the Enlightenment is based on the value of inner-direction

Enlightenment Reason has always rested on premises. The advance of
Napoleonic armies into the Spanish peninsula rested on the premise
that it was the right of France to advance revolution by the force of
arms, a claim that led Goya to protest that 'The dream of reason brings
forth monsters'.

But whether we agree or disagree with the various premises which
have historically been advanced by reasoned strategies, there is one
premise common to them all which bears examination. *Individuals'
goals and intentions should be deliberately planned, calculated and
implemented, so that consequences logically follow.*

We call this *inner-direction.* 'I think therefore I am', said Rene
Descartes. The value common to all celebrations of Reason is that the
human actor should be 'in the driver's seat', to quote the Avis
advertisement—that our conscious purposes should be fulfilled. We

first cogitate, then we act. If our reasons are sound we should get what we want.

At the same time we admit that this is an ideal case. Science is in practice messy and rationally 'bounded' by what we know at the time. Accidents abound. Sheer luck intervenes. Flashes of insight occur to naked philosophers in the bathtub. Many brilliant executives 'fly by the seat of their pants'. Yet whenever serendipity gives rise to a discovery, it must still stand the test of reason. The hypothetico-deductive method states that 'if this is true, this should be the consequence'. In the end it all comes down to prediction and control. All things stumbled over must be subjected to this test or the claim to knowledge fails.

The American philosopher Abraham Kaplan contrasted the Logic of Discovery with the Reconstructed Knowledge.[5] These are not the same. We know very little about how we actually learn and discover. Instead we have reconstructed idealized logics which we then confuse with real learning, substituting one part for the whole. It is hardly surprising if we encounter this lost part of the process of discovery in East Asia. As George Renwick says of the Chinese, they are concerned with 'the further pole of the human', that is furthest from us. But if the economies of East Asia are not as beholden to formal reason and inner-directed operations, what do they prefer?

East Asia is more attuned to outer-direction

Table 6.1 reveals the 'swept up in global change' attitudes of managers in most East Asian cultures. Their destinies are often decided elsewhere and they are less reluctant to admit this than are Western managers, raised to be 'Masters of their Fate, Captains of their Soul'. Managers in six out of nine East Asian business cultures are readier to admit 'it is not always wise to plan too far ahead . . .' Seven out of nine of these cultures are more inclined to thank their luck for 'being in the right place at the right time', rather than their own abilities, while eight out of nine are readier to confess that they do not feel in control.

The exceptions to this rule are also instructive. The Philippines has a largely American educational system and Korea has been caught up in Cold War rhetoric, with powerful military governments, massive *chaebols* and a fateful decision to throw in its lot with the USA against communists to the North. South Korea saved itself by armed resistance and the experience has left it with iron in its soul, a stand-out against the Red tide.

Outer-direction is not, of course, a recipe for success. No single polarity of value is better than its opposite, or sufficient in itself. Outer-directed cultures which have *not* shown aptitude for economic growth include Saudi Arabia, Venezuela, Nepal, Bulgaria and Russia.

Table 6.1   East Asia as more outer-directed than inner-directed

Question 1:
Accepts: 'It is not always wise to plan too far ahead because many things turn out to be a matter of good or bad fortune anyhow.'
Rejects: 'When I make plans, I am almost certain I can make them work.'

Japan	55.97	*Korea*	23.70
Hong Kong	49.21	*Thailand*	23.46
Malaysia	47.72	Ireland	21.68
China	43.77	Italy	20.79
Singapore	42.43	Spain	20.52
Philippines	32.22	The Netherlands	17.39
Indonesia	31.44	UK	16.73
Belgium	27.49	New Zealand	16.28
Taiwan	27.35	Switzerland	15.00
Sweden	27.01	Norway	13.05
Germany	26.10	Australia	10.84
Brazil	25.57	USA	7.39
France	24.90	Canada	5.19

Question 2:
Accepts: 'Getting the right job depends mainly upon being in the right place at the right time.'
Rejects: 'That people do the right things depends upon ability. Luck has little or nothing to do with it.'

Malaysia	76.02	*Philippines*	33.33
Japan	70.98	Ireland	32.71
Indonesia	59.92	New Zealand	29.89
China	46.53	UK	28.90
Singapore	45.98	*Thailand*	28.40
Taiwan	45.71	Sweden	28.35
Switzerland	44.28	Canada	24.48
Belgium	40.43	France	24.42
Hong Kong	39.29	Australia	24.22
Germany	37.31	The Netherlands	24.13
Norway	36.78	*Korea*	23.70
Brazil	33.93	Spain	20.00
Italy	33.71	USA	18.57

Question 3:
Accepts: 'Sometimes I feel I do not have enough control over the direction my life is taking.'
Rejects: 'What happens to me is my own doing.'

China	60.89	The Netherlands	25.11
Singapore	42.66	France	23.89
Japan	36.61	Brazil	23.75
Hong Kong	33.97	Ireland	23.08
Germany	33.47	UK	22.47
Korea	31.79	Spain	21.83
Indonesia	29.58	Switzerland	20.83
Taiwan	29.40	Canada	19.06
Malaysia	29.02	Australia	18.40
Sweden	28.18	USA	17.29
Belgium	28.12	Norway	14.46
Italy	27.97	New Zealand	13.79
Thailand	27.16	Philippines	11.76

Source: The Trompenaars Group, Database. Amsterdam, 1997.

What works is seizing upon inner-directed technologies originating in the West and refining these for Asian and Western markets via outer-directed customer orientation, which combine the best of East *and* West.

Nor have East Asian economies stopped there. They are heavily investing in Research and Development, having no intention of relying upon the West to innovate for a moment longer than necessary. They intend to be inner-directed *too*, to combine this with outer-directed processes at which they excel.

It is very hard for North Americans, Britons and other inner-directed cultures to see outer-directed people as anything other than losers. Almost forty years of research by J. B. Rotter has confirmed as much.[6] So long as the culture consists of a set of Finite Games, the winners will congratulate themselves, while losers will cast around for excuses. It follows that 'the bad workman blames his tools', his luck, his circumstances, his social disadvantage, the referee of the game, everyone and everything except himself. In contrast, winners glow with inner satisfaction. They are self-made men. In the case of Horatio Alger, he was an orphan so he did not have to thank even his parents for his success, only himself!

But the situation in outer-directed cultures is quite different. Those who talk most are children, subordinates and women. The traditional *kanji* (Chinese letters) for woman is 'noise'. People who talk too much, talk too directly, assert themselves and make their requirements known with insistent emphasis are considered immature, child-like, ill-mannered, insensitive and/or coarse. Losers in such a society are those who clamour to get their way, who are desperate and too maladroit to control the expression of their wants and so create disharmony everywhere. It is the willingness to connect your aims to other people's aims, to react to their suggestions in an outer-directed mode, which creates harmony and it is the joining of game to game which creates Infinite Games. Mature behavior in outer-directed cultures connects all personal agendas by attaching our own to others.

The outer-directedness of most of East Asia also helps to explain their late-late economic development. To pioneer capitalist industry requires inner-direction. To create new industries, first in textiles then in steel, chemicals, electronics and biotechnology, takes inner-direction. But recognizing which of these vehicles and trends your nation should attach itself to, and jumping smartly on the best of these bandwagons, which most thoroughly educate your own people, takes outer-directedness.

Moreover, the world of business requires more outer-directedness as industries and services complexify. The day is gone when you could charge ahead in a self-chosen direction like the Titanic. As the environment fills up with players, contestants and complementors, every move becomes a reaction to every other move. The number of initiatives within you shrinks in contrast to the number of initiatives outside you. Those who relate the best and attach themselves most harmoniously to clusters and networks, gain competitive advantage. The huge prototype industries of the industrial revolution which only exist to expand their original purposes across America's vast domestic market, now resemble beached whales.

None of this should be taken to mean that inner-directed, reasoned strategies are no longer crucial. They are. It simply means that these are not *enough*. The ratio of planned action to improvized reaction has shifted in the latter's favor. Curiously the Western democracies are aware of this in their political thinking but less in their business thinking. The follies of government planning and the unintended consequences of the initiatives by state bureaucrats fill books and broadsheets with contemptuous comments. Yet this rarely extends to industrial giants, often larger than the GNP of nations, who carve their way through economic oceans with the same single-minded, one-eyed momentum. So long as power is private we believe

Table 6.2   Dominant cultural characteristics of left and right brain functioning

Left mode USA, Northwest Europe	Right mode Japan, East Asia
Rational, sequential, propositional (if–then)	Relational, connective, appositional (contrast–unify)
Analytic, specific, reductive into parts	Holistic, diffuse, syntheses into wholes
Discontinuous, finite episodes	Continuous, infinite processes
Logical, categorical	Intuitive, esthetic
Verbal, linear time, inner-directed	Non-verbal, circular time, outer-directed

Source: M. Yoshikawa (1989) *Communicating with the Japanese, A Reader.* Institute for Intercultural Communication; C. Hampden-Turner (1981) *Maps of the Mind.* New York: Macmillan, pp. 86–89.

it benign. But the excesses of inner-direction are the same whoever attempts it.

That Japanese culture is more outer-directed than inner-directed has been attributed, by Muneo Yoshikawa, to the greater use of the right-brain hemisphere. Table 6.2 contrasts the two styles using the categories of Yoshikawa, and also Robert E Ornstein, R W Sperry, Michael S Gazzaniga and J E Bogen.

It should be obvious that thinking in terms of specific, rational propositions, projected forward in time, with the purpose of achieving finite objectives is an *inner*-directed mode. In contrast, thinking in terms of apposite approaches and time coordinations that will connect and relate you to others in a continuous, infinite process of esthetic wholeness is an *outer*-directed mode. You have to process many simultaneous inputs and adjust yourself to the surrounding force field.

Where the two processes combine these constitute a continuous improvement through circular reasoning

Outer-direction is *not*, of course, sufficient in itself and may not result in faster economic growth. Not all outer-directed economies are successful, as we can see in Table 6.1. Outer-direction becomes a powerful adjunct to learning only when it *accepts* inner-directed Western initiatives, and 'completes the circle' of reasoning by improving rapidly on those initiatives. In other words, inner- and outer-direction are complementary. To have a genuine conversation with nature you need to listen as well as talk, yield as well as dominate, exercise power not just *over* people but *through* them. In short, the reconciliation of inner- and outer-direction allows you not just to think before you act but to reflect after you act and use that reflection to improve your thought before you act again.

The Infinite Game reads as follows:

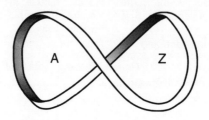

A. Your inner-directed convictions will be vindicated and will be realized, provided...

Z. Your outer-directed adjustments allow you to revise your aims and to renew...

Improvement comes from inside *and* outside. The loops above are not conventional Western rationalism but nor are they unreasonable or irrational. They make very good sense as a logic of discovery, as opposed to the always doubtful claim of being God's agent-on-earth and discharging His will, or seeing science as unilateral prediction and control of a Cosmic Clock.

The double loop above allows emotion to take its place beside calculative reason. This is because the vindication or frustration of our aims will bring us joy and woe respectively. We need *emotional intelligence* to continue, a realization that has come to Americans only recently.[7] Social learning both wrenches and develops emotional muscles. The traditional case against emotion emphasizes the bias which enters our perception when we *want* something to be true which is not. Emotion can impede inner-directed experimentation, so total detachment is advocated. But there is no avoiding our emotions when we learn after the event and reflect on our mistakes before trying again.

Some very famous Western axioms are stood on their head when we examine these closely and combine them with error-correcting logic. Take, for example, Adam Smith's famous dictum that if we all pursue inner-directed self-interest this will be transformed into public benefit without our intending it. Hence if the butcher or baker vies with competitors to supply customers, these inner-directed, Finite

Games take care of customers by indirection. It is, said Smith, as if an Invisible Hand had intervened to serve public ends.[8]

But this entire argument rests on the supposition that we are inner-directed by motives of acquisitiveness as opposed to outer-directed by the pleasures of serving customers' needs and wants. It makes as much sense to say that private self-interest is the indirect result of serving customers well, as to claim that serving customers well is the indirect result of private self-interest. The two propositions join in the form of the Tao, or Infinite Game, so:

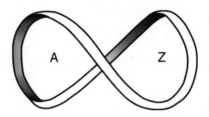

A. The outer-directed pleasure of serving customers better and better contributes to...	Z. The inner-directed pleasure of increasing personal wealth and using this to serve...

In the case above, the increase in personal wealth is more easily sated and gorged than is pleasure in serving customers better and better, which is the more elusive goal. No wonder that the chief value of Japanese economic actors is persistence, while generations of British entrepreneurs dropped out to become gentlemen and would-be aristocrats. Outer-directed cultures create wealth so long as any external needs remain unsatisfied. In contrast, Western producers typically stop at some stage to spend it all or give it away, as did the great American philanthropists.

Thinking in circles, not lines, is a major competitive advantage at which tiger economies excel

In what remains of this chapter we will cite advantages accruing to circular thinking with outer-direction as a way of completing processes often begun in the West but finished and refined in East Asia. We look at:

- concepts of *kaizen* and rapid development;
- skills in harnessing external forces;
- total design;
- deviance amplifying feedback;
- designed and emergent strategies;
- the bottom-up flotation of ideas;
- the crisis of authority;
- middle up–down management;
- knowledge-generating top management;
- the Japanese success of W. Edwards Deming;
- the escape from adversarialism;
- how Singapore responds to MNEs.

All these help 'complete the circle' of accelerated learning.

Concepts of kaizen and rapid development

Kaizen means refinement, getting the product just right for the market place. If inner-directed cultures are better at the first half of product development, at science development and product creation, outer-directed cultures tend to be better at the second half, developing and refining those products and getting these to satisfied customers at the lowest possible cost. Because the West tends to think of 'pure knowledge' which is then 'applied' we tend to celebrate hypotheses and deduction and to stigmatize the pragmatics of getting it right for people through the rapid correction of errors.

Getting it right the first time tends to be more time consuming than making errors and correcting them fast. No wonder, then, that East Asians are fast in their time to market (see Box 6.1). Hong Kong, Taiwan, Japan, Singapore all outstrip the USA, while Malaysia, Thailand and Korea are faster than most of Western Europe.

The truly appalling mistake made by the USA was to license hundreds of its products to Japan, Korea and Taiwan, so that its own inner-directed expertise could be leveraged by East Asian outer-direction. Again and again the East Asians got to market first with products Americans had invented! Robert B Reich commented:

Americans invented the solid-state transistor in 1947. Then in 1953, Western Electric licensed the technology to Sony for $25,000—the rest is history. A few years later RCA licensed several Japanese companies to make color televisions—that was the beginning of the end of color-television production in the USA.[9]

Americans invented video-recorders but the Victor Company of Japan spent an estimated $4 billion on investment in producing the consumer product. Refinement is neither cheap nor easy. The point is, however, that *combining* what Americans invent with what East Asians refine may be unbeatable.

Skills of harnessing external forces

Outer-directed refinement is very much of East Asian culture. Their heroes are not the inner-directed Superman, 'faster than a speeding bullet . . .' etc., but the outer-directed Monkey King, the prankster, the agile utilizer of *other people's* energies and contributions. The Monkey King is everywhere in East Asia, a lothario in Thailand, a martial arts expert in Japanese soaps. Children's books illustrate how this imp of fun is eventually socialized. Leaping into the hands of Buddha, his head is bound by a band which will tighten whenever his tricks hurt other people. But this in no way lessens his agility or outer-directed antics. He is now a trickster for virtue and compassion, side-stepping enemies and allowing them to blunder out of harm's way.

Nearly all Asian martial arts operate in a similar mode, variations of 'the gentle way' of using the momentum of your opponents so that your strengths combine with theirs to propel them in directions of your choosing, inner-direction *by way of* outer-direction. Shintoism may be one origin of this tendency, wherein the amoral force of wind, storm and stream are captured and used by man's inventiveness.

Total design

There is a major difference in what Westerners conceive of as design and East Asian design, which is illumined by both inner- and outer-direction. Too often in Western companies designers are the sole originators, gods on Mount Olympus, sending their gifts some distance down the line to manufacturing, distribution, sales, etc. Designers may even be isolated from lesser mortals in leafy environments which help develop their muse.[10] In this way design or invention *directs* everyone else, originating ideas but not taking them on board.

East Asian corporations put designers in the very heart of the production process. You design not just *for* better products, but for improved processes, cheaper assembly, fewer defects, easier distribution and easier fault detection. Indeed, computers can be designed to help assemblers assemble them, by reading out what is wrong and what still needs adding. Outer-directed design *helps every department* save costs and improve quality. The solution of thousands of problems can be designed into the larger process of production and distribution. Everyone brings their problems to design, which loops around and around in endless iterations, not causing problems 'down the line' but circling and solving.

Deviance amplifying feedback

Currently all or most corporations, East and West, speak much of the value of feedback. By now the complete loop or circle with improvement as its aim is common parlance. But there remains one subtle difference noted by Magorah Maruyama, the Japanese-American cybernetician. Americans use feedback to *reduce* deviance from their original sovereign intentions. They remain inner-directed like guided missiles homing in on a chosen target. The Japanese may use feedback to *amplify* deviances towards the sovereign intentions of their customers. They assume that customers will want something or some*things* different from what the company originally intended to supply, and that such differences must be discovered and catered for. Thus American learning will tend to converge with the path originally chosen by the inner-directed executives while Japanese learning will diverge along paths leading to what various customers now want.[11]

There may be learning loops in each culture, but while one narrows, the other broadens; while one regards any deviance as 'error', the other regards it as a legitimate diversity of demand.

Designed and emergent strategies

In effect, then, outer-directed strategies are 'evolutionary', sending into the market environment hundreds of small differences and allowing those which 'fit' to survive, while inner-directed strategies are more 'biblical', one all-knowing creator. This is very similar to Henry Mintzburg's distinction between business strategies which are designed 'on high' by top management and cascaded down for middle managers to implement. He calls these *designed* strategy. In contrast are strategies which *emerge* at the grass roots from direct interaction with customers who want something different. Although these ingenious responses are often ignored by top management and not dignified by the word 'strategy', they are strategic nonetheless and whole organizations may change this way.

Richard Pascale tells an amusing story about how Honda's campaign for motor-scooters in the USA was written up by the Boston Consulting Group as a triumph of designed strategy, but when Pascale interviewed retired Honda executives who had actually been there, totally the opposite picture emerged. The designed strategy had been abandoned, an emergent one substituted at the last minute.

The original plan was to launch a powerful 300cc bike, but America's much larger, much rougher terrain caused it to break down and leak oil. An emergency meeting was called in Los Angeles. The launch was only months away. The disconsolate Japanese executives arrived at their meeting on 50cc Supercubs—as these were later called—a low-powered scooter which they had no plans to sell in the macho American market of Hell's Angels.

During a break in the meeting they saw a crowd of Angelinos around their parked scooters including a Sears buyer, who offered to sell it through his sporting goods department. The entire strategy changed from that moment on. They launched different bikes in different outlets, to different socio-economic groups, for different purposes. It was an emergent strategy, directed from outside by its customer environment.[12] Whole companies can be run from their peripheries; a fascinating example from Taiwan is Acer (see Box 6.1).

The bottom-up flotation of ideas

This leads us straight to another phenomenon in the 'tiger economies'—their quite extraordinary success in moving ideas, suggestions and improvements up the organization from the grass roots. So pronounced is this tendency that Mitsubishi has claimed 60,000 implemented suggestions a year from its own Japanese workforces. This unusual capacity stems from outer-directed preferences. It is high status for those in authority to listen, to receive, to acknowledge, to approve, to encourage. It is fitting for those who are younger and subordinate to speak up and give wise authorities ideas to judge and to appreciate.

It is precisely the opposite in much of the West. The word 'authority' comes from 'author'. Authorities are supposed to be the authors and originators of ideas and rules, which subordinates follow and obey.

Box 6.1   Outer-directed Acer is Owned by its Peripheries

Acer, the Taiwanese personal computer company, is probably that country's most famous branded product. Its 50% growth in 1995 and 1996 has brought it to world attention. The founder, Stan Shih, calls himself 'Stan' to accommodate Western conventions, for Acer is outer-directed towards the ways customers think and act. Acer puts stress on its components, largely microprocessors, which are then assembled and sold in different countries. Likening himself to a franchisee, he supplies 'the brains' (literally) and nationally based, highly autonomous companies combine quality ingredients according to local demand.

Since microprocessors are light but the context in which they are placed is heavier, Acer distributes lightweight but highly intelligent components at great speed around the world, while letting the locality control the finished product. But local control goes further than even this. He seeks a company *owned by local investors* and quoted on national stock markets. Nineteen public companies are in prospect. He has completely junked the idea of a 'controlling share' in his own company. Such control as he does exercise will be strictly through the skill and quality of the components he supplies. If local management does not want his components, because they are no longer the best, the latest and the least expensive, he will discover this, hopefully in time to reverse the trend. In short, this is a company controlled by *skill not power*, by distributed brains not muscle. Acer was in trouble in the early 1990s when a CEO hired from IBM tried to control-from-the-center in American style. Shih offered his own resignation—modest to the end—but the network was having none of it. The CEO and his team left and Shih persevered in his radically decentralizing strategy.

He is famously tolerant of errors, so long as these are notrepeated. He calls them 'tuition payments'. All subordinates interview and report upon prospective superiors being hired or promoted. He offers up to 15 percent of shares in national companies to employees. No foreign institution may own more than 7.5 percent. He has no wish to *be* controlled either!

Source: 'Twenty-one Ways to Play Acer', *Fortune*, October 30, 1995.

The leader is inner-directed. The follower is outer-directed. But if you want the organization flooded with new ideas, you must reverse this. You must teach authorities to *listen* and subordinates to *participate*. This is essential to the knowledge-generating, knowledge-processing organization.

Outer-directed leadership is not confined to Japan. We visited American-owned Malaysian plants in Penang, managed by largely Chinese leaders. We found the plant walls plastered with 'I recommend' stickers, bearing the names of workers who had made implemented suggestions for improvements in their parts of the factory. These extended far up the plant walls. Framed photographs of prize-winning idea creators and winning teams smiled down at us from corridors and conference room walls.

It was the birthday of Madame Ko, the CEO. The flowers began thirty feet from her office door and we had to fight our way through. That evening she and her senior managers served the food in the dining hall, a gesture of modesty and thanks for all those flowers and ideas.

No crisis of authority

We hear much of the 'crisis of authority' in the West. Leaders are increasingly despised, suspected, rejected. It could be called the 'crisis of inner-directed authority'. The world is becoming simply too complicated and contradictory for 'conviction politicians' to sound off. And the more they talk the less they listen. Being briefed by pollsters and spin-doctors only makes them worse. They now aim their rhetoric like rifles at known opinions, a technique which leaves the rest of us cynical.

Authority in some tiger economies and parts of East Asia is in less trouble because it is the recipient of information and data from beneath. It is not that the Economic Development Board in Singapore is omniscient, it is that MNEs inform it thoroughly and carefully. The Ministry of International Trade and Industry also listens carefully and is very well briefed by industry associations in Japan. Table 6.3 shows that the credibility and public trust in corporations remains very high in most tiger economies. The exception is inner-directed Korea and its giant *chaebol*, which are widely distrusted, as is the political–commercial nepotism in Indonesia. In general, however, Singapore and China have the highest trust of all, with corporations in Malaysia, Hong Kong, the Philippines, Japan, Taiwan and Thailand

Table 6.3 Credibility and public trust for domestically situated corporations survey, rated 0–10

1	*Singapore*	8.04	24	Germany	6.24
2	*China*	8.00	25	*Thailand*	6.16
3	Chile	7.62	26	Belgium	6.15
4	*Malaysia*	7.52	27	Turkey	6.14
5	Finland	7.48	28	Brazil	6.14
6	*Hong Kong*	7.43	29	South Africa	6.07
7	Colombia	7.38	30	Australia	6.07
8	Switzerland	7.27	31	USA	5.77
9	Denmark	7.26	32	France	5.63
10	Norway	7.19	33	Portugal	5.58
11	*Philippines*	7.18	34	Italy	5.56
12	The Netherlands	7.14	35	Argentina	5.47
13	Ireland	6.96	36	Spain	5.41
14	Sweden	6.96	37	Czech Republic	5.37
15	New Zealand	6.87	38	Greece	5.32
16	Iceland	6.82	39	Mexico	5.32
17	India	6.76	40	UK	5.30
18	Canada	6.75	41	*Indonesia*	5.07
19	*Japan*	6.67	42	Poland	4.71
20	Luxembourg	6.64	43	Hungary	4.62
21	Austria	6.61	44	*Korea*	4.60
22	*Taiwan*	6.44	45	Venezuela	4.50
23	Israel	6.38	46	Russia	2.90

Source: *The World Competitiveness Yearbook*. Lausanne: IMD, 1996.

all more trusted than corporations in America, the UK or France. (Malaysia has an annual contest for 'the most caring corporation', nominations from the community only.)

Outer-directed cultures may be developing an *authority based on knowledge*. How else can we explain that cultures we consider 'hierarchical' manage knowledge so effectively? Leaders are not cut off from the real world *provided* they heed upward influences from subordinates. A hierarchy based in knowledge acquisition is shown in Figure 6.1.

But this only works well if the data supplied by workers and customer contact staff help form the generalizations and categories supervisors generate, which in turn provide the information in which middle managers deal, who then inform top managers, the guardians of knowledge. Every successive level *encompasses* the one below in a larger integration, hence the Chinese puzzle box design. Without strong *outer*-direction, or in this case direction from beneath, these knowledge pyramids cannot function. All knowledge *must* be wide

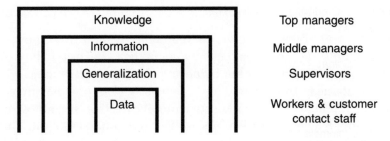

Knowledge	Top managers
Information	Middle managers
Generalization	Supervisors
Data	Workers & customer contact staff

Figure 6.1

open to data qualifying it and challenging it, especially where this originates with customers and the (usually) low level staff who contact them.

Middle up–down management

Support for the idea that upward flowing, emergent plans and strategies are commoner in East Asia, comes from two Japanese professors, Ikugiro Nonaka and Hirotaka Takeuchi, who explain how Japanese corporations use 'middle up–down' management.[13] Long range plans for the corporation are initiated by middle-managers, executives fifteen to twenty years from retirement. Why? Because these are the people who will carry through the plans and succeed or fail by their appropriateness. The role of top management is entirely outer-directed. They receive, critique and eventually endorse these plans once they are satisfied. The plans are made *out* of the data supplied by the junior staff.

The corporation proceeds by a whole management echelon laying the rest of their lives on the line for policies they themselves devised. It is not pure outer-directedness, but a judicious mixture, with top managers as sounding boards for a committed middle management. If we compare this to the chopping and changing Anglo-American management with 'tough bosses' appointed to lay off thousands, we see that our penchant for the inner-directedness of leaders may make everyone below them chronically insecure and uncommitted. People leaving in droves scatters knowledge and information to the winds.

Knowledge creating top management

Nonaka and Takeuchi give us valuable insight into how top managments in Japan manage by *indirection*, by not telling subordinates what they want but by posing riddles and dilemmas which will elicit ideas from below. By using *metaphors* of what they are seeking, top managers can indicate without directing, suggest without specifying, trigger a creative process without commanding it. This is no trick. It is not that senior managers know what they want or know how to create it and are manipulating consent. Top managers know what *values* they want the creation to incorporate and from this they create analogies and metaphors. The creation of the product which will deliver such values remains to be devised.

The metaphors included 'automobile evolution', moving 'beyond Detroit', creating a car 'man-maximum, machine-minimum'. Other analogies were 'The Sphere' and 'The Tall Boy'. All these triggering devices were tossed into *tama dashi kai*, or brainstorming camps. The eventual result was a roomy, space-saving, easy to park, almost spherical automobile, the Honda City.[14]

Another breakthrough came from studying and videoing the hands of master bakers in the Osaka International Hotel, from which was derived the metaphor 'twist and squeeze'. The tacit knowledge of workers was thus incorporated into the dough-kneading machine for Matsushita's home bakery.[15]

Some metaphors enter the brainstorming teams by sheer accident. Cannon Copier were struggling with the problems of maintenance for home copying machines, when beer they had ordered was delivered. They discovered they were holding an analog of the answer in their hands, in the aluminum cans. If the machines had disposable drums, every time they malfunctioned the drum could be exchanged for a new one. The drums could be made of light, cheap aluminum. Spares could be kept at home like light bulbs.[16]

The Japanese process of *ringi* (circling ideas and proposals) typically starts with junior staff and spirals upwards through their seniors with the latter putting their seal of approval on the idea, or not, in which case their reservations are considered again. The role of seniors is to receive and juniors to initiate.

The Japanese success of W Edwards Deming

The father of continuous improvement was, as we might expect, an

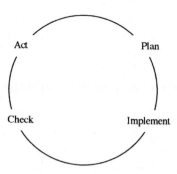

Figure 6.2 Deming's circle of quality.

American, W Edwards Deming. Unable to interest American industry in his ideas, he began consulting to Japanese industry in the late 1950s and stayed on and off for twenty-five years. The Japanese give an annual Deming Prize in his honor to the most improved corporation. The circle of quality which he drew is shown in Figure 6.2.[17]

We can see from this circle why the Japanese found it culturally compatible and most American corporations came round only after continuous improvement was being used against them by the Asian 'tigers'.

In this schema *action precedes planning*. In other words, you—or your competitor—act first and this leads you to plan, implement and check. The circle exemplified action-learning, not the hypothesis and deduction of traditional inner-directed science.

It could be objected that the circle does not really start with action, at top left, but simply revolves infinitely. But this would also represent an outer-directed dynamic, a vortex into which we must step and be whirled around. For many reasons businesses must *act*, usually long before the information is all in. Whoever is first with a product or service, however imperfect, makes the market and has customers with whom to speak. If you improve fast enough, the first product will also be the best, once others enter the market. It may anyway be faster to make mistakes and correct these than work out a perfect theoretical formulation. Businesses use error-correcting or after-the-fact planning *more* than they use scientific reasoning.

In any event *social* learning or learning-from-customers is nearly all trial and error. People want what they want and the reasons may not be found in formal logics. Even if you *could* find formal reasons, the chances are they would change their minds by the time you have finished formulating! It has been noted, for example, that the Japanese do less market research with formal hypotheses but have more conversations with customers. Customer service is outer-directed by definition, as are most sales staff in our research, regardless of national cultures. You offer something and *then* you learn.

The escape from adversarialism

Inner-directed cultures which take seriously the process of formal reasoning tend to get stuck in Finite Games and are unable to escape from adversarial relationships. This is because reason is usually based on the premise of self-interest and advancing your own prosperity, and so two 'lines of reasoning', based on the desire to win and for your contestant to lose, end in a clash of wills and interests.

Paul Watzlawick, the communications psychologist, created a famous analogy of the logical entrapment so common in Western cultures. He called this 'Two Sailors Trying to Steady a Boat Steady to Begin With' (Figure 6.3).[18]

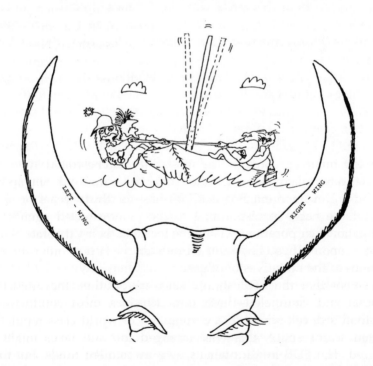

Figure 6.3 'Two Sailors Trying to Steady a Boat Steady to Begin With' (P. Watzlawick).

Note that no amount of formal reasoning or pristine logic can get either of these parties out of their trap. The right-wingers say to themselves, we must lean out to the right or the ship of state will capsize to the left. Were we to compromise and move closer to the mast, and were they to continue leaning left, catastrophe would follow. Of course, the left-wingers have the mirror image of this argument. If they do not retain their absurd posture, with their behinds almost in the water, the ship of state will capsize to the right.

The problem of inner-directed adversarialism is *insoluble by formal reasoning*. Both parties are logically correct. Any concession they made might well be exploited and then they would lose. You simply cannot escape from this impasse without an *outer-directed logic* applying to both parties, which says, in effect, 'move by increments towards the mast and so will we'. Outer-direction permits a logic of whole systems to emerge. Inner-directed rivalry prevents such a logic developing.

It is noteworthy that the only East Asian tiger in serious trouble is Korea, paralyzed at this time of writing by strike action and militant trades unionism. It is surely not a coincidence that the most inner-directed of all tigers has succumbed to Anglo-American style adversarialism between labor and management. It was this kind of defiance that stopped North Korea gaining US assistance. Need we be surprised that South Korea, with close to half a century of confrontation with communists, has now adopted the warrior-stance of the Finite Game player?

How Singapore responds to MNEs

We come finally to perhaps the most finely orchestrated system of outer-directed planning which the world has witnessed. Singapore's Economic Development Board (EDB) has, for thirty years or more, been in the habit of responding to the inner-directed agendas of multinational corporations wishing to locate in their City State. Singapore's economy has been built almost entirely upon outer-directed reactions to the initiatives of others.

It is not that the EDB simply said 'yes'; rather, they deflected requests and channeled these into activities most conducive to Singapore's development. If a corporation of world class reputation wanted scarce space, this was arranged for, and taxes might be deferred. The EDB might offer its own investment funds, but there were conditions. High skilled work must be done on this site, leading edge products created with Singaporeans doing the design and research and participation in a joint training initiative was requested. In this way skilled labor would keep pace with growing demand. It was in the interest of the corporation itself not to bid up the scarce skills.[19]

So while MNEs provided the text, Singapore provided the context; while MNEs 'did their own thing', these 'things' converged into clusters of mutual assistance and cross-hybridization. It is like conducting a huge orchestra to achieve harmony among the international players of various instruments. No wonder the EDB refers to itself as a Knowledge Arbitrageur, a Catalyst, a Vision Sharer and Information Hub. It is the top management sounding board to which the world's mightiest corporations bring their ideas and plans to be finely fitted together.

Box 6.2   The Verdict of Multinational Enterprises on Singapore's EDB

'They (the EDB) were the most knowledgeable government people, who knew exactly what it took to make a business successful, who knew business trends around the world and who had a truly international focus and, most important of all, had a "can-do" attitude... They are driven by a spirit of "let's figure out how to get a win–win situation for both Singapore and DuPont".

'Singapore was unique. Hong Kong was status driven andcorrupt; Singapore had a more a philosophical approach, a general direction which was for the *long term* and not the quick dollar, here and there. They had their eyes set on developing their resources, thinking about the education of their people. They had a real spirit of cooperation with business and a free market philosophy within boundaries. They were democratic but they viewed it as a managed democracy.' (Lubrizol)

'Had Texas Instruments gone straight to the JTC (Jurong Township Corporation) they'd have been laughed out of the office, because even one acre is beginning to be hard to find... So EDB became the roadblock buster... TI would call them and EDB would say "Give us a couple of days". (In 1969 the EDB set up TI's integrated circuit test and assembly plant in 50 days. It is known as "The fifty day miracle".)

Box 6.2   Continued

'The EDB knew more about us than we did. It was the most organized government we had ever dealt with. Other governments mostly did not know much about DEC, partly because we were not a well-known player at that time.

'Our company is a joint venture between EDB Investment Pte Ltd (15%) and Hitachi Ltd of Japan (85%)... EDB had the *foresight*.... supported by strong and prompt actions to ensure the survival of the country's economy. This was evident in their commitment to realize their vision (e.g. Manufacturing—2000, Information Technology—2000. Regionalization—2000) such as identifying and attracting the kind of investment that is desired.

'From the EDB's point of view, Hewlett Packard's twenty-five year history in Singapore is also a prototypical success story in that both HP and Singapore have benefited from HP's presence there. HP has evolved into a major player in the computer industry and its Singapore operations have contributed heavily to that evolution, including some successful product designs executed by local engineering and R&D staffs. In 1995 HP was given the "Distinguished Partner in Progress Award" by the Singapore Government.'

Source: *Strategic Pragmatism: The Culture of Singapore's Economic Development Board*, Edgar H. Schein, Cambridge, MA: MIT Press, 1996, Chapters 8–9.

Praise for how they are received, listened to, served, encouraged and guided by the EDB's one-stop system for all their wants, is detailed in Box 6.2.

Summary

Formal reasoning is not wrong, it is incomplete. It examines what you do *before* you act, but largely ignores any reflecting, correcting, elaborating and diverging occurring after the act. But if you join together inner- and outer-directed processes you get a circular learning system, a true logic of discovery.

The tiger economies and newly developing East Asian economies tend to be more outer-directed and adjust quickly to new Western initiatives and technologies. The tradition of the European Enlightenment is overwhelming inner-directed, underestimating styles of thought not formally reasoned. Inner-direction tends to promote Finite Games and clashes of will between contestants. Typical is the following pattern:

The less convinced and
inner-directed of any two
contestants tends to lose out...

A

To the more convinced and
inner-directed opponent, which
reinforces the moral that...

Z

In contrast, when inner-directed Western corporations venture into East Asia they find themselves used for leverage. Tigers borrow Western skills and add their own to create an unbeatable infinite composite, so:

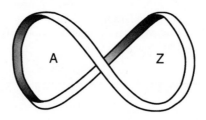

A. License, copy or acquire
innovative pieces of Western
inner-directed technology and...

Z. Through continuous
improvements, refinements,
adaptations and outer-directed
customization win markets and play
host to...

By joining their own outer-direction to Western inner-direction they often 'complete the loops' faster than Western corporations alone.

Inner-directed and outer-directed cultures think differently about the purpose and value of feedback loops. Inner-directed cultures use feedback to persevere with their original intentions and to return to the path initially chosen. Any deviation from these intentions, targets or objections is deemed an 'error' to be 'corrected'. A Finite Game ensues between 'the true path' and 'deviation', so:

Deviations from any intended direction are labeled 'errors' to be 'corrected' and are...

A

Therefore suppressed and eliminated in favor of the actor's inner-directed purpose.

Z

Among tiger economies, however, deviations may be generated in order to discover whether customers prefer some *variations* of what you originally intended to supply. These diverse preferences by customers are sovereign in outer-directed cultures. What matters is not what you intended so much as what they prefer and what variants fit best into the market environment. There is no struggle *against* deviation but rather careful consideration as to whether it better suits customers:

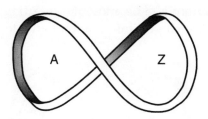

A. You create by inner-directed means the best product you can, studying the feedback from this process...

Z. To see what outer-directed elaborations and divergencies, from your intentions your customers most prefer, then...

This helps to explain the astonishing diversity of goods East Asian tigers offer their customers, and the rapidity with which preferences are discovered.

 Finally, Western insistence upon inner-directed authority, with decisive individualists at the helm, puts an intolerable strain upon 'omniscient' leaders who are typically far from the field of action. A 'crisis of authority' has arisen with many once-famous business leaders, politicians and members of royalty now cast down by popular rebellion and cynicism.

Expectations that decisive inner-directed leaders will save us by the steadfastness of personal conviction

A

Encounter disillusion, cynicism, rebellion and mockery as disenchanted followers topple their leaders.

Z

With the media acting as a popular 'jeering section' it becomes almost impossible to rule (which is why Singapore 'gazettes'—restricts circulation of—magazines which disparage its leaders).

But authority is more likely to survive and be trusted if it adopts an outer-directed listening mode, which draws information from the bottom to the top and allows junior staff to participate in inner-directed ways. Yet genuine wisdom lies with those who receive these inputs and use them to define the Knowledge Society.

Inner-direction from juniors and outer-direction by seniors join in an Infinite Game which gets information to the top of the hierarchy, so:

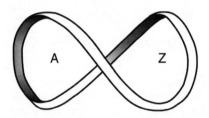

A. Inner-directed data and information from customers and junior staff allow these to participate in a hierarchy...

Z. Of organized knowledge, which outer-directed, listening leaders elicit and integrate, thereby encouraging more...

You are not estranged from a leader whom you inform and he or she values you because you have the data which the theory needs to be truly knowledgeable. Beyond reason lie new ways of discovering and organizing knowledge.

Chapter 7

Beyond Achievement: The Discovery of What is Worth Achieving

If nothing else is sacred, surely achievement is. Are we to judge people by their race, gender, ethnicity, family connections, age, religion, ancestry, politics, ideology or by to what they DO? The Finite Games a person has played gives us access to their *track records*. On a specific date at a specific place he/she finished first or in the top ten placings. The person has 'made it' by so much. All interested spectators know the score. Anyone can enter most, if not all, contests. Choose your Finite Game. There are hundreds of them. Then play hard and win if you can.

That is what the New World of the USA is all about. And if you can count your winning in dollars, so much the better. Well played games are the ones spectators most enjoy. You are being paid for the quality and popularity of your performance. What could be fairer? Persons are rewarded in accordance with their level of appreciation in the Open Society. It is a form of natural justice, harnessing the initiatives of individuals to the requirements of corporations and the demands of markets. Achievement is pragmatism applied to commerce.

We will be arguing that despite the attraction, even allure, of Finite Games these will *not* be sufficient to build a strong economy, any more than bread and circuses were enough to sustain the Roman Empire. Finite Games are certainly adequate for a thrilling calendar of sporting fixtures with our gazes focused on victory and averted from the vanquished, but they are only half of what it takes to build a modern economy and grow rather than shrink in world stature.

There is nothing like being a small, overcrowded country initially left behind in the race to develop to impress upon your mind that *not all achievements are of equal worth.* Singapore cannot admit all businesses which seek entry. There is insufficient room. China faces the choice between mobile phones that may soon be able to bounce signals off IRIDIUM satellites, and stringing the whole country with ugly poles and wires. The choice precedes the achievement. Indeed, Western technologies stand side by side in a global bazaar. Newly industrializing countries ask, 'which of these achievements are for us?'

Moreover, such countries gain *knowledge* of these new technologies some years before using that technology to achieve with. They must first value it enough to gain expertise in its use.

The argument in this chapter is as follows:

- East Asian cultures are more likely to achieve status. Western cultures are more achievement oriented.
- Pure achieving is not so effective as achieving what has first been ascribed as important as a national priority. This enables the group to realize . . .
- The value of superordinate goals, and it places . . .
- *Learned* advantage above *natural* advantage. Where learned advantage is emphasized, accelerated learning can become a national objective . . .
- Not waiting for markets to demand education and assuring a high-skilled labor supply by . . .
- Fine-tuning education and enterprise. The aim must be the development of . . .
- Human potential into a self-fulfilling prophecy. This encourages senior managers to mentor juniors and so . . .
- Leave a legacy behind.

East Asian cultures are more ascriptive of status; Western cultures are more achievement oriented

Table 7.1 reveals that, with some exceptions, tiger economies and newly industrializing economies in East Asia lean towards *ascribing status*. This does not mean that they are indifferent or neglectful of achievement, but that they prefer to define the valuable *and then* achieve this, rather than have achievement defined by winners of Finite Games. Indeed, the idea that achievements shape our values, rather than the other way around, is very much a minority viewpoint.

Only the five English speaking nations, UK, USA, Canada, Australia and New Zealand, subscribe to this idea, plus Norway. East Asian countries occupy ten of the top sixteen places in considering 'the way you really are', a reflection which *precedes* achievement and is more important than achievement.

Alternative sources of ascribed status derive from seniority and from family. On the issue of senior managers being older than their subordinates, nine out of ten East Asian cultures head the list. On the issue of family being an important source of status, East Asia cultures hold the top six places and eight of the top ten. Asian cultures with

Table 7.1   Ascribed versus achieved status

Question 1: *'Is the most important thing in life to think and act in the manner that best suits the way you really are, even if you don't get things done?'*
% agree

Korea	76.01	Singapore	61.41
Spain	75.22	Philippines	60.44
China	71.87	Germany	59.62
Japan	70.34	Malaysia	54.98
Indonesia	69.50	Brazil	55.06
Belgium	67.41	Sweden	53.41
Taiwan	67.35	UK	49.83
Hong Kong	67.13	New Zealand	45.40
The Netherlands	65.95	Australia	44.82
France	65.65	Ireland	44.62
Switzerland	65.35	Canada	44.33
Thailand	63.58	USA	39.11
Italy	62.48	Norway	33.68

Question 2: *'Is it important for a manager that he is older than most of his subordinates?'*
% agree

Japan	53.61	Spain	28.79
Korea	43.64	Brazil	28.73
Hong Kong	40.28	France	28.67
Singapore	39.51	Germany	26.62
Malaysia	36.11	Australia	25.25
Taiwan	36.07	Norway	25.00
Indonesia	36.04	The Netherlands	23.74
Philippines	34.37	Switzerland	21.78
China	33.51	UK	21.72
Italy	32.63	New Zealand	21.26
USA	32.46	Sweden	21.07
Thailand	30.56	Canada	20.90
Belgium	29.03	Ireland	20.58

Table 7.1 Continued

Question 3: *'Is the respect a person gets highly dependent on the family from which he comes'*
% agree

Thailand	48.46	Spain	30.30
Philippines	43.96	*Malaysia*	30.22
Hong Kong	43.75	Brazil	29.98
Indonesia	41.94	*Japan*	29.48
Korea	37.00	France	29.03
Taiwan	36.82	Sweden	26.22
Germany	36.32	USA	25.91
China	36.24	Canada	24.87
Belgium	35.78	Australia	24.21
Switzerland	34.36	UK	23.34
Singapore	31.98	Norway	20.79
Italy	31.49	Ireland	19.27
The Netherlands	31.43	New Zealand	18.39

Source: The Trompenaars Group, Database. Amsterdam, 1997.

high exposure to the West, e.g. Singapore and Japan, and cultures where most of our respondents worked for US companies, e.g. Malaysia, are less emphatic about ascription by family. Japan persists in emphasizing age.

Of course, simply preferring age or seniority to achievement confers no necessary competitive advantage. Such cultures could be nepotistic or gerentocracies without becoming successful. Among cultures which ascribe status yet have achieved scant economic development are Egypt, Uruguay, Hungary, Bulgaria, Nepal, Romania and Kenya. Giving status to Communist Party members in China and East Europe was clearly of limited value. Tribal status is probably no better.

What concerns us here is the capacity to first choose your values, technologies, industries and then achieve these. You need some form of ascription to escape from the Finite Games into an Infinite Game.

Pure achieving versus Achieving what has been ascribed as important

Where achievement is defined by the relative prominence of success-ful contestants then markets become the sole arbiters of what is true and beautiful. As Frederick Winslow Taylor said to one of his experimental subjects in the science of shoveling, 'Are you a high-price man, or a low-price man?'. We speak of 'selling' others on our proposition, of 'marketing' ourselves to employers and of getting subordinates 'to take ownership' of a new policy by 'buying into it'. Achievements get to be acknowledged by fighting and winning, but they never really stop contending. Why should soccer champions not be more admired than American football champions? Even when you are the champion, publicity for your game vies with other games.

All claims to fame are relative. Nor is the society ever agreed on what is valuable and cannot therefore give its wholehearted support to any cause save defense or national survival. The Red Scares, the Prohibition amendment and moral majorities which have struck America periodically, represent desperate yearnings to reach beyond the subjectivism of markets to something higher, infinite and transcendent.

The Finite Game reads as follows:

No value can ever be genuinely agreed upon. All are temporary, relative achievements in a market place of...

A

Contenders for popular acclaim, which eventually eclipses even the brightest...

Z

Nothing lasts in this culture—you are 'as good as your last film', as interesting as a week-old newspaper. Where once British Royalty stood for values above the fray, they are now trapped in the games of fame. Did the Prince of Wales' handlers outsmart the publicity agents of Princess Di? Could she have won a larger divorce settlement?

You can only create an Infinite Game if you *first* agree on what is valuable and then set out to achieve this. There is no problem in setting up contests to see who best achieves these common aims, but these are not contests *among values* but among those attempting best to fulfill these values. The Infinite Game as played among most Asian tigers reads as follows:

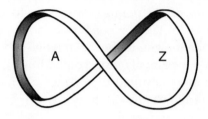

A. Values *ascribed* to the Developmental State and to the Learning Society are superordinate goals by which you...

Z. Inspire, encourage, and motivate all citizens to *achieve* such aims so as to fulfill those...

It is possible to come up with superordinate goals for reasons rehearsed in Chapter 4. Some technologies catalyze whole clusters of other technologies. Microchips and machine tools for example join game to game as infinite connectors. It is in the interest of all industry and all citizens that these superordinate technological objectives succeed, as it is in the interest of Japan, its religion, its esthetics, its environment and its economy that it be the first to harness the renewable power of the sun. You make your own country pollution-free and then sell these solutions to the world.

The value of superordinate goals

There is the old story of the three medieval craftsmen working on the same edifice, who were asked what they were doing. 'I am earning two groats an hour', said the first. 'I am a master stone-mason demonstrating my craft', said the second. 'I am helping to build a cathedral', said the third. Only the third had a superordinate goal which transcended his own being. Only he could claim to dedicate his life to a value beyond himself and take pride in a legacy of a thousand years.

Our work in building an economy is not chiseled in stone but our contributions can last, even if improved upon monthly, for several decades. Growing more knowledgeable, more skilled, more prosperous year by year is a potentially exciting experience. Seeing your own work built upon, your own techniques enfolded into larger systems, your own ideas put to a use beyond your own imaginings is to be in touch with the infinite. Seeing your children growing beyond your own powers, seizing opportunities you never had, yet passing on the strength and affection you gave them to grandchildren and beyond is what makes the games of life infinite. 'Where there is no vision the people perish', says the *Book of Proverbs*. Without superordinate goals life lacks meaning.

A Singaporean man who was 70 years old in 1997 has seen the City grow from a malaria infested swamp of colonists and coolies to a nation far, far surpassing its one-time masters economically and industrially. Our Singaporean might even have been the husband and father of one of the mothers so poor and desperate they flung themselves with their babies into the waters of the harbor—as reported in the British press in 1950. It is difficult to imagine what it means for three million people to reorganize their lives so completely, with their values and brains as their only real resource.

There are, of course, good reasons for tiger economies to have superordinate goals. South Korea confronts North Korea. Taiwan confronts China. Singapore is surrounded by Muslim nations and when it seceded from the Malaysian Federation many doubted its viability as a City State. Hong Kong lived until 1997 on borrowed time. Japan had been incinerated by conventional and nuclear bombs and lost an empire. In no case was survival guaranteed without huge efforts of rebuilding, redefinition and a new ascribed identity and purpose. In no case was business-as-usual an option.

Nor are superordinate goals always benign. The Thousand Year Reich was pathological and genocidal. Mao's 'Catch up Britain by 1963' is seriously behind schedule and 'The Great Leap Forward' was a great stumble. Even Japan's Fifth Generation Computer project and its HDTV fizzled. There can be no guarantees that superordinate goals will succeed and their failure saps confidence, yet without such goals who will submerge factional interest for the larger good? How else can contenders see the connections between their games? How else would companies share R&D and then compete in achieving an outcome? Without superordinate goals economic development becomes a struggle between interest groups, shareholders who want to know the real cost of management share options, managers and CEOs who want to disguise this, and accountants who do not want to be sued by either side. These finite

Table 7.2 Extent to which the values of society support competitiveness survey

1	*Singapore*	8.46	24	Turkey	5.82
2	*Hong Kong*	8.12	25	France	5.74
3	*Malaysia*	7.63	26	*Thailand*	5.68
4	*Japan*	7.37		Denmark	5.68
5	Chile	7.19	28	India	5.54
6	Canada	7.06	29	UK	5.53
7	Finland	7.01	30	Austria	5.50
	Israel	7.01	31	Brazil	5.43
9	Switzerland	6.98	32	*Indonesia*	5.26
10	Iceland	6.92	33	Czech Republic	5.17
11	Belgium	6.77	34	Italy	5.12
12	*Korea*	6.69	35	Portugal	4.94
13	New Zealand	6.60	36	*China*	4.89
14	USA	6.54		Colombia	4.89
15	*Taiwan*	6.53	38	Argentina	4.88
16	Ireland	6.46	39	Mexico	4.83
17	Philippines	6.25	40	Spain	4.68
18	The Netherlands	6.13	41	Greece	4.38
19	Australia	5.93	42	Hungary	4.11
20	Norway	5.91	43	Russia	4.08
21	Luxembourg	5.90	44	Poland	4.05
22	Germany	5.87	45	South Africa	3.71
23	Sweden	5.83	46	Venezuela	2.90

struggles never end and there is no common objective higher than sectional interest.

Is there any evidence that creating superordinate goals of developing through knowledge and learning and achieving higher complexity wins over the populace and employees so that their morale is high? *The World Competitiveness Year Book 1996* asked whether the values of society supported competitiveness or whether these detracted from competitiveness. The national rankings are given in Table 7.2. The first four—Singapore, Hong Kong, Malaysia and Japan—are all East Asian. Korea is 12th, Taiwan 15th and the Philippines 17th; China, Indonesia and Thailand have yet to complete reforms. Five East Asian economies score higher than the USA. Eight score higher than the UK. All score higher than Mexico, America's NAFTA partner. It is clearly easier to use superordinate goals with smaller populations than larger ones. Thirteen of the top fifteen have populations of 21 million or less. Of those with populations over 40 million only Japan, Korea, the USA and the Philippines make it into the top twenty. Five of the six largest nations, China, India, Indonesia,

Brazil and Russia, fare poorly. Ex-communist countries do not yet have their values together. Poland is best at 19th.

Learned and natural advantages

It has long been the endeavor of economists to keep their 'science' free of values, as cold and as hard as celestial clockwork. To that end Riccardo proposed that nations specialized in different products, not so much because they valued them, but because of natural advantage in producing them. Hence Britain uses its damp meadowlands to raise sheep and produce wool, while Portugal uses its sunny slopes to grow grapes and produce port wine. The two nations exchanged wool for wine over the centuries.[1]

What this theory does *not* explain is why Britain prospered mightily in the 18th and 19th centuries and Portugal did not. One possible answer is that Britain *learned* to weave wool in its factories and cotton from its empire to produce a textile industry, while wine production remained substantially unchanged. Theories of natural advantage had little attraction to East Asian economies, beginning with Japan because they had virtually no such advantages. All they really had were people, lots of them, and so they set them to the task of learning. Learned advantage is the secret of the tiger economies as Bruce Scott and George Lodge have pointed out. It was also the secret of the United Kingdom's industrial revolution, but we invented a different explanation and lost the thread.

Not waiting for markets to demand education

An obvious characteristic of both late developers (Germany, France, Scandinavia etc.) and late-late developers (the Asian tigers) is that they do *not* start at the beginning of the industrial revolution with shoe and textile factories, but cut straight to the leading edges of their eras.[2] Hence Germany went for steel, chemicals and machinery and Singapore, Malaysia, Thailand etc. have gone straight for advanced electronics. All this means that you educate yourself first and then use that knowledge to create market opportunities by offering yourself to multinational organizations for prime manufacturing and research sites.

The belief that education should be left to market forces may be the biggest mistake that Western economies ever made. It takes up to a quarter of a century or more to train a human being, and the idea that markets signal the trends of education demanded so that students spontaneously prepare themselves for these positions, is highly implausible. There are, of course, some short term, strategic shifts. America's large number of lawyers originates from the late sixties, when student loans replaced student grants. Students needed jobs that would repay loans quickly, and the Finite Games lawyers play beget more lawyers. But the idea that higher salaries for scarce expertise attracts recruits and is self-balancing does not bear close examination.

There are several problems with this argument. The first is that the skill shortage which raises salaries has *already* slowed down the process of knowledge intensification. Those who fail to get the scarce talent cannot climb the knowledge ladder and do not enter complex markets. The second problem is the time-lag—four years or more. With this long interval between signal and response, the economy is slowed. An additional issue concerns the likely surplus of recruits if all respond to the same signal. By the time they all graduate their skills are in surplus and their salaries are down! A final problem is that companies rarely *know* their needs five years hence, especially if skill shortages are blocking their way.

All these problems are but variations upon one central misconception. *Markets create knowledge more slowly and less certainly than rising knowledge creates markets.* You cannot grow fast if highly skilled employees are not abundant and hence relatively cheap, and if consumers are not educated enough to use your products. Trying to bribe individuals into more years of schooling by the distant promise of higher salaries is the hard, slow path to growth. By putting achievement ahead of knowledge, we expect knowing to be pulled in achievement's wake. We have it back to front. It is knowledge that adds value to achieving.

If you put learning first as an ascribed value, then people will use it to achieve with, and the more knowledge and skill that is around the more they will use. Knowledge intensive products will arise because it is boring and unfulfilling to do anything less. Moreover *the workplace will be where you learn and grow*, as opposed to the Western concept of learning at school in order to achieve in the workplace, and buying in smarter people when you need them via head hunters.

Knowledge surpluses rather than scarcities also affect the design and implementation of new technologies. In Japan, according to recent surveys, technologies are used to *upgrade worker skills*. There is so much skill that technology counts on being able to use it.[3] The ideal is 'automotation', in Taichi Ohno's words—the progressive extension and elaboration of the human nervous system through electronics and machinery.[4] But in the typical situation of many Western economies, with severe skill shortages, technology is designed both to save labor *and to save skills*, thereby reducing the costs of labor. Technological design responds to market forces by making labor dumber.

The evidence that rising levels of knowledge *precede* rapid economic development rather than follow it comes from a major study by Barbara Heinzen, then in Shell's planning department. She used World Bank and UNESCO figures to plot rises in education, health care and community provision, and found major surges in economic activity coming 10–15 years later.[5] While growth in knowledge is not a *sufficient* condition for economic take-off, it appears to be a *necessary* condition. The values of health, education and social responsibility are ascribed first and achievement follows, *not* the other way around.

According to the American economist Lester Thurow, the economic pay-off to the achieving individual of getting an American education is no longer big enough to tempt him or her.[6] As more and more people enter higher education the pay-off falls and those who only study to achieve more have ever fewer reasons to invest privately in schooling. Thus a college education plus forgone earning costs about $180,000 up. Sixteen years of schooling costs around $250,000, yet $1 invested now is worth only $0.16 sixteen years from now. Given that 26 percent of all American white college graduates earn less than white high school graduates, the pay-off in achievement of a college education is not simply uncertain but quite low. While college education does pay handsomely for those near the top, it is a questionable investment for most graduates. They would get more by investing the price of their college fees in equities than by trying to earn their money back. If male wages continue to fall, as they did in the US in the early 1990s, while equity returns improve, the hard-nosed capitalist should logically question the personal utility of higher education.

Thurow is, of course, having fun with us. The one-time Dean of the Sloan School at MIT is not questioning the value of education but the value of Western economic orthodoxy. The question, 'Does college education help me personally to achieve more money?' is the wrong question, posed by the wrong economic unit. The pay-off for knowledge acquisition *has always been communal and social,* he argues. America has subsidized public education from the start with lavish land-grants to colleges, GI bills, post-Sputnik bonanzas and so on. Only now are we out of excuses for such economic unorthodoxies.[7]

The reason for getting knowledge through a college education is that everyone who engages you for the rest of your life stands to learn more as a result. Knowledge is infectious and contagious. It spreads through the culture like a benign virus. One reason that the children from tiger economies are already outperforming North American and British children by age six is the *superior educations of their mothers* in largely intact families, who stay at home.[8] The role of the Japanese 'Education Mama' is well known. Knowledge is an Infinite Game spread by affection and other close relationships. To see in it only pre-match training for competing achievers shrinks its value to a fraction of the whole. Cultures thinking in this way are in grave danger of falling behind.

Fine-tuning education and enterprise

We have seen that it is essential to value knowledge and to increase the supply of knowledgeable workers and managers before they can achieve at tasks with higher value added. Knowledge is more the propellant of achievement than the result of it. But this raises the crucial question of how you get specialized knowledge to varieties of complexifying jobs in timely fashion.

If waiting for the market to attract higher talent with higher salaries is too slow, too costly and too encumbered by perpetual scarcities, then what other ways are there? Fortunately there are detailed studies of how Singapore, at least, channels the needed know-how to the right industries so that they can use it to grow fast. We are indebted, for much of what follows, to David Ashton and Francis Green.[9]

The process begins with the negotiations by MNEs with the Singapore government upon locating in that state. Even companies resident in Singapore for some years may have the Economic Development Board (EDB) as an investor, currently or historically. They need to negotiate expansions, regionalization and especially access to skilled manpower. It is the availability of these skills that attracts industries in the first place and during the negotiation stage they are encouraged to site their most ambitious, innovative and complex activities in Singapore.

As an investor, the EDB has the right to know future plans in detail, and as a host country making room for such plans will require advance notice in any case. Bankers and large investors have always had superior and more intelligent access to the plans of industry than have ordinary shareholders in equity markets, to whom a legal minimum is revealed. Large investors or lenders are privy to long term strategies and have generally delivered a lower cost of capital.[10]

Hence the Singapore government is able to compare and collate the projected manpower needs for all or most MNEs and Singaporean companies on the island. It is in the interests of each company to keep the government informed if it wants its own specialized skills in good supply and wishes to avoid bidding up the price of scarce skills. With manpower requirements known two to five years in advance, the Ministry of Trade and Industry (MTI) plots future manpower resources and compares these to projected needs. The EDB creates a nationwide target for skills development and passes this to the Council for Professional and Technical Education (CPTE). The CPTE breaks these down into smaller targets for each university, junior college and technical institute, which then prepare the requisite courses using equipment, software and 'teachware' supplied by the companies needing those skills. Plans are made five years ahead by the ITE (Institute for Technical Education), responsible for the bottom 25 percent of the job market. But plans are rolled over every two years, because of unpredictable events. Hence you never stop anticipating, yet you frequently change your mind! You think five years ahead not because you will be right, but in order to stay alert.

Does readying recruits for plans laid by corporations a few months earlier require massive dragooning of 'work-fodder', so that students must shift with every global wind-change? Certainly American and European institutions of higher education preserve an almost total autonomy from government, and regard the true and the beautiful as their own province, which business would be lucky to share or emulate.

The only insight we have been able to obtain from students being prepared for knowledge-intensive businesses comes not from Singapore, but from neighboring Malaysia. At the Penang Skills Center, jointly funded by forty-five multinational corporations in the

Free Trade Zone, we found an extraordinary level of interest and excitement about future jobs in the leading edges of technological innovation. Students had very clear aspirations to work on certain developing technologies in certain key companies, on whose equipment they had already trained. Among the favorites as of 1993 were Intel's Pentium Processor, Seagate's latest disk-drive and Toshiba's new PC.

The students' interest and enthusiasm were shared by sponsoring companies who were anxious to get the best students for their money. Students had a planned rendezvous on graduation with the industrial processes and the companies of their choice. The transition from training to work was almost seamless. No one was being prepared in seedy government training institutes for already obsolescent jobs, as is common in parts of Europe.

But such efforts are insufficient without the re-training of adult workers. Ninety-four percent of companies in Singapore, all but the very smallest, offer on-the-job training. And 30–90 percent of re-training costs are paid by the government, depending on the size of the company. A great deal was learned from Japan's Human Resource Development Law (1985) and from industry associations in Germany, Switzerland and Scandinavia which organize in-house training. In Table 7.3 we see that Japan, Singapore, Korea, Malaysia, the Philippines and Taiwan occupy six of the top fifteen places, along with their European mentors. The USA is 22nd, the UK 38th and *laissez-faire* British-run Hong Kong, 26th.

Singapore's ITE has recently launched its Adult Cooperative Training Scheme aimed at coordinating in-house, on-the-job training with more ambitious off-the-job re-training, in jointly financed industrial institutes. The emphasis is on making the original employer responsible for trainees on both sites. To that end, a version of the German *Meister* oversees the development of a given number of apprentices in both locations, assuring the re-employment of workers at higher skill levels back in their original companies.

For larger, multinational companies with more entrenched systems the Skill Development Fund (SDF) promotes and assists company-based training schemes, providing funds which top up what companies themselves provide. There is an especial interest and provision for innovations in training and a Training Grants Scheme is run by the National Productivity Board to aid experimentation. Under such auspices the number of training places increased from 32,000 in

Table 7.3   In-company training

1	Japan	7.71	24	Brazil	5.18
2	Germany	7.11	25	Italy	5.12
3	Finland	6.93	26	Iceland	4.97
4	Sweden	6.90		Hong Kong	4.97
5	The Netherlands	6.82	28	Czech Republic	4.91
	Denmark	6.82		Colombia	4.91
7	Singapore	6.81	30	India	4.86
8	Korea	6.79	31	Canada	4.82
9	Austria	6.78		Spain	4.82
10	Switzerland	6.51	33	Greece	4.75
11	Norway	6.38	34	Indonesia	4.71
12	Malaysia	6.26	35	Venezuela	4.65
13	Philippines	6.25	36	Argentina	4.64
	Taiwan	6.25	37	Thailand	4.63
15	Chile	6.23	38	UK	4.61
16	Australia	6.07	39	South Africa	4.58
17	Belgium	6.04	40	China	4.56
18	New Zealand	6.03	41	Turkey	4.53
19	Luxembourg	5.91	42	Russia	4.49
20	Ireland	5.64	43	Mexico	4.29
21	France	5.63	44	Hungary	3.93
22	USA	5.43	45	Portugal	3.68
23	Israel	5.19	46	Poland	2.95

Source: *World Competitiveness Report*. Lausanne: IMD, 1996, p. 568.

1981 to half a million by 1996. Few workers are not at some time involved.

None of this could work in Singapore or other tiger economies if the overriding goals of the nation were not given preference over the more sectional achievements of educators, professional associations, unions and companies. To this end, personnel are regularly exchanged between government, employers, unions and schools. This practice, long common in Japan, allows leaders to see their own position from many different angles.

In Singapore the head of the National Trades Union Council (NTUC) has become head of the National Productivity Board (NPB). It is indicative of how much unions have gained through the high skills route rather than through strikes and disruptions.

Human potential and self-fulfilling prophecies

Another vital reason for ascribing status to people *before* they achieve is that human potential precedes achievement. The skeptical attitude 'prove to me that you are worth what I pay you' demands winning achievements from day 1, before any respect is shown or status conferred. Cheerleaders for American-style achievement, like George Gilder, cite mostly uneducated achievers. The poorer your education the less you owe to anyone else but yourself. You made it *despite* the ridicule of others!

But if we are to be serious about the Learning Corporation, or even the Learning Nation, then we must recognize that its first duty is to the potential latent in all employees and all citizens, in whom it is necessary to invest heavily before they achieve. It is not that we consider achievement unimportant. It is inseparable from overall competitiveness. Our point is rather that achieving is a prophecy that fulfills itself and that prophecy must ascribe status to all actors in the economy in order for achievements to be generated. Moreover, within a learning environment the leaders are the coaches and mentors of those who achieve, not achievers themselves, although they may have achieved in the past. In such learning environments the top people define excellence and ascribe status to it. Their subordinates excel and fulfill the corporation's faith in their potential.

Such systems follow the Japanese in paying employees for the number of skills they have mastered. Reward is for their *potential* value to a team in which many different roles may be required and many different problems solved. This is also the pattern in Korea and Taiwan. Your value lies less in your latest achievement than in the breadth and versatility of your capability to achieve, the range of your mastery. This is also the reason for the recent emphasis in Singapore on basic skills, a platform of general education beneath which no one may fall and whose lowest rung was recently abolished.

Singapore is now following Switzerland and Japan in *skills deepening* programs.[11] The idea is to train workers in the theoretical base which *joins their old jobs to their new ones*. In this way any changes they must make have one coherent meaning, an underlying theme of continuity. For example, several different jobs using numerically controlled machine tools and precision engineering are variations in the possible settings of the machine. Workers learn how to program and reprogram machines for work of ever greater complexity. They are learning not just about their own potentials but about the potentials of precision engineering machinery.

It is well known that small companies have cash-flow problems. By paying its contribution to re-training costs up front, the Singaporean government helps to ease these problems while promoting the training it seeks. It was the objective of Singapore's NPB, announced in 1993, to double company investment in on-the-job training from 2.0 percent of payroll costs to 4.0 percent, excluding the government's contribution. This had been met by 1996. It is only fair to warn, however, that calculations *can* go wrong. When Japan's real estate bubble burst in 1993 badly damaging those banks who held property as collateral, a large number of manpower plans collapsed too.[12]

Seniority and legacy

It is the habit in Japan (less so in Korea) to promote employees by their seniority, so that whole 'year groups' ascend the ladder together, and you can locate schoolmates in other companies at almost identical levels of authority. Respect for age and seniority is also a feature of Chinese culture, where political leaders retain authority into their 80s or beyond. While Japan has an official retirement age of 55, senior executives may advise, consult or move into liaison between government and industry, remaining active indefinitely. To Westerners such respect for age rather than achievement appears perverse.

Yet there are a surprising number of advantages when the system is examined closely. First, promoting by seniority creates a system in which top people can create an environment for achievement, a culture of excellence, without having to prove or to achieve themselves. They can listen, encourage, guide, advise and manage values, while their subordinates can consummate those values by achieving them. Steady promotion by age does not prevent executives competing; rather, it ensures that they compete *in their contributions* rather than in gaining personal rewards. Because everyone ages, everyone's time will come.

The achievement system provides a useful pretext for ridding the company of non-achievers. It also allows the supervisor to attribute successes or failures to particular subordinates, as opposed to his *relationship* with those subordinates and the culture of his workplace. In 'firing' the person, i.e. pressing the trigger and have him fly away, the supervisor only *appears* to have rid himself of the problem, which is often right there in his office, not hurtling conveniently into the sky. It is usually better for the productivity of an organization not to rid itself of symptoms but to deal with the malaise of a low achieving environment. In a system which respects age and promotes by seniority it becomes harder to dump your 'losers' and drop them from the game. Such organizations fear being lumbered with dead wood, but this fear has a paradoxical result. If it is difficult, not easy, to get rid of people, you are more likely to *invest in their training and improvement.* Instead of always blaming the non-achieving person, you ask what more the company might do to bring out the human potential of its employees. Dumping losers prevents you learning how you might have helped them win.[13]

Promoting by seniority also increases the admission of past mistakes and the opportunity to learn therefrom. If a person is appointed leader because of his brilliant track-record, he is likely to forbid criticism lest it undermine his authority. If he is appointed for his age, modesty, humility and judgement, all errors will be pored over for possible lessons. Japanese retired presidents often tour the plants of their company speaking of their past mistakes. If, as we argued in Chapter 6, after-the-fact learning is one of the secrets of tiger strength, then the most senior employees are best qualified in such philosophic views. As you grow older more of your knowledge is of the past.

We have all by now heard of mid-life crisis. It is especially likely to hit Western executives moving up into the highest reaches of the corporation. It is often a crisis of meaning, a confrontation with the futility of winning the Finite Game for promotion. There you are with the key of the executive washroom. Your bodily needs screened from the *hoi-polloi.* You have 'made it', whatever 'it' entails. You have reached the summit of your ambition only to experience a profound anti-climax. Before long you will retire. After that comes one, perhaps two, heart-attacks and then it's all over. Is that what you lived for, to climb to the top of a heap before competitors? It is, of course, a spiritual vacuum. Our corporations rarely give us ways in which to continue to live through others. Charles Handy recently likened it to a modern sculpture, 'The Empty Raincoat', a ghost in protective clothing.[14]

This helps to explain why the better American multinationals, e.g. Motorola, but also Ford, have begun to ask their senior officers, *what is your legacy?* What do you seek to leave behind you, as a lasting gift to your corporation, your customers and your country? What will be the signs that you passed this way? The form this legacy takes is the

Box 7.1   An American Text in a Malaysian Context

Motorola's Malaysian facilities in Penang, Kuala Lumpur and Seremban have all achieved successes that have harmonized positively with the context of Malaysian cultural values and development policies.

Motorola has been responsive to numerous aspects of the '2020 Vision Statement' of the Malaysian Government. This remarkable document visualizes Malaysia pursuing excellence in all domains, including the techno-economic and sociocultural. Under the plan, Malaysia will continue to rapidly upgrade its human and technological resources, and will be making greater contributions to world science and knowledge, while at the same time continuing to build an ethical society deeply rooted in the strength of local cultural values.

Motorola contributes to the realization of these 2020 objectives by adhering to two key values in its own corporate culture, namely 'Uncompromising Integrity' and 'Constant Respect for People'. Thus Motorola has installed state-of-the-art technologies at all its Malaysian facilities, transferring technology rapidly, promoting 'home-grown' R&D and sharing its learning with local organizations.

More specifically, Motorola has taken the following initiatives:

- Instituted an 'empowerment process' for its employees, result-ing in the formation of several hundred teams of employees (often joined by vendors and customers) dedicated to improving productivity and quality, in pursuit of Motorola's 'Fundamental Objective' of attaining Total Customer Satisfaction with its products and services.
- Helped design and build Quality Control Circles for local organizations.
- Co-founded the Penang Skills Development Center to help upgrade local technological skills.
- Provided Malaysian Motorolans with fully paid opportunities for further education through in-house programs, including under-graduate and graduate degree programs.
- Co-created joint advanced graduate engineering programs with a local university.
- Sponsored joint technical research projects with local universities.
- Made its Land Mobile Products R&D Center in Penang the design headquarters for all of its Asia-Pacific operations.
- Continuously developed the skills of Malaysian Motorolans and 'exported' key local talents to its facilities worldwide.

Box 7.1   Continued

- Pioneered industrial waste treatment practices, including
  the elimination of all use of chlorofluorocarbons.

By such means, through the years Motorola has expanded its
workforce to over 12,000 Malaysians, who now account for an
appreciable portion of the total value of the nation's
manufactured exports.

Source: R. S. Moorthy, Motorola University, Schaumberg, IL.

---

creation of values, ideas, visions and a sense of mission which *other
people* will continue and consummate after you have gone. The frantic
takeover plots among Western corporations testify to the desperation
of executives in the last months of their power, vying with each other
to make a startling impact. The final winning smash. That in doing so
they smash whole social contexts which have given thousands of
employees identity and meaning deters them not at all.

But all this masks the real crisis, that they have not yet discovered
what is *worth* achieving, and so identify with stratospheric numbers
and whole companies as retirement presents and monuments to their
infighting prowess.

So the final important reason for discovering what is worth
achieving is to leave a legacy to the people and companies we care for
and see parts of ourselves incorporated in the continuing quest for
knowledge and service. It is interesting that where major US
multinationals locate themselves in East Asia they live up to the
ascribed values of that nation (see Box 7.1).

Summary

We have seen that there is a natural tendency for countries coming
from behind to develop economically, to ask themselves 'Which
technologies should we adopt? Which among this variety of tools is
worth studying and using? What will our culture express with such
tools?' In this way developing countries ascribe status to a business
activity and *then* set forth to achieve it. Achievement remains essential
but as a vindication of values already selected.

Superordinate goals which reconcile many sectional interests are the form which value ascriptions take. They give a larger meaning to all economic activities and allow citizens to dedicate their lives to a transcendent purpose.

Markets do not demand knowledge as effectively as knowledge creates new, innovative markets. Attempts to drag knowledge in the wake of market demands, leads to the following Finite Game:

Companies who cannot hire enough scarce knowledge workers are gravely weakened...

A

In battles with complex, innovative market leaders and so these remain...

Z

So long as severe scarcities of knowledge persist, many or most companies must lose, especially against economies which supply knowledge in abundance. With knowledge in abundant supply all or most companies can get enough, and an Infinite Game develops:

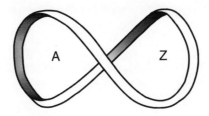

A. The more knowledge workers are supplied with the more technology and strategy will utilize them and the...

Z. More contestants will be able to achieve at complex innovative tasks, enabling them to hire...

Knowledge is the medium in which novel achievements are expressed.

The second major issue had to do with the uncertain pay-off for education in terms of personal enrichment accruing to the individual achiever. With more and more Americans and Europeans going to college and the general decline in the standards of public education, can private markets supply college education and is it smart to buy it?

The calculation does not favor college education with any real decisiveness. Knowledge acquisition struggles with alternative uses of the money. The Finite Game reads as follows:

The expense and time taken to acquire a college education pays back the achieving individual too little and too uncertainly...

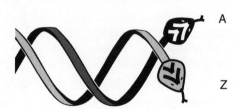

A

To compete successfully with alternative uses of the time taken and other investments, which throws doubts on...

Z

But all doubts upon the value of knowledge disappear if we remove it from the context of *individual* achievement and place it in a societal context. Education enriches everyone touched by knowledgeable persons and generates itself among them. The Infinite Game involves the community and reads as follows:

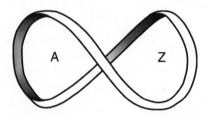

A. Because knowledge is the ascribed value of a society, it self-generates among...

Z. Its members and all achievements are the more complex, scarce and valuable...

The great advantage of a City State like Singapore is being able to anticipate its manpower needs in just those proportions which the growing economy needs—a challenge more difficult in larger countries and with highly autonomous sectional interests. Our final issue had to do with leaving behind you a legacy of yourself to others. When one approaches retirement in individualistic Western countries, even the triumph of getting to the top of your 'game' rings somewhat hollow. The Finite Games are suddenly over, yet you have 'risen without a trace'. You are yesterday's scoreboard, by now surpassed easily, like one-time Olympic stars.

Triumph in the struggle to achieve promotion rings oddly hollow when you have finally 'made it' and

Look down from the edifice you climbed to see only your replacements, your retirement, your death.

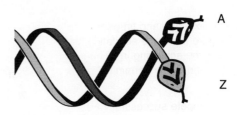

A

Z

East Asian economies may have surpassed us in finding meaning in the Learning Society and its infinite spread of knowledge.

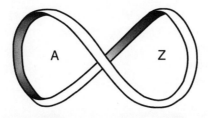

A. Genuine and lasting value lies in the vision and legacy you leave behind with those...

Z. Whose potential growth and learning you nurtured and whose achievements you elicited to make possible...

Chapter 8

Beyond Contract Compliance: Dynamic Reciprocity

The demise of European modernism will revive other overshadowed value systems, triggering an intense rivalry between the old certitudes of the West and resurgent norms. The dispute over democracy is a case in point. Is a political system that guarantees individuals the freedom to engage in all kinds of activities really the best? It strikes me that it is no longer axiomatic that Anglo-Saxon democracy is the ultimate form of governance. Our increasingly inter-related world needs new paradigms of 'freedom' and 'democracy'.

M. Mohamad and S. Ishihara, *The Voice of Asia*.

If we ask what makes our Western Finite Games so fragmented, so easily insulated from larger meanings, the answer is compliance with contracts. We use contracts to *define*, 'to put an end to' business activities, so that we conceive of these as separate games and finite episodes.

'What do you need if you find five lawyers up to their heads in sand?' 'More sand.' Lawyer jokes abound in America these days, because when they win too many of us lose. The rules of Finite Games are typically drawn up by lawyers before we start to play. In fact the battle starts before the rules are agreed. Each side wants the agreement adjusted to their own advantage. How smart are *their* lawyers, compared to *ours*?

Ideally, with good enough lawyers we should win *whatever* happens. If our product sells in Japan we have a fat royalty, if it fails to sell there is a large minimal payment. We cannot lose. We have cleverly secured the rewards but shifted all the risks to the other party. Heads I win, tails you lose. Never give a sucker an even break. And once the game starts what do we want? No favors please, no charity!

We want what is *due* to us. In the title of that monstrously kitsch novel by Jeffrey Archer we want *Not a Penny More, Not a Penny Less.* If the rules are even slightly vague or ambiguous, we all know what will happen. Our opponent will seize advantage of the slightest ambiguity to tilt the table towards him. For make no mistake about it, both contestants are poring over the small print to wring any concession they can from the other. Since they are doing this so must you. The legal expense is unavoidable as both teams square off.

And so everything *must* be spelled out, every contingency foreseen, every strategy anticipated. If appropriate penalty clauses are not inserted then the unconstrained, unharnessed self-interests of each party will run amok. This is especially important in dealing with foreigners where the scope for cultural misunderstandings is so broad. Unless all details are nailed down in black and white and signed and witnessed, both sides will claim that the understandings within their respective cultures should prevail. Legal penalties are a good way to cut through the cackle. Pain is pain in all cultures at all times, and it concentrates the mind wonderfully upon the objectivity and precision of legal language.

But above all, contracts force foreigners to play *our* game, by *our* rules, in *our* ways which greatly clarifies communication! In a very real sense we use contract law as a defense against anxiety. East Asia confronts us with so much perplexity and ambiguity, and with so many strange sights and sounds that their impacts may overwhelm us. (We might even learn.) Better by far to pull our partners or agents into a definitive legal cage, designed to reduce their range of 'bizarre' behaviors. It is difficult to control foreigners, but possible to control the games we play with them by stipulating all permissible moves.

But, as this chapter will argue, all such defenses are erected at a severe cost to our opportunities to prosper and compete. In most of East Asia the *relationship comes before the contract. Wa* (harmony), *quanxi* (mutual relationships) and dynamic reciprocity, where favors escalate on both sides, are considered more important than the small print. Of course contracts are still to be seen as useful, but these are at best good illustrations of what the parties intended at the time they were negotiating. Where changing circumstances render contract terms onerous to one or both parties, let the terms be changed. The mutual relationship which *made* the contract initially takes precedence over the terms negotiated.

Moreover, each party may strive to go *beyond* contract terms to bestow greater benefits than those legally obligated. All employment contracts in Japan are for one year, so that lifetime employment becomes a favor to employees, for which they must reciprocate with devotion also beyond the expectations of their employer. Indeed, doing what the contract specifies is the *minimum* allowed; both sides will practice trying to do more, improving with every new effort, in a *system of escalating favors.*

After all, a relationship is of infinite duration; where you mingle your genes or products you are for ever joined through the next generation of offspring. Contracts are mere milestones, recordings of your progress along the way, joint understandings reached at finite moments of time. It follows that the Infinite Game, which is your developing relationship, will define, and if needed re-define, all contracts between you. Contracts are soon surpassed as your relationship improves far beyond what you once promised.

The argument in this chapter is as follows:

- Contracts are finite, relationships are infinite. Negotiating contracts tends to be a Finite Game, as does imposing contract terms on partners.
- East Asian cultures, given a choice, are relationship oriented, rather than principle or contract oriented. But when you *combine* contracts with relationships, then you come to regard . . .
- Contracts as the floor—reciprocity as the ceiling.
- Contracts as closed—reciprocity as open.
- Relationships as flexible—contracts as brittle. This is partly because . . .
- Relationships include new information which contracts exclude. Illustrations of dynamic reciprocity include . . .
- Sacrificial pricing and saving reciprocity, which happens when a customer saves a supplier from the consequences of his generosity by, for example, doubling his order. Also . . .
- Tough reports—strong rapport. In this case the rapport within the relationship is strong enough to carry the most painful truths. An orientation to particular relationships also has an effect upon . . .
- Ambiguity and clarity. In a contract culture each party articulates ideas very precisely and makes law from these. In a reciprocity culture, ideas may start as fuzzy and inchoate and be

clarified *through* the relationship. Another angle on this distinction is . . .

- Congruence or consensus. Those who seek contractual clarity typically seek consensus on precise terms, but those who seek to make their aims congruent with another are content that the other's aims are different yet mutually compatible with their own. Acceptance that the other party is different helps the process by which . . .
- Latent and tacit knowledge become articulated, as each party explores together what he really wants and what his latent needs might be. This leads to . . .
- Learning from customers, not 'selling' them on your pre-calculated pitch. Buyers and sellers, customers and suppliers help to discover and articulate each other's needs.

Contracts as finite, relationships as infinite

The Finite Game of contract-terms-before-relationships sees good relationships as the product of contract compliance, of 'keeping your word'. Note the idealized specificity of this phrase. There are not several words but one! Your 'word is your bond'. It is said to be 'coin of the realm', i.e. not adulterated or debased, but precisely what you promised. A relationship may form between you but only after clear demonstrations by both of you that you have kept your word to each other and are doing so even in inconvenient circumstances.

Unfortunately this code of literal compliance becomes a weapon of finite game playing.

By forcing my partner and potential opponent to play by my rules, on my terms, in my way,

I aim to wrest advantage from him by legally or morally enforcing contract terms.

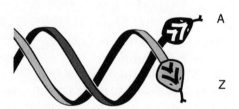

A

Z

This game ends with the threat or reality of courts certifying my victory and if the relationship is thereby forfeit, too bad. I am ahead on the deal and there are many more fish in the sea.

But in the Infinite Game it is our *relationship* which wins, and by extension both of us, with our contracts periodically adjusted so that both of us can benefit. The game reads as follows:

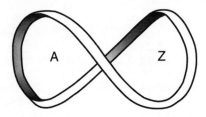

A. Each partner gets all contracts complied with by going beyond the contract to a process of mutual . . .

Z . . . Enrichment wherein escalating favors are reciprocated, relationships deepen, performances improve and . . .

The Infinite Game transcends successive contracts in one developing relationship that includes them all. In this process contracts are important guidelines but not occasions to quarrel. Like banisters on stairs, they are to be gripped only in emergencies. Far more important is the growing satisfaction of both parties and the capacity of their relationship to learn and accumulate information.

East Asian cultures, given the choice, are relationship oriented, rather than principle or contract oriented

We asked three questions which pitted contracts, plus the principles embodied in those contracts, against particular human relationships which were close and intimate. The purpose was to see whether managers would uphold the principle and contractual obligation at issue or would show loyalty and support for close friends and associates. It is important to remember that *we forced this choice* on respondents through posing dilemmas. They did not *want* to sacrifice friends to principles, or principles to friends! We were trying to dig down to the origins of their judgements.

In Question 1, in Table 8.1, 'You are the doctor for an insurance company examining a close friend who needs more insurance.' Your friend is in pretty good shape, but you have doubts, two minor points, difficult to diagnose. Would you shade your doubts in favor of your friend or stick with your obligation to the insurance company?

Table 8.1   Universal contractual principles or loyalty to particular friends?

Question 1: '*Would I shade my doubts in favor of my friend?*'
% agreeing

1	Korea	57.21	14	Italy	39.86
2	Belgium	52.11	15	Spain	38.87
3	Thailand	52.00	16	USA	38.41
4	Singapore	49.20	17	UK	38.24
5	Taiwan	49.18	18	Malaysia	37.48
6	Germany	47.26	19	Brazil	37.25
7	The Netherlands	46.04	20	Switzerland	35.52
8	France	45.71	21	Sweden	35.40
9	China	43.57	22	Canada	34.97
10	Indonesia	43.13	23	Australia	33.64
11	Hong Kong	42.86	24	Norway	31.29
12	Philippines	41.80	25	Ireland	31.15
13	Japan	41.68	26	New Zealand	25.23

Question 2: '*Would I testify for my friend?*'
% agreeing

1	Korea	63.53	14	Brazil	28.81
2	China	48.50	15	Germany	21.29
3	Indonesia	48.24	16	Italy	20.88
4	Hong Kong	46.43	17	The Netherlands	18.93
5	Thailand	43.09	18	UK	17.17
6	Japan	38.22	19	Canada	16.28
7	Taiwan	38.00	20	Ireland	15.14
8	Philippines	37.61	21	Australia	13.54
9	Beligum	34.62	22	USA	13.11
10	France	34.58	23	Sweden	13.05
11	Singapore	33.84	24	New Zealand	12.07
12	Malaysia	31.91	25	Switzerland	10.71
13	Spain	29.83	26	Norway	8.20

Question 3: '*Has a friend a right to expect me to go easy . . .?*'
% agreeing

1	Korea	55.82	14	Germany	40.07
2	Hong Kong	54.46	15	UK	39.79
3	Japan	47.09	16	Canada	37.05
4	Singapore	46.97	17	Sweden	35.94
5	China	45.55	18	USA	35.31
6	Indonesia	45.53	19	New Zealand	35.00
7	Malaysia	42.00	20	Ireland	34.76
8	Taiwan	41.96	21	Italy	34.49
9	France	41.94	22	Norway	34.10
10	Spain	41.04	23	Brazil	33.76
11	Belgium	40.96	24	Australia	33.74
12	Thailand	40.86	25	Philippines	32.50
13	The Netherlands	40.25	26	Switzerland	29.81

Source: The Trompenaars Group, Database. Amsterdam, 1997.

East Asian countries occur in four of the top five places in preferring relationships and nine of the top thirteen. Only Malaysia is adrift and most of our data come from US-owned companies there, who probably taught their legal–contractual orientation to employees.

In Question 2 a much more serious dilemma is posed, one going to the foundations of civic virtue. 'You are riding in a car with a close friend, and he hits a pedestrian.' You know he was breaking the speed limit. 'His lawyer says if you testify under oath that his speed was only 20 mph, it may save your friend from serious consequences. There are no other witnesses.' Should your testimony support your friend?

The more serious the issue the more completely it divides the West from most of East Asia. Here East Asian cultures occupy the eight highest places and ten of the top twelve. Koreans are nearly eight times more likely to side with close friends than Norwegians, and five times more likely than Americans. Before we conclude that East Asians are barely moral at all, let us consider the third question.

This was about a journalist writing a column on restaurants, whose female friend has sunk her life savings in a restaurant where the food is *not* good! Has she a right to expect her close friend to go easy on her new restaurant? Once again the top eight cultures most inclined to put friendship first are East Asian.

Let us remind ourselves that there are *no right answers*. To stick with principle and your contract with the insurance company, with your newspaper and its readers and with fellow citizens, is self-evidently 'right' in Western traditions, but not so self-evident in East Asia. We could argue that if personal friendship and family were the social ideal, then most people would tell the truth most of the time, as one would to a good friend or family member. You can generalize a Golden Rule to particular cases, or you can discover and rediscover within particular relationships, your golden rules. Both ways of thinking work.

Nor is being particularist and supporting close friends enough to guarantee fast economic development. Among national cultures which are relationship orientated but *not* growing fast are Yugoslavia, Nepal, Venezuela, Russia, Bulgaria and Kuwait. The ideal which develops the economy is neither rules-without-relationships nor relationships-without-rules, but contractual rules *within* improving relationships. The reason East Asian economies are growing so fast is that they go *beyond* rules to build up relationships around these, which develop ever higher levels of reciprocity. The rules they have learned from us. But have we learned relationships from them?

Contracts as the floor—reciprocity as the ceiling

Most contracts among major Japanese corporations and some 'tiger' corporations use these to make a minimal 'floor', below which the contract has been breached. But standards specified in the contract are *not* the ideal, but rather indicate the lowest level of acceptable performance, the springboard from which the supplier or contractor is expected to gain higher elevation after each try.

Motorola recently struggled hard to come up to tough specifications set by Toshiba. There was general rejoicing when they made it, in which congratulations Toshiba joined. After all, the specifications were exacting. But when Motorola again met the same specifications three months later, Toshiba had stopped smiling. 'When are you going to improve?' they asked.[1] Meeting the contract is rarely enough. You are expected to do *more*, whereupon Toshiba does more for you, and dynamic reciprocity takes off into the stratosphere, leaving the contracted terms far below both of you.

Going beyond contracts is a moral rather than a legal act, something for which you feel grateful, not entitled; something that indebts you to your benefactor so you strive mightily to repay. This is one reason why East Asians are at best lukewarm about 'human rights' and 'human entitlements'. If something generous and kind is a 'right', the recipient will not be grateful, will not feel the need to repay, will cease efforts to surpass previous performances, will rest content when dues are paid. Relationships are renewed and maintained by feelings of indebtedness, which are shifted off one's own shoulders and onto one's partners, when your reciprocity exceeds the original favor. Now your partner must think of a way of surpassing *your* generosity, and so on.

We recall the bewilderment of a Chinese CEO on receiving instructions from his American parent company that all local employees must receive from their supervisor attentions 'due' to them. There was, said the Human Resource protocol, an 'implied contract' between superiors and subordinates under which subordinates had 'rights' to a list of 'entitlements'. 'It doesn't translate into Mandarin', said the CEO worriedly. 'If I translated this literally, there could be a riot. We give to each other what each *deserves*. No one gets anything up-front because he stands there breathing. I'm sure it makes sense in English but we don't *think* this way.'[2]

Contracts are closed—reciprocities are open

The problem with carefully specified contracts is that you get what is 'due' to you, and *that is all you get*. Contracts are closed systems. The worker promises to work an eight-hour shift, to be punctual, to obey instructions, to keep busy and to receive a set wage in consideration of this. The only ethic involved is 'a fair day's work for a fair day's pay', to quote the cliché of Western industrial relationships. It is not a prospect which inspires.

And what is not expressly forbidden may be done, such as the unannounced lay-off of large parts of the work force by the very managers who made the errors necessitating this. Employment contracts are designed so that the company, not the employee, will win any finite conflict which may break out. This is true of nearly all corporations, East or West.

The important difference is that escalating reciprocity leaves employment contracts far behind. We consulted with P Y Lai, then the CEO of Intel in Malaysia. On his own initiative, and fending off inquiries from HQ, he organized a free bus service to bring his employees and other employees in the zone to work and back. He set up a kindergarten in the grounds of the company, where working mothers could leave their children, together with an adult activity center, a sports center, etc. He started an in-house shop so employees did not have to travel half a mile to local shops. From the profits of this venture he started a credit union, from which employees could borrow. The funds of the union were invested in medium tech. companies in the area. Why?

So anyone who cannot keep up with the complexities needed to make the Pentium processor has another job to go to, a job in a company partly owned by the union. No one, I repeat *no one*, since I took charge has left without a job to go to. If they all do their best, we look after them.[3]

What puzzled us was how the company could possibly afford the additional costs of all these amenities, the rose garden where the kindergarten children sat learning English, the equipment in the gymnasium. How could management justify this by the usual payback criteria? We discussed this somewhat confusedly. We do not think Lai understood us properly, nor we him. But when he described the reciprocal *process* by which these amenities were offered and the iterated response of employees, we could understand. Following each new initiative, employees would organize spontaneously to do something for management and shareholders, who had just done something for them. This took the form of campaigns to reduce maintenance costs, to bring down the costs of waste metal and silicon scrap, week by week, to keep a perfect record of on-time deliveries, even if this meant volunteers working late. One way or another they *more than repaid the costs of each successive amenity*, with the result that they got another and then another.

While in contracts you get only what you originally bargained for, in dynamic reciprocity you get what your partners have devised for your benefit. It may be novel, unprecedented and far beyond your expectations. It requires that they identify with your needs and purposes, imagine themselves running the company, as with Japanese 'voluntary management' groups, and provide something their supervisors may not even have thought of, or thought necessary. There are more things in an engineering workshop than are dreamed of in a lawyer's contract. Relationships, but not contracts, are wide open to infinite possibilities.

This helps to explain why taxes, welfare burdens and costs of government regulations tend to be far lower in tiger economies. Relationships rise above litigiousness. Business includes more social activities. The work bargain between managers and workers is *much more broadly defined*. While contracts are narrow: 'I do this and you do that and that settles our account', dynamic reciprocity is broad: 'I will do anything for which you are so grateful as to return my favor'. Companies build social infra-structure *not* for reasons of 'paternalism', but to provoke employees into imaginative reciprocities. The broader the work bargain and the more social amenities it includes, the less is left for governments to do, and the more of what humans live for is *connected* to their work. P Y Lai did not put a single Intel worker on the unemployment rolls.

Flexible relationships—brittle contracts

One consequence of relationships being open is that they are flexible and can change as events and situations change around them. But contracts, being closed systems, are brittle. Circumstances change but contracts insist upon compliance with superseded logics. In most cases these changes elevate the fortunes of one party while depressing the fortunes of the other. Contract terms become a bonanza for the first and a crushing burden for the second, who tries to escape his obligations while the first tries just as hard to box him in. A Finite Game breaks out which, whatever its outcome, ruins the relationship.

The one favored by the changing circumstances argues that he gambled and won. His forecasters read more correctly the changing scene. His lawyers were the more far-sighted. The one harmed by the changing circumstances searches desperately for a loophole or technicality in order to escape. No one expected this to happen. Circumstances alter cases. Ruin is in prospect.

Just such a scenario arose in the mid-seventies between Japanese sugar importers and Australian sugar refiners. The ink was hardly dry upon the contract when the world price of sugar tumbled by over $10 per ton. The Japanese had signed long term contracts to buy Australian sugar at $5 below world markets price only to find themselves obligated for many years to pay $5 above the world price. In keeping with Japanese custom, the importers asked for the contract to be re-negotiated. Surely the Australians could not want the Japanese sugar industry to collapse under so massive a disadvantage? Surely the mutual satisfaction of both parties and their ongoing relationship was what really mattered?

In keeping with Australian custom, the answer was blunt. The Japanese importers had miscalculated and must pay the penalty. The Australian refiners had fairly bargained and fairly won. Had the price risen not fallen, Australians would not be crying and the Japanese should practice the same intestinal fortitude. You get paid in business for risk-taking and it ill behoves players to try to escape the price of losing.[4]

Such tough talking is, of course, the song of the Finite Game. You win some, you lose some, and to ask to have the score changed at the end of the match is for wimps.

In vain did the *Japanese Economic Newspaper* complain: 'It is true that a contract is a contract, but when customers are in a predicament, we believe that assistance is routinely extended . . .'[5]

It was especially galling that most Western governments took Australia's side. Japan had just reeled from the first oil shock and was about to reel from the second. Nearly all her energy was imported. Surely Australians could not *want* her to suffer such reverses? Australians did not appear to mind at all . . .

Relationships include new information which contracts exclude

In all the fuss around learning organizations and learning nations we routinely forget to ask *who learns?* The traditional Western corporation, especially in Britain and North America, states that *individuals* learn. You hire and you fire until you have all the 'units of intelligence' you need. As challenges come and go, you off-load those you no longer need and on-load those you now require, forming the requisite networks of expertise. It works rather like Legoland construction. It is the job of schools and universities to produce the intelligent units.

But this greatly simplifies and underestimates how intelligence actually works and how knowledge is used in business. It makes more sense to say that knowledge is stored in *relationships*. I know what I know, but I also know *that* Tom, Dick and Mary are knowledgeable about certain work-related issues. I do not know what they know, that would be duplication, but knowing that they know means that this knowledge can be retrieved. We do not even know what the books in our own libraries say, but know enough about them to pull them from the shelf on cue. Again the knowledge is in our relationships to information sources not 'inside' each one of us.

It follows that relationships are not simply open-ended and flexibly changing, they can store and access knowledge in any one of their nodes. For example, in a team of ten people with ten different skills, each could, in theory, make nine factorial two-skill combinations, or 240—a large number and a very versatile capacity. A learning organization resembles a fractal super-brain, a brain *of* brains with neural connections inside each brain and relationships between brains capable of accessing what these know. No wonder that Japanese auto-producers average 28.9 suggestions per worker of which 23.0 are implemented, compared with 1.3 in the USA with 0.7 implemented

Plants with suggestion schemes

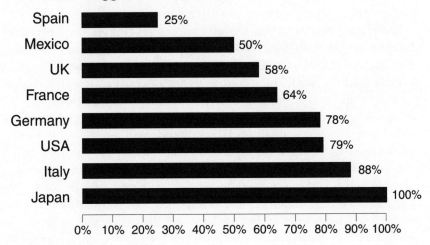

Suggestions per person

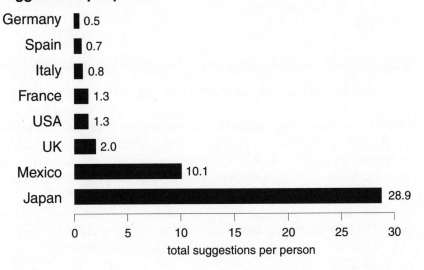

Figure 8.1 Suggestion schemes and their relative success in worldwide automobile manufacturing. Suggestions are incentivized in the USA, UK and Germany, with the average worth of around $225, rising up to $4,500. Japanese incentives are symbolic at around $20. A thousand-person Japanese auto plant could expect to make 23,000 changes in its workplace per annum out of 29,000 suggestions. Source: *Worldwide Manufacturing Competitiveness Study.* Andersen Consulting, 1994.

(see Figure 8.1). Japan does not simply elicit fourteen times more suggestions than the UK but implements 80% of them, while implementation ratios are around 50% for other nations.

In contrast, contracts and the way we interpret them present a very different proposition. Much energy is given over to *excluding* all issues save those deemed relevant to deciding the finite contest. One of us recently had the misfortune to lose a case in court concerning a legal partner who sued for a share in the proceeds of our business. We contended, as defendant and witness, that the partner had done nothing to help us at all; that we could find no client that had approached us at his bidding and he should not be paid for doing nothing. The court found that indeed he had done nothing but the contract *had not specified anything he should do* and that therefore his 'good will' was sufficient to earn him $300,000. It must be the most expensive vibration ever beamed in our direction, but it serves to remind us that contracts are no substitute for relationships, especially when the former are so narrowly interpreted and the latter are a potential cornucopia of benefits.

Sacrificial pricing and saving reciprocity

One of the commonest accusations made against Japan, Korea and other tigers is 'predatory' pricing. These people have no idea about the necessity of making profits and no concept of unit cost structures. We have in our files an extended complaint from an American parent to a Korean subsidiary that it was 'giving away the store' and seemed to think that 'we're a charity'. The Korean subsidiary had actually priced below the current per unit cost of the product. 'We cannot countenance this reckless disregard for pricing guidelines', the memo concluded.

'Predatory' would be the right word if we were playing Finite Games. The contestant is attempting to destroy all other players. But 'sacrificial' is the better description of those trying to set an Infinite Game in motion. To price below cost is, in fact, sacrificial to the point of suicide *if* your customer does nothing but accept your offer. Suppose, however, that the customer knows full well the cost to you of so low an offer and decides to save you from the consequences of your generosity by quadrupling his order? Now you can supply him profitably after all—who says that cost-per-unit is the decisive issue? What about the *value of reciprocity*?

If a woman goes into a Tokyo drug store to buy a shade of lipstick not in stock, the staff may motion her to a chair and deliver the product by dispatch rider within twenty minutes. Now the cost of running a single tube by motorbike across town is at least five times the cost of the lipstick, but you still oblige and if the customer later reciprocates the favor, you may both still profit. In any event, the focus of value is the human relationship, not the material lipstick. The hope must be that the relationship mediates additional trade.

The psychological impact of this deliberate vulnerability is of some consequence. Suppose you have supplied a customer several times at sacrificially low prices and high cost to yourself? In that case the customer's appreciation of your offer and his reciprocity has literally saved you, repeatedly. People who have made themselves dependent on other people's gratitude and returned kindness establish *close bonds of trust*. If I save your economic life, you are mine. If we save each other's we are blood brothers, partners for ever, infinite players.

This helps to explain the non-tariff barriers the West encounters in doing business in parts of East Asia, especially Japan and Korea. Coming in with a tempting offer or a better product may not be enough to break existing relationships. Instead one partner will urge the other to match the Western product's price and quality so that they may continue a lifetime's mutuality without loss of competitiveness. There is nothing much governments can do about such practices, which are cultural. Hence 'market opening' initiatives and promises generally fail to work out in practice.

A notorious case is the one of Japanese rice, up to eight times more expensive than American rice, yet hard to distinguish in quality. Rice in Japan has ancient historical roots as a staple for food, drink and paper. It symbolizes connection to the earth in a land increasingly urban. Rice is the centerpiece and sponsor of cultural festivals which preserve the endangered life of traditional villages. The Japanese architect Kisho Kurokawa has called rice a 'sacred zone' of culture bonding town and country.[6]

Despite fierce American pressures the Japanese government refused to allow the low price of American rice to compete with the expensive social bonds of Japanese rice. Perhaps they feared the outcome of a Finite Game between loyal relationships and a price differential so vast. Loyalty might lose, as it does so often in the West. Instead, the

Japanese allowed imports of a fixed quota of American rice and *blended* it with Japanese rice, thereby selling it more cheaply than would otherwise be possible. It was an ingenious if unorthodox solution to preserving relationships at a cost borne by all domestic rice consumers equally. At the same time Americans were, in part, mollified.

In the case just cited it proved expensive to preserve relationships rather than let American rice capture the whole market, but tenacious loyalty among partners who have 'saved each other' is, in most cases, very effective. It marries reports with rapport, an issue we now consider.

Tough reports—strong rapport

A characteristic of contracts is the accurate, signed reports they give of what both parties promise to do. There it is in writing. Where contracts are not written down, courts will infer from the behavior of people, reported in evidence, that implied contracts existed. In contrast, relationships are all about rapport, the enjoyment of another's presence. Deborah Tannen, an American psycho-linguist, found in her studies that American men leant heavily towards reporting and American women more to rapporting. If a wife complains because she wants comfort and sympathy, the husband immediately treats the complaint as a report and tries to find solutions to her problem![7]

If the two styles are polarized, each has its weakness. Reporters fail to relate. Rapporters try to protect their relationship from 'the truth', say a simple solution to the complaint being made, or the money saved by buying American rice. But, and this is crucial, rapport can, like relationships, *include tough reports within it*. Businesses survive by facing and communicating accurate reports with very dire consequences, tough upon the parties concerned. If, for example, you have a long relationship with a partner who is not now improving fast enough, your report of this will potentially distress both of you. Your rapport must be very strong to survive such reports. Any hope of influencing him to change needs a toughness about the predicament joined to a tenderness about your relationships of *equally strong intensities*.[8]

There are issues so personal and so threatening that only your best friend will tell you and which are only believable coming from such a friend. Here truth and friendship intertwine, while in the enforcement of contracts truth has cast out friendship and one version of the truth must be victorious over another.

Menthe tells the story of American and Japanese negotiators starting off their session with speeches in which each side begged the other to be 'sincere'. Unfortunately their definitions of sincerity differed widely.[9] What the Americans meant was that they would express their feelings and beliefs honestly and without reserve, straight-from-the-shoulder reports. What the Japanese meant was they would make a *bona fide* attempt to be so hospitable, kind, attentive, correct and polite and be such assiduous hosts that the Americans would reciprocate with equal sincerity, and rapport would be established, each side being now obligated to the other. It is only *later* that the Japanese try to encompass report within rapport. This is the stage when *tatamae* — surface politeness and etiquette—gives way to *honne* — the sharing of deep feelings.

Of course, the meeting was not exactly a success. Americans told hard truths which devastated Japanese attempts at good etiquette. So, far from reciprocating the trouble the Japanese had taken, Americans seemed intent on puncturing it. The American view was that there was 'too much bullshit and rigmarole'. They had tried to 'talk turkey' but the Japanese became upset.

Ambiguity and clarity

East Asia and much of the West differ in their relative evaluation and communication of ambiguous versus clear statements. Sino-Japanese discourse is famously indirect, aphoristic, metaphorical, indirect, tangential, analogical and fuzzy.[10] The Japanese have even made major technological breakthroughs in 'fuzzy-logic' microchips.[11] In these cultures you imply what you mean, to see if the other wishes to participate in the clarification of that meaning or has, perhaps, a different meaning, which qualifies yours yet is connected to it. It is *not* that cultures prefer unclarity or expect to develop economically by being vague, it is rather a difference in the process of clarification itself. Western cultures, especially English speaking ones, prefer the individual to articulate clear and precise ideas. The clarification takes place in the mind before speaking. East Asian cultures, for the most part, prefer more vague and tentative statements, clarified through *dialog and relationships.*

In other words, meanings and precise formulations are negotiated. It is considered ungraceful and uncouth to confront other people with completed and predefined propositions of your own, so that in effect you shove these down their throats to swallow or regurgitate.[12]

The vagueness of indirect speech necessitates longer pauses between statements. The person responding must interpret what was said and then connect his own meaning to that statement in a constructive manner, not 'yes . . . but', but 'yes . . . and'. Such discussions tend to enlarge meanings and construct whole patterns of interconnected meanings. When English speakers put a proposition to Japanese speakers there is often a very long pause. In part this comes from the need to translate the structure of one language into another, but it also comes from the Japanese idea that they must *fit their response to your statement* so as to confirm and build upon it.

Two habits English speakers have which upset the Japanese is to make incisive, challenging, confrontational statements and then *not wait for the reply* but add more such statements.[13]

It is notorious that when Westerners try to negotiate with the Japanese the former try to clarify the contractual agreement point by point while the latter give off vague assurances and subtle hints intended for later clarification, but not *in themselves* clear. Westerners are trying to build a solid edifice out of agreed pieces, like laying bricks; the Japanese are inviting you to jointly mold a lump of soft clay into an esthetic and elegant shape, going back to the parts Westerners thought had been agreed hours ago and modifying their shape.

Each side has a different mental model of negotiation. For the Japanese mutual satisfaction, mutual benefit and ever improving reciprocal relationships are the key. To this end, items and specifics are best left to the goodwill of the parties and should fit the circumstances at the time of delivery. If the whole is to be harmonious the pieces should be flexible enough to fit that whole.

For many Western cultures each item is an essential component in the structure of the contract, where even if *one* term is ignored a precedent may be created for ignoring others, especially those costly to one party. If you try to alter one piece, late in the negotiations, the whole edifice could collapse, since one part stands upon or balances another. Japanese vagueness is seen as an attempt to evade compliance with negotiated contract terms, a sure sign of unreliability.

Yet vagueness followed by relationships-which-clarify may give East Asia advantages in building the networks and alliances so crucial to late capitalism, since these are based on congruence.

Congruence versus consensus

There are two approaches to the psychology of agreement, according to Bill Ouchi.[14] Cultures in the West tend to idealize *consensus*, as enshrined in contracts voluntarily entered; while East Asians, especially the Japanese, think more in terms of *congruence* among the goals being sought by various parties, as enshrined in reciprocal relationships. Consensus means you 'want the same things' and is a 'celebration of sameness'. Congruence means you want different things and is a celebration of diversity but that both or all such objectives are congruent with one another.[15] Dynamic reciprocity in which favors escalate on each one is clearly a cause that is congruent, not consensual. Contracts where both sides sign up to a single statement of terms are clearly consensual.

Of course not all clauses in the contract are equally attractive to the parties, who might prefer to gain the benefits while avoiding the obligations, but by agreeing to the document as a whole they have put their pledged word ahead of self-interest. In cultures motivated by self-interest there may be no better way.

In contrasting Japanese with American labor relations, Ouchi points out that in American labor relations both sides are, in theory, bound by contract to pursue the objective of the enrichment of shareholders. It is somehow difficult to conceive of American workers greeting the dawn of each day with the happy prospect of making shareholders wealthier, especially since the same shareholders may have bought or sold their shares before lunch. It is more realistic, Ouchi argues, to assume that workers want to improve the lot of themselves and their families, but that this goal is seen as *congruent with* paying returns to shareholders and investing more in the company.[16] The stakeholder vision of East Asian capitalism is based upon a dynamic reciprocity among stakeholders. The profit-maximizing vision of Anglo-American capitalism is based around an assumed consensus upon the employment contract, in which top managers 'represent shareholders' to their organizations.

This difference between consensus and congruence becomes even more important as we move further into the Learning Society. People who agree with each other are redundant as far as information is concerned. You learn something new from someone different from yourself, and widen your horizons by learning to reciprocate to needs not your own. Learning Networks consist of different agendas congruent with one another and benefiting from aid and trade.

Magorata Maruyama examined the spontaneous formation of Japanese youth groups. He found they organized themselves to draw upon the widest variety of pastimes. Hence the group would admit members for their knowledge of videos, music discs, baseball, telephone cards (collected like stamps), video games, pachinteo parlors etc. Instead of duplicating consensual interests, they diversified congruent interests so each new member brought new knowledge to the group.[17]

Congruent objectives explain why Singapore's Economic Development Board is such a good host to Western multinationals. It does not really matter if Western corporations locate there with the objective of making profits and repatriating these to Western shareholders, if in this process Singaporean skills are utilized and upgraded. Receiving dividends does not teach you very much. Learning higher and higher skills means that you make yourselves invaluable to all corporations in the knowledge race. There is a dynamic reciprocity in which both parties get what they value. The problem for the West may lie in what it values, and the advantage for Singapore may lie in its different perspectives.[18]

Latent, tacit and articulated knowledge

Knowledge varies considerably as to whether it is coded and articulated, in which case it is clear and definitive, or whether it is latent and tacit in which case it is vague and easily modifiable. Max Boisot and John Child contrasted the uses of knowledge in America, the United Kingdom, China and Japan and found that the two Western nations had a pronounced preference for codified knowledge of the kind used in computers, bond prices and the Dow Jones averages in 'market' cultures. Chinese and Japanese managers had more respect for tacit and uncodified knowledge of the kind exchanged in close relationships.[19]

While Sino-Japanese culture saw latent, uncodified knowledge as the well-springs of knowledge itself, Western cultures felt this barely qualified as knowledge at all, unless it was in the process of being codified in which case it would literally 'count'.

Codified knowledge was also much more likely to lead to conflict with other rival codes, each trying to force re-definition upon the other. Because of its sheer size and wealth, the USA has usually won these conflicts. It is no coincidence that the International Dialling Code for the USA is 1, or that world time zones start at Greenwich (a suburb of London) Mean Time. Boisot observes:

> Codifying is conflict-laden. To assert A is also to reject not-A and thus by implication to reject those . . . who have a stake in not-A as an outcome. New knowledge is always, . . . to a degree, a threat to the established order, to the stability of at least part of the old order.[20]

In contrast, starting from tacit and latent knowledge, sharing this in reciprocal relationships and agreeing ultimately on a common code is a far less quarrelsome mode of operating. Ikujiro Nonaka and Hirotaka Takeuchi describe this difference between US and Japanese corporate cultures:

> Japanese companies . . . have a very different understanding of knowledge. They recognize that knowledge expressed in words and numbers represents only the tip of the ice-berg. Their view of knowledge as being primarily 'tacit' is something not easily visible and expressible. Tacit knowledge is highly personal and hard to formalize, making it difficult to share and communicate with others . . . (it is) deeply rooted in ideals, values or emotions . . . schematic, mental models, beliefs and perceptions, so ingrained we take them for granted.[21]

Owing to the difficulty in communicating latent knowledge people move very close to each other in their attempts to share, hence 'clan cultures' and 'fief cultures' in which non-verbal behavior is common, including *haraga* or 'belly talk'. Nonaka and Takeuchi argue that whatever deficit the Japanese suffer from in their lack of individualism and their reluctance to stand out from the group is more than made up for by the processing of tacit knowledge within close relationships and a genuine capacity to co-create new meanings, by moving together from tacit to codified forms.

An interesting example of this is 'latent need analysis', a process originated by Japanese electronics firms in engaging their customers and makers of original equipment. In this process you describe what an envisaged microchip or semi-conductor could do and then explore with customers their latent needs for such a device. The need is 'latent' because, until told of the possibility, the equipment maker would not know that such a device was possible. He needs to be informed that traffic congestion can be detected ahead of one's vehicle, police put on the trail of a stolen car by use of a transmitter, or that the car can self-seal on hitting water. If indeed there is a need for such functions, intimate plans are laid to install them two or three years from now. Translating the technical capabilities of chips into the vehicle capabilities of autos involves the exchange of tacit knowledge, personal confidences and shared secrets. It is perhaps the closest customer relationship of all.

Learning from customers and 'selling' them

Throughout this book we have stressed that Western cultures have seen and even originated many of the 'ways' of East Asia but without internalizing these or, if finally internalizing them, doing so belatedly and reluctantly, after seeing them work well elsewhere. An interesting example of this is an experiment conducted by Tim Gallwey, the Californian-based writer and consultant with IBM sales forces in the mid-eighties.[22]

For years sales people had met together quarterly to compare selling records. Contests were staged in who had closed the most sales and written the most contracts. But there were problems. The harder sales staff pushed to close sales, the more customers resisted and delayed. 'It's like pulling teeth', one salesman said.

Gallwey conducted an experiment in which sales staff competed in *what they learned from customers* in the previous quarter. They would come to the platform in turn and tell all the other sales staff what they had discovered, who then voted on the value of this knowledge. Pushing contracts upon reluctant customers ceased to be the object of the game. Listening to them and gleaning valuable information became the focus instead.

And, of course, sales rose and customer resistance melted. The contract had been swallowed up in broader relationships of reciprocity between customers and sales representatives. Look after the relationships and the sales will take care of themselves.

Stories like these can be multiplied indefinitely. American culture has been shown again and again that broader reciprocity works better than grim struggles to sell contracts. What is missing is the cultural programing which can easily absorb such lessons. Trying to qualify contractual orientations is like swimming upstream. A sale is only a sale if you have 'sold him' on your proposition.

Summary

We have seen that contracts have the effect of chopping relationships into finite episodes, each independent of the other. Those negotiating contracts too often try to slant the rules so as to give the advantage to their own clients. Contracts confine parties to stipulated obligations and benefits and are designed so as to be successfully enforced through adversarial procedures in a court of law. To this end the words used are literally interpreted.

The first set of issues we addressed was that while for Westerners the contract terms were the end point, for East Asians the contract forms the starting point, the floor which escalating reciprocities could raise to ever higher ceilings. While contracts were closed, brittle, frozen in time and largely confined in their information to what the contract originally stated, relationships were open to new ideas, flexible in the face of new environments, forever contemporary and able to store information accessible to all parties.

The Finite Game pits both parties against a literal reading of the contract terms to which both are subordinated. The contract 'wins':

Both parties are subordinate to
and confined within, a strict
interpretation of contract terms . . .

Frozen in time, closed to new
ideas or information and blind to
changing environments.

The Infinite Game, on the other hand, reads as follows:

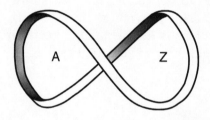

A. Specification of a floor for minimal contract compliance acts as a spring-board for a series of reciprocal initiatives, which progressively raise performance . . .

Z. Ceilings via relationships open to new ideas, flexible in the face of new events, always contemporary, and storing crucial information so as to surpass . . .

A second set of issues argued that sacrificial pricing followed by reciprocity which saved the supplier from his own perilous generosity engendered mutual trust and very strong rapport, so that relationships in East Asia had a durable tenacity, constituting 'non-tariff barriers'. While offers of cheaper products easily severed old relationships between suppliers and customers in some Western countries, East Asian companies maintain their relationships, using strong rapport within those relationships to match or surpass Western offerings.

The Finite Game the West is accustomed to reads like this:

Whenever a customer receives a
report that the unit price of a
product from his regular supplier
has been surpassed by a rival
bid . . .

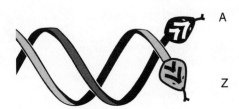

Then his *rapport* with that supplier
is severed and is sacrificed so that
the better offer can be
accepted . . .

The Finite Game between personal gain and personal loyalty leads to gain winning and loyalty losing.

But the Infinite Game both takes notice of the more competitive price *and* works to preserve the original relationship by persuading the regular supplier to match or surpass the new price. It reads as follows:

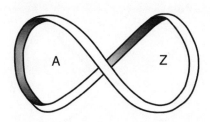

A. Sacrificially low prices from
suppliers evoke a saving reciprocity
from customers, engendering
powerful rapport . . .

Z. And deep trust on both sides
which can countenance tough
reports of price differentials and
by . . .

Finally we see that most Western cultures prefer the clarity of argument and confrontation which leads to the consensus around the articulated, codified knowledge, typical of contracts and the need to 'sell' people these contracts. Codification is inherently quarrelsome, however, since finite game players wish their own rules and codes to prevail. They are more competitive if they can carry with them the codes under which they successfully operated in the past.

The Finite Game often goes something like this:

It becomes possible to 'sell'
customers on a contract and beat
down rival codes, provided we
confront these . . .

A

With a clearly argued, boldly
articulated consensus around a
highly codified system of superior
knowledge.

Z

The Infinite Games preferred in East Asia start with vague, ambiguous, tacit knowledge learned from customer and colleagues. These *become* more precise, more clear, more refined, better articulated selling propositions as a result of dialog, and of constructive participation which progressively defines and polishes these propositions. Instead of seeking consensus on the value of a contract, the two parties look for the congruence between quite different needs, which through dynamic reciprocity can deliver ever more value.

The Infinite Game reads roughly as follows:

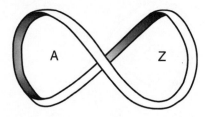

A. Latent, tacit, tentative and vague
ideas are exchanged between
confidantes in a process of mutual
refinement and constructive
co-definition . . .

Z. So that manifest articulated,
finished and clearly defined
products can emerge with excellent
prospects of pleasing customers,
with whom originated the . . .

The answer to so many problems facing the West lies in 'the Between', not in things or in people but in the spaces between these. Phil Slater ended his book *Earthwalk* with the words:

We keep searching for the star-gate but it is not hidden. Hovering delicately in the spaces between things, it has been there all the time . . .[23]

Chapter 9

Beyond Time and Motion: Designing with Time

The future began yesterday

In my early childhood, I always wondered why we only learn from the past . . . Couldn't teachers teach something of the future? . . . Holistic anticipation of the future through the use of Ethnographic Futures Research by many informants with varying backgrounds can provide useful frameworks for policy makers.

S. Ketudat, Former Minister for Education of Thailand, in R. B. Textor (ed.), *The Middle Path for the Future of Thailand.*

How cultures think of time has always provided important clues—to those cultures, for time itself is a social construct. You cannot see, hear or touch time, although you can do all three to instruments used to measure time. In Ancient Greece there were two gods of time, representing two conceptions of time. Chronos was the god of seriatim time, that is time as passing increments; seconds, minutes, hours, days. Kairos was the god of time and opportunity, or the god of 'good timing'.[1]

The Chronos view of time, from which we get chronometer, is linear and sequential:

Time like an ever rolling stream
Bears all its sons away

Time is digitalized. Time flies. Time thunders towards us like an express train, rushes past and then recedes. Clock time has always had a powerful grip on the Western imagination. Sir Isaac Newton conceived of the cosmos as a celestial clock, wound up by God and left for the faithful to discover.

Eastern philosophies conceive of a cycle of eternal return, a wheel of time, a mandala which revolves, a seasonal Tao of shifting night and day, summer and winter. Buddhism teaches that there are timeless moments of enlightenment, a nirvana in which time is suspended, an 'eternal now'. In East Asia, then, we have an orientation to time as timing, a search for infinite moments when time stands still.

Time plays a crucial part in the history of Western industrialism. Frederick Winslow Taylor, the engineer–inventor of carbonized steel tools, developed time and motion study, an attempt to calculate the most efficient motion of hands and tools in a given interval of time. This gave rise to Scientific Management and to Fordism. Vehicles proceeded down a central assembly line whose speed had been calculated, while workers performed stipulated tasks and motions. Work was 'machine timed' and liable to speed-up. Completed vehicles came off the assembly lines every few seconds.

For a number of economic and historical reasons Scientific Management took American industry by storm, and paid back very handsomely indeed. Standardizing production is profitable provided there is a mass market of sufficient size, and America's was the largest the world had ever witnessed. Mass manufacturing geared to this market was spectacularly successful in lowering production costs.[2]

Scientific Management also made profitable use of immigrant laborers, then pouring into the USA. Many did not speak English but were able-bodied and eager, even desperate, to find work. With tasks reduced to a few simple hand motions, workers could be trained in hours and easily replaced if they asked for higher wages. By keeping jobs simple and machines complex, Taylorism kept the price of labor down. He even called a Dutchman, Schultz, the subject of his shoveling experiments, 'ox-like and stupid'—ideal traits for his purposes.[3]

What finally undid the Taylorist strategy of mass manufacturing with replaceable human and machine components was the globalization of markets and the huge increase during the 1980s of international competition. Newly industrializing countries could buy entire factories from the West and man them with workers earning $50 a month. Semi-skilled blue-collar employment in North America, Britain and Australia went into free fall. Trade unions operating domestically were outmaneuvered by corporations acting globally. The world search for cheaper wage rates was on.[4]

The argument in this chapter is as follows:

- Finite sequences contrast with infinite circles. In the Taylorist mind-set you seek to complete sequences fast.
- East Asians are more oriented to synchronous time, to coordinating circles and cycles. This helps to explain . . .
- The psychology of long termism. If time revolves, the past, present and future are all now with decision-makers. The future is not distant. Asian orientations to time are typified by . . .
- Just-in-time delivery, which keeps inventory and carrying costs low while mandating the parties to synchronize activities. This also facilitates . . .
- Customization and short runs, which require careful pre-synchronizing of production processes. This also facilitates . . .
- Parallel processing and flexible manufacturing. East Asian planning is also based on synchronous thinking, hence . . .
- Planning for hybridization and fusion deliberately steers disciplines towards cross-fertilization. If you keep your eye on the rendezvous between yourself and the customer at some future date, then you may benefit from . . .
- Pull strategies and faster time to market. All funds and efforts are concentrated in getting to market, just in time for your customer's requirement. The logic is synchronous.

Finite sequences, infinite circles

A sequence, or a straight line, is necessarily finite. You compete in a race and pass the winning post. Game over. But a circle never ends. If you make a line into an arc and join two arcs you get a circle, an Infinite Game going around for ever.

The same principle applies in the workplace or factory. While it is obviously better to complete jobs in the shortest interval of elapsed time, this is only half the battle. The faster such sequences move, the greater the challenge to coordinate them. It is no use raising the speed of fork-lift trucks to 20 mph if they collide or bury employees in produce. It is no use jumping a traffic intersection to get home before dark if you thereby lock up large parts of downtown Manhattan, a condition known as gridlock. In such games nearly everyone loses and activities grind to a halt.[5]

Nor is sheer speed the answer if this de-skills workers and keeps them stupid, divided and cheap. 'Making a quick buck' may not be conducive to the development of complex products, built to last. As with all 'single principle imperialism', many other values can be sacrificed to the singular goal. You get what you want but then wish you had not wanted it.

Racing against the clock is more implacable than racing against competitors. At least you can take a breather if your competition is not as fast as you are, but the clock never concedes a second, never lets you rest, always demands more. As they sang in the American musical *The Pajama Game*:

When you're racing with the clock
When you're racing with the clock
The second hand, doesn't understand
That your back's all ache
And your fingers break
And your constitution isn't made of rock.

In the middle of the stage loomed a huge clock, with the jerking movements of the dancers keeping time with the ticking seconds on the clock. Clock-time ordered everything: life, work, play—all of it in jumpy increments of time.

The race-against-time is a popular motif throughout Western cultures. Time wins. People and their values lose. The movement of the clock's hands becomes an idiot's rhythm, a dance of marionettes:

Employees grow stupid,
coordination breaks down and
gridlock threatens...

... When protagonists make 'fast
bucks', 'quick killings' and race
against time

A

Z

In the race above, employees' development is stunted, their nervous systems wrecked, their socio-emotional skills atrophy, and their knowledge and complexity are sacrificed. Talking to other workers becomes 'wasting time', pausing for reflection is punished and any activity not foreseen by the time and motion engineer is illegitimate. In the end, even speed itself is sacrificed because sequences jostle each other and collide. The fast-footed opportunist scatters rival players.

Inevitably these failures lead to *re*-engineering, which you do when engineered sequences smash each other up. Except that the logics of re-engineering are more of the same, processes streamlined by purging people and omitting steps.

In contrast, the Infinite Game works by synchronizing the faster of several alternative sequences so that, like relay runners, these pass the baton to each other in carefully timed coordination. The game reads as follows:

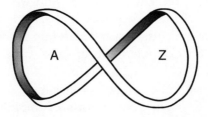

A. To really speed up production accelerate the sequences, and...

Z. By lightening synchronization run these in parallel so as...

Overall time taken to complete a production process equals the speed at which processes move *divided by* the number of processes performed in parallel, rather than in sequence; and to run processes in parallel requires synchronous approaches to expert timing.

Many schedulers begin with the fallacious belief that some 'racecourse' has been set out in advance which they must run, neck and neck with their competitors. In fact, no such racecourse has been decreed in advance, save by the habits of our minds. The best pathways to satisfying customers are *designed by* supplying corporations. Such pathways may be long, where sequences are connected lengthwise, or short, where sequences overlap and are coordinated.

East Asians are more oriented to synchronous time

While we are convinced that sequential versus synchronous time is a crucial bifurcation between cultures, and while there is considerable

Figure 9.1

anthropological writing on this contrast, we are *not* well satisfied with our attempts to measure this difference. We have been using a projective test devised by Tom Cottle, wherein the subjects are asked to express past, present and future by arranging circles of any size on a quarter sheet of paper. We leave the subjects free to decree the relative sizes of past, present and future, and we measure the extent to which the three circles *overlap* or stand *apart* from each other. We conceive overlap as synchronous and standing apart as sequential. We discovered early, for example, that Japan and the USA have highly contrasting styles, as portrayed in Figure 9.1.

Unfortunately, we failed to get confirmation that the rest of East Asia also preferred a synchronous form of thinking about time. We routinely discuss with respondents why they answered as they did, and during our inquiries we were frequently told that Chinese, Singaporean and Hong Kong Chinese felt their future would be radically different from the present, and that therefore they had placed the future far apart from the present to designate 'a great leap' in wealth, living standards or, in the case of Hong Kong, political control. East Asian economies, with the exception of Hong Kong, *do* overlap past and present, but those undergoing rapid economic change face a discontinuity, a race into the unknowable future.

We therefore devised an alternative question. We asked managers about the relative time horizons of the past, present and future, i.e. 'my future starts seconds/minutes/hours/ days/months/years from now'; 'my past started . . .' etc. We were trying to discover to what extent the horizons were discrete, separate and so sequential, or the extent to which they overlapped, fused and were synchronous. Table 9.1 shows the degree to which all three categories overlapped synchronously and the degree to which present and future overlapped to generate long term thinking.

The results are interesting. Five of the top ten in overlap are East Asian cultures, including the first three, yet Malaysia and the Philippines score sequential. Overlap is an even more pronounced trait in East Asia if we consider the-future-within-the-present. Six of

Table 9.1

	Overlap of past, present and future			Overlap of present and future	
1	*Hong Kong*	5.82	1	*Hong Kong*	6.17
2	*Korea*	5.46	2	*China*	5.28
3	*China*	5.31	3	*Korea*	4.44
4	Sweden	5.23	4	*Japan*	4.23
5	France	4.90	5	Sweden	4.12
6	*Japan*	4.88	6	France	4.06
7	Switzerland	4.85	7	*Singapore*	4.00
8	New Zealand	4.75	8	*Indonesia*	3.88
9	Norway	4.74	9	Canada	3.69
10	*Singapore*	4.70		Germany	3.69
	Germany	4.70	11	Switzerland	3.59
12	The Netherlands	4.67	12	The Netherlands	3.58
13	Australia	4.60	13	*Malaysia*	3.57
14	Canada	4.58	14	New Zealand	3.51
15	*Thailand*	4.57	15	UK	3.50
16	*Indonesia*	4.56	16	Norway	3.49
17	UK	4.55	17	USA	3.24
18	Italy	4.48	18	Australia	3.23
19	Belgium	4.37	19	Italy	3.20
20	USA	4.34	20	*Thailand*	3.18
21	*Malaysia*	4.25	21	*Philippines*	2.93
22	Ireland	3.92	22	Ireland	2.91
23	Brazil	3.86	23	Belgium	2.71
24	*Philippines*	3.62	24	Brazil	2.52

Source: Trompenaars Group, Database. Amsterdam, 1997.

the top ten are East Asian, but Indonesia and Singapore turn out to score lower on total overlap because they detach themselves from the poverty of their past. Their present and their future they grasp in a strong synchrony. It is interesting how differently Hong Kong managers think from the stereotype of their short term, laissez-faire Western-type economies. Perhaps they anticipate Chinese rule. Perhaps they never really changed.

Quite apart from the statistics, however, there is a growing body of anthropological research upon the two forms of time (see Table 9.2).[6]

Let us now turn to some of the more profound of these differences.

The psychology of long termism

If only the present is measurable and objective then the future becomes

Table 9.2

Sequential	Synchronous
Do one thing at a time.	Do many things at a time.
Time is objective, tangible, divisible.	Time is inter-subjective, ideational.
Keep carefully to schedule. Concerned with running late.	Time is more elastic. Concerned to complete transactions.
Conflicts solved by 'first come, first served' and forming lines.	Conflicts solved by meeting multiple needs from minimal set of actions.
Accustomed to many short term relationships, easily formed, easily broken, highly flexible.	Accustomed to longer term bonds, renewed through re-acquaintance, tested by shared criticism.
Concentrates on the job, dislikes interruption.	More easily distracted, juggles assignments.
It is good manners to *keep* to time. 'Time and tide waits for no man.'	It is good manners to *give* time. 'What goes around comes around.' Circles,
Straight lines, i.e. 'line organization' 'bottom line'.	i.e. 'quality circles', *ringi.*
Time extended.	Time telescoped.

regarded as uncertain and hypothetical. Money made *now* is worth far more than future prospects, and the further away such futures are, the more they must be discounted. Present value analysis is a popular financial calculation used in Western economies to compare future fund flows by estimating their present value. Hence $1 million of investment starting to pay back at $200,000 per annum after five years will *not* break even in ten years. If we discount cash flows for inflation on, say, 3.0 percent per annum, and for uncertainty, say 7.0 percent, $1 million is worth less than $600,000 five years hence and the present value of $200,000 halves in six years!

Indeed, those using present value analysis are not too inclined to invest in the future at all. It is much too hazardous! Hurdle rates for new investments of 15–40 percent payback, starting as soon as possible, are typical of British and North American corporations. RCA sold its consumer electronics division to Philips because it could not make 15.0 percent ROA. This is the psychology of short termism. Never release substance for shadow. The 'present value' of money is substance. The future is shadow and if you do not meet shareholder expectations in the coming quarter there may not be any future at all!

But suppose past, present and future visions are really *ideas*, whether memories, observations or expectations, all of which are in the meeting room with you at this moment, so that your *idea* of what the future may bring shapes policy. In that case the future permeates present discussions, enlivens current strategy, alters your present direction and watches over you like a Buddhist ancestor reincarnated through your children and grandchildren. Shintaro Ishihara speaks of being haunted as a young man by reading *Camille* by Alexander Dumas. The part he hated most was the digging up of the decayed skeleton of Margarete Gautier, the courtesan heroine. For him Margarete was always alive and beautiful and in the imaginations of readers, ever reborn. To dwell on her material decomposition rather than her eternal youth was spiritually repellent and deeply repugnant.[7]

If the future is aimed at the development of knowledge and the elaboration of core competencies, you can no more afford to stop investing than to stop thinking or gathering knowledge. Long before your investment has paid you back in profits, vital knowledge has reached you which could change everything, including profitability.

That the nations of East Asia save a far greater proportion of their GDP and invest this in the futures of their own nations is made clear in Table 9.3. Eight East Asian economies head the list. Nine are in the top fifteen, only the Philippines lagging. In contrast is the 'spend today' short termism of the English speaking developed economies. Australia at 29th saves only one-third as much as Singapore. The UK

Table 9.3 Gross domestic savings as a proportion of GDP

1	*Singapore*	48.00	19	Norway	21.90
2	*China*	40.50	20	Belgium	21.60
3	*Indonesia*	38.70	21	Israel	21.00
4	*Thailand*	37.20	22	New Zealand	21.00
5	*Malaysia*	35.60	23	Brazil	20.50
6	*Korea*	35.10	24	Germany	19.60
7	*Hong Kong*	33.00	25	Ireland	19.30
8	*Japan*	32.50	26	Spain	18.70
9	Russia	31.50	27	France	18.10
10	Switzerland	29.60	28	Italy	18.00
11	Chile	28.75	29	Australia	16.70
12	Czech Republic	28.71	30	Mexico	15.80
13	*Taiwan*	26.00	31	*Philippines*	15.40
14	Austria	24.20	32	USA	14.90
15	Portugal	23.70	33	Canada	13.30
16	The Netherlands	23.30	34	UK	12.70
17	Poland	23.00	35	Sweden	12.30
18	India	22.10	36	Venezuela	10.80

Source: *World Competitiveness Report*. Lausanne: IMD, 1996.

saves only a quarter as much. The three NAFTA partners, Mexico, the USA and Canada, are 30th, 32nd and 33rd in the savings league. Rich although Singapore, Hong Kong and Korea have become, their savings rates are climbing, while that of the USA, the UK, Australia and Canada are falling.

Up to and including 1989, *The World Competitiveness Report* measured 'The Capacity of Manager to take a Long term View'. After that date the question was rephrased to commend governments who had 'Restructured the Economy for Long term Competitiveness', an attempt to highlight privatization and welfare cuts. In the original question about the culture of managers, Japan scored 1st, Singapore 7th, South Korea 11th, and Taiwan, Thailand and Malaysia 13th, 14th and 15th respectively. No country in East Asia save Hong Kong fell into the bottom half of the table, and Hong Kong, reverting to China in 1997, should not have been asked that question. The USA scored 19th, the UK 22nd and Canada 25th.

Why the longer term orientations in East Asia? The communitarianism we examined in Chapters 4 and 5 must play a part. After all, the country, the corporation, the community and the family all survive our own deaths. Saving is not just for the future of the economy but for the future of all those to whom we have committed our lives. What we have saved transcends our lives and in Buddhist religion could both facilitate and enrich our rebirth.

Long term orientations are also involved in the making of 'remote connections' over time. For example, the current standards of public education today will be crucially important to the effectiveness of a skill-intensive economy thirty to forty years hence. No one denies this, but most East Asian economies follow the Japanese in giving prime importance to elementary and secondary education. Indeed, Japanese colonialism, cruel and oppressive though it was, considerably boosted school literacy in Malaysia, Taiwan, Singapore and Korea. The status ascribed to schoolteachers is generally high throughout the region.[8]

The situation in the English speaking developed economies is in marked contrast. Britain's public education sector is starved because the elite educate their children privately. The USA uses property taxes to fund education and a majority of property owners do not have children of school age. Voters have been campaigning to roll back property taxes for some years. In California, as of 1995, spending on prisons and crime-fighting overtook spending on education for the first time in the history of the state and is expected to exceed education by 20 percent in the year 2000.[9]

Most property owners are understandably more concerned with avoiding robbery than with educating other people's children. The Finite Game known as 'The War Against Crime' is sucking up more and more resources, but crime is itself fueled by 'losers' in Finite Games with grudges against the rules by which they lost.

Just-in-time delivery

If Americans invented ever faster motions in ever less time, then the Japanese brought to this calculation JIT (or just-in-time synchronization). Until quite recently corporations carried large inventories so that mass production machinery could be kept in continuous operation. The costs of running out of raw materials or components were considered to be much higher than the costs of funds tied up in large inventories.

It was all part of the economies of scale. A large number of standardized products were cheaper than smaller numbers, and large numbers of standardized supplies were cheaper too, so 'pile 'em high and sell 'em cheap'. The piles of inventory were not simply in the storeroom but lay in heaps around the factory. Every separate operation was buffered against another operation by large stocks of work-in-process. You did not have to speak to operators working on later stages of a process, you had only to leave them a pile of sub-assemblies, from which they could pick the less obviously faulty and work on those. Inventory had become the universal salve of poor coordination.

Led by Taichi Ohno of Toyota, Japanese industry declared war on excess inventories, thereby exposing uncoordinated workings.[10] Ohno was famous for wrathfully kicking piles of inventory whenever he encountered them. He kept inventories, and hence carrying costs, way down by having suppliers deliver stocks minutes before they were needed, or just-in-time. Without work-in-process inventories the activities of the whole plant needed fine-tuning and precise coordination, and the reliance of every team on other teams was immediately apparent. Work now resembled a choreographed dance. It could be, and was, speeded up to become an 'ever faster dance', but coordination was never sacrificed to speed.

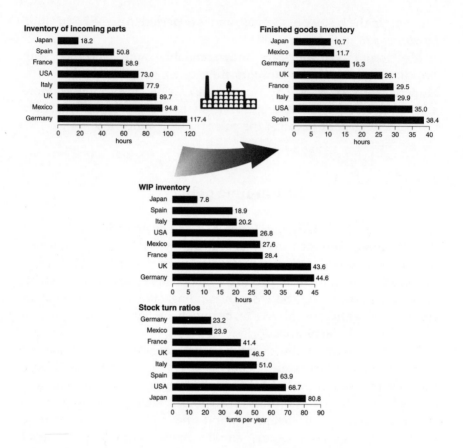

Figure 9.2 Inventory sizes and stockturns in international automobile companies. Source: N. Oliver *et al.* (1994) *World Wide Manufacturing Competitiveness Study*. London: Andersen Consulting.

Ohno described how the fast and skilled workers were given more to do than the slower and less skilled workers who were learning from them. Yet the larger and the smaller cycles were timed so as to synchronize precisely. You do not go as fast as you can but as fast as timed coordination requires.

The capacity of Japanese auto companies to keep inventories lower than European and North American rivals is detailed in Figure 9.2 in a study of worldwide manufacturing competitiveness sponsored by Arthur Andersen. Here we see that Japanese companies hold only 18.2 hours worth of stock. US companies hold nearly four times as much. Japanese finished goods inventories are a quarter the size of US companies. Japan's work-in-process is 20 percent of that in UK plants, while Japanese companies turn over stock nearly four times faster than Mexico and Germany and twice the UK's rate.

Because defective parts from suppliers are unusable and there is no inventory with which to replace them, pressures for lower defect rates are much stronger in lean, fine-tuned systems. Arthur Andersen found that defects from suppliers and defective autos delivered to customers were considerably lower in the Japanese plants sampled than in plants in other cultures (see Table 9.4).

Some of these differences are vast. The USA and UK plants have over six times more defects in their supply chain than Japan, and the UK has over eight times the number of defective deliveries in their distribution chain.

One of the ways of improving synchronous activity and getting everyone in time is via suppliers' clubs. Seventy-five percent of all Japanese auto companies, both at home and abroad, run clubs in which their suppliers have membership. (Honda is a notable exception.) These clubs exchange information, share training activities and coordinate among themselves delivery schedules and compatibility of parts. Sixty-six percent of all suppliers' associations to Japanese auto producers share benefits from improvements. The comparable figure in the USA is 5 percent, in France 55 percent, in the UK 30 percent and in Mexico 15 percent. Germany, Italy and Spain operate no clubs at all.[11]

Seventy-five percent of Japanese suppliers *to* suppliers are club members also, but there are only 5 percent in the UK and France and none elsewhere in Europe. However, suppliers' clubs are springing up in several SE Asian countries. Motorola's Penang facility recently reported on 'extended early supplier involvement' which provided training to the supplier, obtained training *from* the supplier and got

Table 9.4

Average number of defects received from suppliers		Average number of defects in delivered units	
Japan	900	Japan	193
Spain	1,800	USA	263
France	3,733	Spain	314
Germany	4,700	Germany	885
UK	5,900	France	897
USA	6,100	UK	1,650
Italy	7,433	Italy	1,976

both to sit down with the designer so as to be more effectively synchronized. As a result

> suppliers acquired in depth understanding of Motorola's quality requirements. Material quality improved steadily. There were fewer rejects, an increase in direct-to-stock lots (by-passing inspection) and improvement in on-time delivery. Engineering support was extended to suppliers who needed it. Each supplier gets regular quality reviews.[12]

But equally important is *reverse training*, suppliers to customer. This is because of periodic improvements in materials, new trends in engineering and new capabilities suppliers are willing to develop *if* the customer will buy them. Motorola Penang is well known for its sponsorship of supplier fairs, a way of getting in touch with the Malaysian supplier base and publicizing its needs for at least 500 different parts. It also helps the company keep ahead of local content laws which decree that an escalating proportion of supplies be Malaysian.

Customization and short runs

The need for careful synchronization rises and rises as customization increases and shorter production runs become necessary. American inspired high-speed, standardized, mass production is in general decline among wealthy economies because long runs are typically suited to simple goods, and lower wage economies have captured these markets.

As economies and markets mature the demand for niche products and highly specialized customer-specific products increases. The shorter the run, the more tool changes necessary, the more specialized components need to be ordered and the greater the demand for lightening synchronization. Vehicles, for example, may have the same chassis, but come in thirty to forty different variations as far as other combinations of components are concerned. Sunroofs, tape-decks, heated seats and shields on headlamps may be optional.

James Abegglen and George Stalk reported that Japanese competitive advantage rises very sharply with the number of 'manufacturing steps'. In the making of men's dress shirts there were only 25 steps and Japanese productivity was almost identical to American, but in the manufacture of fork-lift trucks there are over one thousand steps and here Japanese advantage was much greater. In ascending order, paper mills, iron foundries, color TV and auto engines have more steps, and Japanese competitive advantage increases steadily with complexity.[13]

What is curious is that Abegglen, an American based at Sophia University in Tokyo, never questioned his own use of the word 'steps'. Steps are, of course, sequential and the real advantage of Japanese corporations in complex operations is that they do *not* take 'one step at a time' but take many.

Parallel processing and flexible manufacturing

To the Japanese belongs most of the credit for teaching the world flexible manufacturing. So long as you think only sequentially, in Taylorist terms, manufacturing cannot be managed flexibly without great losses of efficiency. Every time you wish to add a new component, or develop some variety of output, the capacity to charge straight ahead suffers serious delays. The original Ford model Ts were all black. In time, it because possible to develop 'add ons' such as white-wall tyres, different colors and different seats, but standardization remained vital. Vance Packard, writing in the 1960s, called this minimal variety 'marginal differentiation'. You added the frills after production was complete and stuck them on the outside. Mass production was still the engine of growth.

But in Tokyo from the late 1950s onwards a hybrid process was emerging which was to reconcile *both* concepts of time, faster sequences *and* better synchronization. This is illustrated in Figure 9.3, the diagram coming from Taicho Ohno's own publication *The Toyota Production System*.

Note that each one of the small cars is drawn in a way which makes it different from the others. Taylor or Ford's final body assembly line remains a central feature.

The arrows represent messages sent from the main line to feeder lines. When vehicle 20 is five places from feeder line E, a message goes to E and the appropriate engine converges with the central line. All conveyors travel at the same speed, so synchronization can be calculated to the second. Visual control panels assure operators that

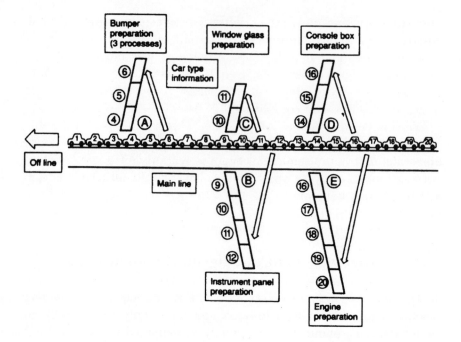

Figure 9.3 Toyota final body assembly line. Source: T. Ohno (1978) *Toyota Production System: Beyond Large Scale Production*. Cambridge, MA: Productivity Press.

everything is in order, with vehicles moving along at the greatest practicable speed.[14] But what was new in the 1950s, although a common feature of all automobile plants today, are the processes leading into the line. The arrows show messages sent to the engine preparation process, the console box preparation process and so on. The appropriate console box and the appropriate engine etc. reach the final assembly line just-in-time for perfect coordination to occur.

Because of such expert timing, a large variety of automobiles can come off the final assembly line *with almost no loss of speed*. The line moves as fast as it ever did, but combinations of different components reaching the line mean that every car is customized. Cars can be ordered from showrooms and manufactured in a few hours in precisely the mix that customers have specified.

Economies of scale have not disappeared. It may still pay you to standardize key platforms, but flexible manufacturing qualifies the economies of scale with those of *scope*. How cheap is it to increase variety? If customers want variety, and they increasingly do, the company whose scope is 'highly economic' will prevail.

Products as families which procreate

Are products simply lines of widgets with a cost, a price on the market and resulting per-unit return to the supplier? This is our conventional wisdom and it keeps cost accountants busy. Every additional unit has a variable cost, which must be added to the fixed costs of setting up operations in the first place. The 'contribution to overhead' of every product 'line' and the incremental contribution of extending that 'line' are then calculable.

Generally speaking products which do not 'pay their way', like people in the same condition, should be dropped. There are exceptions, as when customers require a full service from a whole product range, not all items of which it pays you to supply, but these circumstances are unusual.

Products, like profit centers, make individual contributions to the bottom 'line' from separate 'lines' of their own. It is all immaculately logical and sequential. The US Congress even has a special fund to sponsor 'orphan drugs'. These are drugs needed to keep patients alive and healthy, but whose diseases are so rare that it does not pay the drug company to supply them.

But cultures who think in a synchronous way and not in straight lines, and cultures who see major gains in the advance of knowledge, need to consider that products are like families. They procreate. The question is much larger than whether product A 'wins' and product B 'loses'. What if the *combination* of A and B in a second, third or fourth generation of products were more effective still? If you discontinue a product because it 'lost' a Finite Game for this or that market, you may lose a whole line of thought which might have contributed to knowledge development.[15]

Each product may be thought of as carrying knowledge genes, which, joined with the genes of a product partner and passed on to the next generation of products, develops the core competencies of the company. There is growing evidence that this is how the Japanese think of their products, especially in electronics and materials sciences, and that this style of thought accelerated Samsung's breakthrough in microwave technology in Korea.[16]

Just as families turn outwards to strangers to avoid the incest taboo, so products cross-fertilize with different products to procreate offspring. We are back again to the unity of differences: the harmony among those singing different tunes, the coincidence of opposites, the two Finite Game players joined together in the Infinite Game of creation.

Planning for hybridization and fusion

We have by now convinced ourselves in the West that planning, in the form of straight-line forecasting, is a pretty hazardous process. We still do it because the only alternative would appear to be drift. We generally frown on governments doing it. An interesting alternative is scenario planning, which envisages three or four alternative futures and invites strategists to ready themselves for each. Scenarios have important elements of synchronous thinking. Each future is an internally consistent and coherent 'scene'. The Global Business Network in Emeryville, California, is a good example of American adaptation to synchronous ways of thinking.[17]

But for the furthest development of synchronous thinking in planning we need to look to Japan's Ministry of International Trade and Industry (MITI) and Singapore's Economic Development Board (EDB). Synchronous planning steers corporations towards hybridization and fusion. Instead of saying 'we plan to produce this specific product by this specific date', synchronous plans cross-fertilize technologies and businesses with very high predispositions to 'mate' and then wait for something to happen.

There are some interesting examples. The area of 'mechatronics'—a fusion of mechanical with electronic engineering—is highly developed in Japan and has been taken up in Singapore, Korea, Malaysia and Taiwan. Magorah Maruyama has argued that while creativity is attributed to the interaction of single ideas within one mind by most Western thinkers, the Japanese view creativity as the interaction of many ideas within a team or group, especially where its membership is cross-occupational or cross-disciplinary. Hence the Japanese bullet-train was created by locomotive engineers working with aircraft engineers, unemployed because the Japanese aircraft industries had been dismantled by the Occupation government.[18]

The aircraft engineers established that resonant vibration at high speed was caused by air turbulence, not friction with rails, and used wind-tunnels to create the optimal train. Seiko's breakthrough in watchmaking via the resonant quartz circuit was the result of jewellery experts who could cut quartz in a zig-zag pattern, working with quartz experts.[19] As early as 1986 the Japanese patents in electronics exceeded those of the USA. As of 1993–1994 Japan still leads the USA in the average number of patents granted to residents—75,034 versus 54,652. This means that on a per-capita basis Japan is three times more productive of patents. Taiwan also exceeds the US on a per-capita basis, with 13,828 in a population of 21 million, which is only about 8.0 percent of America's population.[20]

What planning authorities do in East Asian economies is deliberately steer industries into creative collaboration. The EDB does this with its Cluster Development Fund described in Chapter 3 and its joint training institutes to which partners are required to donate their latest equipment. This has the effect of 'showcasing' all up-to-date production processes side by side. Inevitably the best features of each are soon borrowed and combined, and skilled workers are hired who can work on all the latest systems. Synchronicity is everywhere.

MITI in Japan has gone so far as to create an Inter-industry Technology Fusion Index, illustrated in Figure 9.4, which they call 'The Fundamental Outline of the Twenty-First Century Industrial Society'. This matrix does not tell us what is going to happen; that would be foolhardy. But it does suggest that the marriage of chemistry with machinery will be fecund, and that makes sense. Eric Drexler, the father of nano-technology, tiny engines capable of being injected into the bloodstream and with myriad additional uses, recently gave a seminar for corporations at Stanford University. Ninety percent of the corporations represented were Japanese. Nano-technology is not just miniaturization, a process Japanese culture values, but synchronous by definition, engines within engines.

Pull strategies and time to market

'Time to market' has become a major preoccupation of business strategists. Getting to market faster than competitors means that you may be first with a new product, that your customers may have a

Hybrid and Fusion Technologies

The Japanese Approach to Hybrid Technologies

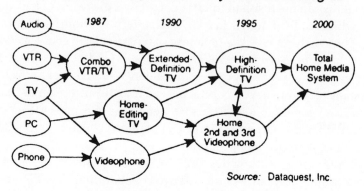

Source: Dataquest, Inc.

... and to fusion technologies

Interindustry Technology Fusion Index

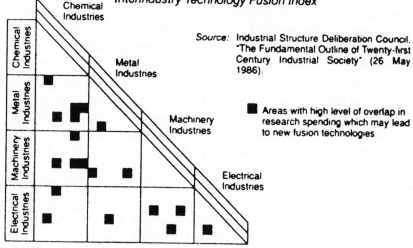

Figure 9.4 Hybrid and fusion technologies. Source: S. M. Tatsuno (1990) *Created in Japan.* New York: Harper & Row.

competitive advantage over their competitors, or that you get feedback faster and so make needed modifications sooner. Generally speaking a company with faster 'cycles' from product conception to product delivery, or to product improvement and re-delivery, will win

Table 9.5 Time to market: launching new product takes: more time than foreign competitors (10) . . . less time than foreign competitors (0)

1	Hong Kong	7.71		22	Colombia	4.84
2	New Zealand	6.76		23	Greece	4.79
3	Taiwan	6.66		24	Norway	4.78
4	Japan	6.44		25	Turkey	4.73
5	Singapore	6.19			Hungary	4.73
6	Israel	6.07		27	Switzerland	4.70
7	USA	5.97			Philippines	4.70
8	Iceland	5.95		29	UK	4.60
9	Chile	5.94		30	Australia	4.53
10	Sweden	5.89		31	Spain	4.45
11	Malaysia	5.73		32	Argentina	4.31
12	Denmark	5.88		33	Poland	4.30
13	The Netherlands	5.73		34	Mexico	4.20
14	Finland	5.60		35	Brazil	4.02
15	Thailand	5.43		36	India	3.93
16	Canada	5.29		37	Venezuela	3.92
17	Korea	5.28		38	South Africa	3.85
18	Belgium	5.06		39	Indonesia	3.77
19	France	4.98		40	Portugal	3.25
20	Ireland	4.95		41	China	2.89
21	Austria	4.89		42	Czech Republic	2.44
				43	Russia	2.32

most business. It is conceived as a Finite Game with speed the essence of victory. Table 9.5 compares time to market for forty-three nations. Four 'tigers', Hong Kong, Taiwan, Japan and Singapore, are among the top five. All four lead the USA despite time to market being a top issue there. Smaller companies may have an advantage, which could explain the high placings of entrepreneurial Hong Kong and Taiwan. Nine East Asian economies are ahead of the UK and Australia. Ex-communist and still-communist countries fare poorly, e.g. Hungary, Poland, China, the Czech Republic and Russia.

Once again, simply moving fast and racing to market is insufficient. Projects which are accelerated tend to relegate projects not accelerated, which become later still. Studies of Toshiba, NEC and Mitsubishi reveal that Japanese corporations prefer 'pull strategies' to the more conventional 'push strategy'. A company 'pushes' when it schedules tightly and engages in 'progress chasing', sending out staff to chivvy and accelerate operations. A company 'pulls' when it *counts backwards from the time the customer wants the product and synchronizes the time of the rendezvous*. Motorola has now adopted pull strategies, influenced by its partnership with Toshiba.

The advantages of a pull strategy are several. You save time and effort in getting products to customers before they are actually needed. Regardless of what the contract says, customers may fall behind schedule themselves. Hence products delivered 'on time' are early from the customers point of view and entail carrying costs. Moreover, the products are sitting in the storehouse, when that time *could* have been used to improve them, to provide a 99 percent solution to making as airbag open in time instead of a 95 percent solution.

The advantage of pulling includes shifting resources from customers who are running late to customers in most urgent need. Projects accelerate or slow depending on the numbers of people and resources allocated. The object is *not* to beat some abstract conception of time, or to keep the promise made in the contract which is now history, but to get the product to the customer just-in-time for use, thereby shaving the costs and increasing the quality of the customer–supplier relationships. Despite its name time to market is not racehorses rushing towards a fixed winning post, but rather spaceships docking in outer space by a series of careful mutual adjustments as the time of their rendezvous approaches. Just-in-time is not objective but inter-subjective. Speed is only half of it. Synchronicity is the rest.

Summary

We have seen that the psychology of long termism versus short termism depends on whether past, present and future are seen as objective increments passing in sequence (short term) or as overlapping ideas with which to design your strategy (long term). You are more likely to save domestically if 'the past' and 'the future' are with you in the same room to deliberate with 'the present'.

The synchronous viewpoint of the more successful East Asian economies is typified by just-in-time delivery, i.e. delivery synchronized with the customers' needs. This has the effect of lowering inventories and hence carrying costs. By thus spurring much closer, coordination defects are also kept down and punctuality increases.

Where projects race each other higgledy-piggledy to market, a highly inconsistent pattern of winners and losers needs to be buffered by large stocks of inventory, lest production be halted by the most tardy. The Finite Game reads as follows:

Uncoordinated, inconsistent patterns of late and timely deliveries lead to knock-on effects and must be expensively buffered...

By carrying high inventories and surplus stocks used to absorb these fluctuations and assure continuous production.

A

Z

In the struggle above, large inventories overwhelm ragged deliveries and save the company becoming hostage to the worst suppliers, who hold up everyone else.

The Infinite Game, in contrast, holds every supplier to both fast *and* timely deliveries through finely tuned synchronization. This assures lower defects, the training of suppliers by the customer and of the customer by suppliers, and the development of supplier associations, who share information and share in any benefits arising from improvements in the supply chain. The Infinite Game reads approximately as follows:

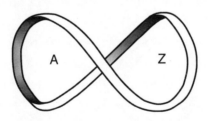

A. High levels of synchronization, just-in-time delivery and lower defects increase shared information and benefits...

Z. Lower inventories and carrying costs, and assure fast delivery of supplies to customers, by reason of...

The need to synchronize keeps everyone stepping smartly in time with the overall rhythm.

We also saw that the more developed an economy becomes and the more it encounters complexity, the more customization and short runs become necessary and hence the more synchronized activities occur.

How fast you move is nothing like as important as how smartly you design activities in parallel processes.

In the traditional Taylorist model the economies of scale fight against the economies of scope and flexibility. You can go fast only if products and processes are standardized and are mass manufactured in long runs. The Finite Game reads as follows:

The economies of scope, together with variety, flexibility, customization and short runs...

Are sacrificed to the economies of scale, with standardized mass manufacturing in long runs.

You can, of course, accommodate variety, but it is expensive. There is too much stopping and starting, more a job-shop than an efficient operation.

But where sequentialism is married to synchronous timing we get *flexible manufacturing*, in which feeder lines are synchronized with the main assembly line. Considerable variety and the economies of scope can now be processed, at much the same speed as the mass production assembly line of old. The Infinite Game reads as follows:

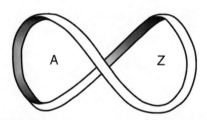

A. With feeder lines converging at synchronized intervals, variety, scope and customization...

Z. Among the products assembled can be combined with the fast movement of the final assembly line...

Another issue was whether products should compete with each other as lines and incremental units, to be discontinued if they were 'losers' and continued if they were 'winners', and whether planning activities, which simply extrapolated current trends and assumed more of the same in the future, were adequate to the job. The Finite Game reads as follows:

Product lines which lose or make insufficient money and straight-line extrapolations...

A

Tend to get beaten by winning products and by forecast trends in opposition to them...

Z

But Japan and probably the rest of East Asia tend to see products not as single lines but procreating *families* of products, passing on knowledge genes and giving birth to product generations. This includes the products of most American electronics companies and constituted a cogent argument put forward by John Sculley of Apple in the late 1980s. MITI in Japan, the EDB in Singapore and the Malaysian government also encourage fusions and hybridizations of products by clustering these in geographical proximity, in Free Trade Areas, industrial parks and industry clusters like Malaysia's Multimedia Corridor. The aim is to sponsor generativity and spontaneous connections, *not* some specific breakthrough foreseen by all-wise bureaucrats. Mix mechanical with electrical engineering and you get 'mechatronic' innovations. Below is the Infinite Game which can result:

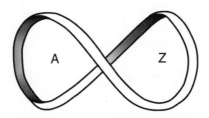

A. By combining products into families and cross-fertilizing procreative trends...

Z. New lines and rapid trend development will form, which will 'win'...

The final issue had to do with 'push strategies' for getting to market faster versus 'pull strategies'. With 'push strategies' some projects get priority *over* others which then run later and later. Push may also get the product there before the customer, who is running late, really needed it. 'Clock time' or 'scheduled time' tends to compete with 'real time' present needs.

Pull strategies, in contrast, combine speed with an arranged rendezvous with the customer in the future. Resources are 'pulled' into the planned convergence and the countdown synchronized. Resources can be switched towards the most pressing rendezvous and switched away from customers running late. The Infinite Game is constituted so:

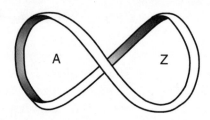

A. Time to market is shortened by synchronizing your rendezvous with your customer at some future time...

Z. And 'pulling' in enough resources to speed your development, make the rendezvous and so decrease...

'Designing with time' consists of synchronizing fast sequences in parallel and constructing the most effective pathways to serve your customers expeditiously. How well you synchronize activities is at least as important as how fast you move. Shortening the 'racecourse' is a good start to fast completion. Whether the nations of East Asia have yet begun to match Japan's lead needs to be discovered.

Let the last word be from the Japanese philosopher Takeshi Umehara:

Modern science has demonstrated that all life is basically one, and it has shown that living things and their physical surroundings are all part of a single ecosystem . . . Even though the individual dies, his or her genes are carried on by future generations in a lasting cycle of rebirth . . . The human race has finally realized that it can survive only in peaceful co-existence with other life forms.[21]

We have now considered eight strands in the development of human relationships. In Chapter 2 we introduced the idea of a 'way' or a 'game' that was infinite. In Chapter 3 we saw that economic actors

Box 9.1   The Silent Black-Robed Horsemen

Japan appears on the world scene like 'a strange band of black-robed horsemen', half-smiling, ambiguous yet somehow demonic. Kisho Kurokawa would make a virtue of the strangeness and has proposed the Philosophy of Symbiosis, an area of interdisciplinary study now installed at several Japanese universities.

Symbiosis is a form of cooperative competing and extols the Life Principle, as opposed to the West's vision of Universal Mechanism, otherwise known as modernism. Symbiosis, then, is post-modernist. It differs from *wa*, the traditional ethic of harmony, in stressing the unique, the idiosyncratic and the sheer varieties of life forms. Symbiosis grows from oppositions among cultivated sensibilities. It moves beyond quantities to ever new qualities of combination.

Especially vital are 'intermediate zones' between things, people and principles. Sometimes these are sacred zones, as with tea ceremonies, or the culture of rice-growing. Vitality lies *between* concepts and mediates these creatively. Examples include *Ma*—intervals of space or time, as in good timing; *Engawa*—the verendatis joining living spaces; *Senu Hima*—the moment of silence betwixt thought and action; *Rikyu*—gray, the subtle blend of black and white; and *Wabi*—the splendour within simplicity. 'Consciousness only', an expression of Mahayana Buddhism, is a symbiotic discipline. The spirit of *alaya* seeks 'not one . . . not two' but the movement between them. The 21st century will see a new age of fusion, connectedness and dialog among cultures in which Japan's subtle virtues will be appreciated and symbiosis will spread.

For the world is growing sick from Western logocentrism (one best way) codified abstractly and then imposed. In place of the domination of the Western values of economy, simplicity, precision, purity, multiplicity, function, abstraction and clarity must come a realization that we shall *never* understand each other completely and must rather learn to respect in one another what is unique, sacred, untameable and esthetically diverse.

Dr Jekyll and Mr Hyde was pathological because of his split values. The West dichotomizes and polarizes all nature, good versus evil, part versus whole, science versus art, intellect versus feeling, 0 and 1. Every Western philosophy can only advance itself through refuting others. All this dualism and dialectical strife destroys the middle ground. Yet within this excluded middle lie the subtleties and synthesis of a new Age

---

Box 9.1   Continued

of Life, which Kurokawa sees reflected in Japan's earlier Edo period.

The author endorses Arthur Koestler's concept of the *holon*, that which is simultaneous, a whole and a part to life 'below' or 'above' it. He finds inspiration in the Diamond Sutra, the fabled bracelet, each precious stone of which reflects the bracelet in its entirety.

But symbiosis has its critics. J Dowling of the Japan–US Economic Council wrote that symbiosis was 'a violation of the US anti-monopoly and anti-trust laws', which is where we came in . . .

Source: *The Philosophy of Symbiosis*, Kisho Kurokawa, London: Academy Editions, 1994.

---

could be joined to each other through knowledge intensification. In Chapter 4 we looked closely at clustering and shared catalyst technologies. In Chapter 5 we saw how competition *could* be made into a game of cooperative inquiry, a search for the best available solution. In Chapter 6 we saw that whether our reasonings were proved or disproved, we could still learn after-the-fact in responsive networks of mutuality and improve continuously in working together. In Chapter 7 we looked at the capacity of superordinate goals to symbolize what was *worth* achieving. In Chapter 8, escalating and dynamic reciprocity among people was seen to go beyond contract compliance, in performances higher than specified.

A crucial aspect of cooperating effectively was designing with time so as to act in synchrony, as we saw in this chapter.

Is there a single East Asian philosophy that epitomizes all these strands of mutuality? The nearest approximation among East Asian thinkers to what we have been trying to outline is *The Philosophy of Symbiosis* of Kisho Kurokawa, a leader of the Metabolist Group of Architects. His philosophy is summarized in Box 9.1.

Chapter 10

The Cross and the Double Helix: The Great Integrations of Culture

> *He knows that he must vote always for the richer universe, for the good which seems most organisable, most fit to enter into complex combinations, most apt to be a member of a more inclusive whole.*
>
> William James.

This final chapter tries to reach beyond East–West rivalries, even beyond the concepts of 'game' or 'way', to explore the processes of development itself and how human beings supply each other with what they value. For we are not going to create wealth successfully unless we pour into the goods we make and the services we provide all the knowledge, values and commitments at our command. Modern competitive conditions demand of us nothing less.

For it has never been the case that it would be wise for Westerners to try and copy the cultures of East Asia. Even were we to try, which is unlikely, there is no way to become Japanese, Singaporean or Malaysian by an act of will. Culture programs our minds from childhood onwards, and its influence is tenaciously strong. There is no way that Americans, Britons or Netherlanders are *ever* going to lose their cultural individualism save through some cultural crisis, and perhaps not even then. There is something almost blasphemous in attacking cultural predispositions which have given meaning to generations of Americans and Europeans, and have shaped their history. Culture grows from what has worked well in the past and no nation can forget its history.[1]

Nor has it been our case that East Asian value preferences are somehow 'better' than our own. There is no reason to suppose that particular and esthetic exceptions are better than universal rules, that communitarianism is better than individualism, that thinking broadly and holistically is better than thinking specifically and analytically. Our point is far more subtle and some may think elusive. What accelerates economic development is *reconciling* rules with the exceptions that 'prove' them, reconciling individuals with groups, narrow criteria with broad criteria, and achieving that to which value has been ascribed.

The problem is *not* that East is right and West is wrong. Were this so, the West would not have jumped off so early or got so far ahead. Nations like Singapore have learned assiduously from the West. The Economic Development Board (EDB) and much of the government is squarely founded on the traditions of the British Civil Service, with business and technological acumen added to this. The problem is that East Asians are learning much faster from us than we are from them. Knowing that they were behind, they studied us. Knowing we were ahead, we first colonized, then patronized and now lecture them. The results have been seen in this book.

But if the pioneer economies of the West are to learn from East Asia, it must be in our own way, based on our existing strengths. If East Asians can start with communitarianism and learn from the West how to make that community responsive to each individual through democratic means, then North America, Europe, Australia and New Zealand can start with their own individualism and learn from East Asians how better to form groups, teams and communities in the workplace and in civic society.

For there is a great variety of individualism in Western societies. Dutch and Scandinavian individualism puts far more stress on individual responsibility to others. New England Puritans were highly individualist but still formed tight, worshipful communities. English Quakers doffed their hats to no man, contributed to the industrial revolution and entrepreneurship in a ratio *forty times* greater than their numbers, gave women unequaled rights, formed small groups linked into networks and gave a proportion of their profits to train apprentices.[2]

The New England transcendentalists—Ralph Waldo Emerson, Henry David Thoreau, Margaret Fuller, etc.—were individualists through and through, but believed that this spirit 'transcended' the person to become part of nature, biological and social. Henry Ford read Emerson's *On Compensation* before he decided to double the pay of his workers and face down shareholder complaints. Soon the workers bought the cars. The anti-slavery movement, growing in the same New England soil, taught that no man could be free if his fellows were in chains. The spiritual heirs of these campaigners helped to de-segregate the South and demonstrated against the folly of American intervention in Vietnam. America and much of the individualist West will always *start* with the individual but they do not always *end* there. Most of the great robber barons ended by giving millions away to foundations which still bear their names. You can start with finite game playing, but as the coming of death concentrates your mind, you search for more infinite meanings.

And the notion of 'play' is firmly rooted in the West and elsewhere. It was the Dutch historian Johan Huizinga, in his classic *Homo Ludens: A Study of the Play Element in Culture*, who argued that cultures learn by *simulating* events which would otherwise traumatize them and wreck lives. The Dutch today have the highest levels of peaceful political demonstrations in the world, known as *aktie*. You play out the sufferings of people on whose behalf you demonstrate. It is an important expression of compassionate individualism: 'I am simulating the horror of what has been done or may happen'.[3]

And of course individually expressive plays are as old as Greek tragic drama. Terrible tragedies, such as a mother killing her own children, were told in dramas like *Medea*, but the aims were paradoxical. See tragedy in play so as *not* to enact it in real life. Our mentor, the psychotherapist and Greek scholar Rollo May, described to us how audiences in Greek theaters sat with their shoulders touching. As the tragedy reached its climax, a huge *frisson*, a cathartic shudder, rippled through the audience. The imagined victims were dead, but the parental audience was alive, vowing *never* to let their quarrels cripple the lives of their own children. The tragedy *on* stage and the elation *around* the stage were as one; paradox indeed, but inspired moral teaching.

It matters, then, to all those aspiring to civilized society *how* we play and what meanings that play expresses. Competition that never moves beyond finite plays is what has earned Western businessmen their reputations for philistinism, has made business writing so impoverished, and brings us that ever running saga 'The Crisis in Economics'. We have to learn how better to create wealth *without* inflicting so much damage upon each other and arranging for half or more of the population to 'lose'. In this respect we believe East Asia is showing the way and, because losers are expensive—one quarter of a million dollars for each *child* sent to a 'secure unit' under Britain's recently proposed penal system[4]—cultures with fewer losers will prevail economically and morally.

All great cultures, East and West, are treasure troves of contrasting ideas and traditions. We cannot learn by deprecating these treasures, but rather by looking within them for different patterns of behavior and thought. So many are the byways, the labyrinthine corridors, the winding interstices, the subcultures and the minority persuasions that our dominant system of beliefs must be challenged from *inside* the culture, not outside of it. Labeling ideas as 'foreign' or Asian is a way of resisting them.

Consider the idea of paradox and complementarity, so strong in East Asia. We cannot import this world view wholesale, but we *can* search Western tradition for equivalents. It was William Blake in his art and poetry who pleaded for 'the marriage of heaven and hell'.[5] It was Scott Fitzgerald who said 'the test of a first rate intelligence is to hold two opposed ideas in your mind at the same time, and still retain the capacity to function'.[6] In the dialogical philosophies of Martin Buber and the 'encompassing reason' of Paul Tillich we see shadows of the Infinite Game.[7]

In the great struggle of theoretical physics in the 20th century we find complementarity at the base of our hardest discipline. In research on the brain and the two cerebral hemispheres we find complementarity again. In the rebellious writings of post-war existentialism, culminating in the dream of Martin Luther King, we find contradictions enthroned. Finally in biology we find 'a double helix', clockwise and anti-clockwise winding past each other in opposite directions.[8]

Or consider our own democratic institutions, probably the West's most durable contribution to a better world. These are not the expressions of paradoxical theories, but rather experience added gradually to experience. Yet their final shape *is* paradoxical. Consider . . .

We have parliamentary *oppositions* which are nonetheless *loyal*. House members *disagree* with what others say, yet *agree* on their right to say it. We persuade each other *openly* on political issues, yet we vote *secretly*. *Groups* of electors return their members to parliament, who then vote their *individual* consciences, not necessarily the beliefs of their constituents. In legal processes, we hold trials in *public* so that justice is seen to be done, yet juries deliberate in *private*. Defendants are *indicted*, yet even so presumed *innocent*. Parliamentary debate allows you to *fight* but do so *peacefully*, a great improvement on being impaled on swords.[9]

All this is a marvellously contrived *synthesis of contrasting values*. It is upon such masterful integrities that all great cultures depend. The real danger is consistency! If electorates voted publicly we could punish non-compliance. If juries voted publicly we could corrupt them more easily. If defendants were assumed guilty no genuine trial could occur.

There are, then, hundreds of strands within Western cultures which have anticipated the dynamics of the Infinite Game. In this book we have encountered Western scholars who originated the concepts East Asians now use: the Continuous Improvement of W Edwards Deming, the cluster development ideas of Michael Porter, Peter Senge's *The Fifth Discipline*, which is required reading in Singapore's EDB. With its circular, cybernetic feedback loops, it comes close to representing East Asian thought patterns while also being a 'New Age' bestseller in the USA. Arguably the concept of 'double loop learning' by Harvard Business School Professor Chris Argyris[10] is very close to our Infinite Game, as is Donald Schon's *The Reflective Practitioner*, who thinks both before *and* after acting.[11] Singapore has recently taken up the 'lateral thinking' concepts of Edward De Bono and plans to incorporate them in the secondary school curriculum. His books have sold by the million in the West, lacking only official cultural sanction. Much of this book could have been written using the ideas of Western thinkers.

But it is one thing to write about such processes and another thing to adopt them and adapt them enthusiastically. What happens when an idea runs against the cultural grain of a culture is that it makes slow headway, as has Elton Mayo's Human Relations School. Its ideas are taken up with far greater alacrity in cultures where relationship is more important.

The Scanlon Plan was invented in the late 1940s by an American trades unionist, Joe Scanlon.[12] It consists of a plan which measures the input–output ratio in a work unit and awards employees a bonus of around 50% of the added value they create by working smarter and devising better practices. The rest goes to shareholders. Although extolled by Douglas McGregor of MIT, there were only fifty Scanlon plans operating in the USA by 1960. A few years later the Japanese took it up with some modifications. In reaction to the plan being used by Asian competitors, America now has 5,000 such plans. American corporations have also taken up Deming's ideas, but after a thirty-year lag! There are *propensities* to try out those ideas most consistent with one's culture while resisting those which are less consistent.

The lesson Westerners can draw from such incidents is to use the creative products of their own culture *before* these are used against us by East Asian economies, who find those ideas more compatible with their values. We need to rediscover community in the West, which writers such as Amitai Etzioni have advocated.[13] Many Western thinkers have pleaded for more holistic ways of thinking and have inveighed against reductionism. We should dust the cobwebs off our own dissenters, rather than run always with popular stereotypes.

There is also at the center of most Western cultures the heartbeat of Judeo-Christian beliefs. These have grown fainter of late. We have expressed some reservations about the ongoing quarrels between scientific skepticism versus unquestioning faith. We also queried whether our values could survive if the 'other world' remained the major source of moral authority.

But none of this is to deny the vital meanings that Christianity and Judaism bring to people's lives and the great inherent value of building on such beliefs. Take, for example, the Christian symbol held before the 'closing eyes' of millions. The cross stands for the divisions in our souls. In Figure 10.1 we have slightly altered the image of the Finite Game, removing the snakes' heads and substituting a crucifix.

In hope that the West can summon up its own religious impulses, we point out the Christian paradoxes at the center of faith, the breaking of Christ's heart, blood and water separating, a splitting of the veil, darkness at noon, death in which life is reborn.

Is not our habit of finite game playing both the basis of our humanity and the occasion of our sin? We seem doomed to display our will power in competition with each other, so as to inflict defeat and obscurity on opponents. In so doing we bring benefits to markets

Figure 10.1   The finite crucifix.

and to the world, yet we also bankrupt, frustrate and marginalize opponents, who may have intended us no harm.

Is there, then, some way of moving from the finite to infinite concerns before our race is run? We believe there is. The English author attended Trinity College, Cambridge, when Harry Williams was chaplain there. Williams argued that the life of the mind and the creation of values involved a form of mental crucifixion among opposed values. Among these were faith and skepticism, mind and body, determinism and freedom, autonomy and dependence, finiteness and infiniteness, dispassion and passion, thinking and feeling, etc. (see Figure 10.2). So long as we place one of these value pairs *above* the other, we make for ourselves a mental prison, in which Faith must *conquer* skepticism or vice versa. For we are more than we are aware of, says Williams—there is an Unknown Self:

> The root of sin is the identification of my total self with the self of which I am aware. Two consequences follow from this identification. First the known self is too narrow to be satisfying to me and is felt in its constriction to be intolerable. Second, the unknown self which, for mistaken reasons of security I keep imprisoned and in exile, becomes a savage as a result, like a man locked in a dark dungeon seeing nobody.[14]

It is only when we allow the hidden, infinite depths of our submerged values to *qualify* our dominant values—mind, determinism, objectivity, skepticism, reason and finiteness, etc.—that a 'crucifix' forms in our mind beyond which is an understanding which redeems. To cross cultures is to discover this unknown self within our own beings. Foreigners may have in abundance what has grown weak and faint within ourselves, like family and community values.

Christians worship a savior nailed upon a cross in great agony. The cross bars symbolize our rival fanaticism, from which we are redeemed when infinite meanings are created from finite conflicts. This reconciliation heals shattered minds and grows value systems. In chapter after chapter in this book we have shown how Finite Games representing seemingly intractable conflicts are not necessarily destructive. They can become synergistic to reach beyond our selfhoods, beyond even our lives, towards the great integrities of culture.

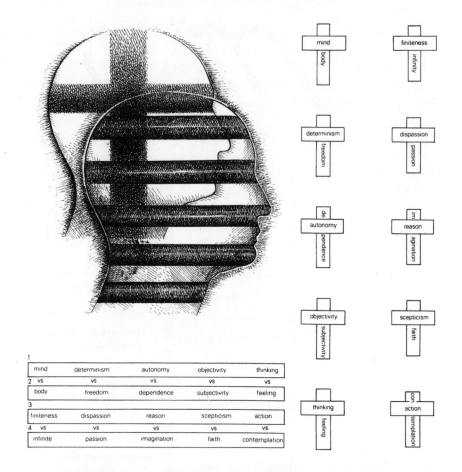

1				
mind	determinism	autonomy	objectivity	thinking
2 vs	vs	vs	vs	vs
body	freedom	dependence	subjectivity	feeling
3				
finiteness	dispassion	reason	scepticism	action
4 vs	vs	vs	vs	vs
infinite	passion	imagination	faith	contemplation

Figure 10.2 The cross and the prison. Source: C. M. Hampden-Turner (1981)
*The Cross and the Prison: The Psychotheology of H A Williams in Maps of the
Mind.* New York: Macmillan; H. A. Williams (1962) 'Theology and Self-Awareness',
in M. Eric Vidler (ed.), *Soundings.* Cambridge: Cambridge University Press.

The ideas expressed in Figure 10.2 are in a Christian idiom. But the
Infinite Game is as much Taoist, Buddhist, Confucian, Shintoist,
Dionysian or Jewish as it is Christian. The search for meaning and
transcendence is the *true* universal as opposed to 'the American Way',
neo-classical economics or Western Capitalism.

So we come, at last, to our final image and to one of the great
scientific triumphs of the West. Look closely at our model of the
Infinite Game and you see something looping back on itself for ever;
'chasing your own tail', as one of our critics put it, rather ungenerously.

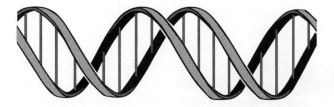

Figure 10.3 The double helix.

Generate more *diffuse* knowledge so as to create...	**Chapter 3** Knowledge Intensive Strategy	more scarcity, more *specific* profits, with which to...
Catalytic and horizontal technologies promote...	**Chapter 4** Cluster Development Strategy	the survival of the 'fittingest' joined by...
Competing, which is friendly and non-traumatic, leads directly to...	**Chapter 5** Coopetition Strategy	*cooperating* based on the victorious idea shared by all to sponsor...
Inner-directed data and information from junior staff allow...	**Chapter 6** Continuous Improvement Strategy	*outer*-directed senior staff to integrate this knowledge and elicit...
Value being *ascribed* to the key aims of the Learning Society...	**Chapter 7** Strategic Superordinate Goals	motivates citizens to *achieve* such aims so as to fulfill the...
Contracts with *universal* and legal obligations are texts within...	**Chapter 8** Making Relationships More Valuable	the context of *particular* relationships whose mutuality and warmth cement the...
Faster delivery of products and accelerated *sequences* are abetted by...	**Chapter 9** Designing with Time	lightening *synchronization* of parallel processes which facilitate...

Figure 10.4

But, in fact, this is an illusion. The Infinite Game is a metaphor for a part of the double helix (Figure 10.3).

What appears to wind back on itself in fact goes on in two helices, looping around each other. Consider also the 'spliced rungs' on the twisted ladder. These include the opposites we have dealt with from Chapters 3 to 9. Untwist the ladder and we can summarize the themes we have explored, as shown in Figure 10.4.

If we then re-twist the ladder, it portrays an ascending series of Infinite Games, as portrayed in Figure 10.5.

We are *not*, of course, claiming scientific status simply because we have borrowed the metaphor of the DNA molecule. Values synthesis is not protein synthesis, seven pairs of bases are not four. DNA is an analogy which will soon break down.

But borrowing metaphors from the hard sciences and popular mechanics has always been the habit of the social sciences. Economics

Figure 10.5

is based on 19th century concepts of mechanism, then the wonder of the populace. Even Freudianism is suspiciously similar to the operation of a steam engine's boiler. Soon after holography was developed, the human brain was said to operate like a hologram.[15]

At least we borrow consciously from the life science of development in order to argue for the development of values. We suspect the so-called 'market mechanism' is closer to an organism and that economics would be less dismal if it had modeled itself on something alive and growing.

For, of course, we grow by differentiating ourselves (finitely) and integrating ourselves (infinitely). All cultures everywhere are laboriously trying to spiral upwards, sometimes gaining, sometimes slipping back. There is a never ending search for the next integrity and the expansion of meanings which such integrity brings. This book is, we hope, a modest step along the way.

Notes

Introduction

1. See debate in *Prospect*, March 1997 between Segal and the British author.
2. See J. Rowrer (1996) *Asia Rising*. London: Nicholas Brealey; M. S. Grindle (1991) 'The New Political Economy: Positive Economics, Negative Politics', in G. M. Meier (ed.), *Politics and Policy Making in Developing Countries*. San Francisco, CA: International Center for Economic Growth, pp. 41–67.
3. R. Findlay (1991) 'The New Political Economy: Its Explanatory Power for LDCs', in *Politics and Policy Making in Developing Countries*, op. cit., pp. 13–40.
4. M. Lipton (1977) *Why Poor People Stay Poor*. Cambridge, MA: Harvard University Press.
5. World Economic Forum (1989) *World Competitiveness Report*. Geneva, p. 261.

Chapter 1

1. L. Robbins (1946) *An Essay on the Nature and Significance of Economic Science*. London: Macmillan.
2. J. Maynard Keynes (1930) 'The Economic Possibilities for our Grandchildren', in *Essays in Persuasion*. Cambridge: Cambridge University Press.
3. See debate in *Prospect*, March 1997, op. cit.
4. Editorial (1990) 'Takeshi Umehara: Japanese Philosopher', *New Perspectives Quarterly*, **7**(3), 22–31.
5. See R. E. Allinson (1989) *Understanding the Chinese Mind*. Hong Kong: Oxford University Press; Fung Yu-han (1996) *A Short History of Chinese Philosophy*. New York: Free Press.
6. See D. Riepe (ed.) (1981) *Asian Philosophies Today*. New York: Gordon & Breach, pp. 236–249.
7. *Asian Philosophies Today*, op. cit., introduction.
8. E. van der Haag (1957) 'Of Happiness and Despair we Have no Measure', in B. Rosenberg and D. White (eds), *Mass Culture*. New York: Free Press.
9. Chang Chung-yuan (1963) *Creativity and Taoism*. New York: Harper & Row; T. Cleary (1961) *The Essential Tao*. San Francisco, CA: Harper.
10. Quoted in K. van Wolferen (1989) *The Enigma of Japanese Power*. New York: Alfred Knopf, p. 240.
11. See F. Capra (1975; new edn 1991) *The Tao of Physics*. Boston, MA: Shambala.
12. *The Tao of Physics*, op. cit., p. 148.
13. D. Bohm (1993) *On Dialogue*. New York: Pegasus Communications.
14. C. Hampden-Turner (1993) *Charting the Corporate Mind*. Oxford: Basil Blackwell, Introduction.
15. Ibid., p. 14.
16. G. E. Moore (1903) *Principa Ethica*, held that the definition was eternally

elusive. To try and derive an 'is' from an 'ought' is called the 'naturalistic fallacy', a term coined by David Hume.

17. E. de Bono (1994) *Water Logic*. London: Penguin, 1994. See also E. de Bono (1979) *Lateral Thinking*. New York: Harper & Row, 1979.
18. Oxford University Press (1972) 'The Second Coming' by W. B. Yeats, in *The Oxford Book of English Verse*. Oxford.
19. See F. Trompenaars and C. Hampden-Turner (1997) *Riding the Waves of Culture*. London: Nicholas Brealey.
20. J. P. Carse (1992) *Finite and Infinite Games*. New York: Ballantine Books.

Chapter 2

1. See the opening chapter of M. Friedman and R. Friedman (1981) *Free to Choose*. New York: Avon, for the triumphalism which would later turn to a flood.
2. Here we follow James P. Carse, to some degree, while applying some of his distinctions more to business than he did.
3. This point about the unit of survival features prominently in G. Bateson (1972) *Steps to an Ecology of Mind*. New York: Doubleday, Anchor.
4. *Harvard Business School Case Library*, Motorola, 1–5.
5. M. E. Porter (1980) *The Competitive Advantage of Nations*. New York: Free Press, pp. 411–413.
6. R. H. Frank and P. J. Cook (1995) *The Winner Takes All Society*. New York: Free Press (a Martin Kessler Book).
7. I. Nonaka and H. Takeuchi (1995) *The Knowledge Creating Company*. New York: Oxford University Press, p. 267.
8. *Fortune* (November 1988) 'Are Europe's Bosses Underpaid?'.
9. Complexity Theory is now being advocated by the Santa Fe Institute as an economics model.
10. R. Reich (1987) *Tales of a New America*. New York: Times Books, pp. 141–146.
11. C. S. Allen (1987) 'Germany: Competing Communitarianisms', in G. C. Lodge and E. Vogel (eds), *Ideology and National Competitiveness*. Boston, MA: Harvard Business School Press, pp. 81–85.
12. *Financial Times* (1993) 'Germany's Green Credentials', *Financial Times*, March 3.
13. Personal communication with Steve Jobs.
14. R. B. Reich (1991) *The Work of Nations*. New York: Alfred Knopf.
15. M. T. Jacobs (1991) *Short Term America*. Boston, MA: Harvard Business School Press, p. 9.
16. R. L. George (1992) *The East–West Pendulum*. Singapore: Woodhead-Faulkner, p. 52. For a Western vision of 'Double Swing' see B. Johnson (1994) *Polarity Management*. HRD Press; D. K. Hurst (1995) *Crisis and Renewal*. Boston, MA: Harvard Business School Press.
17. Quoted in J. S. T. Quah (1990) *In Search of Singapore's National Values*. Institute of Policy Studies, Times Academic Press, p. 56.
18. S. Addis and A. Y. Seo (1996) *How to Look at Japanese Art*. New York: Harry N. Abrams.

Chapter 3

1. Personal communication and presentation at SRI International Values and Lifestyle Forum, 1983.
2. *Essays in Persuasion,* op. cit.
3. *Understanding the Chinese Mind,* op. cit.
4. B. Scott and G. Lodge (1985) *American Competitiveness.* Boston, MA: Harvard Business School Press.
5. D. Sainsbury, personal communication.
6. William Morrow (1996) *The Future of Capitalism.* New York.
7. E. Schein (1996) *Strategic Pragmatism.* Cambridge, MA: MIT Press.
8. EDB Yearbooks, 1992–3, 1993–4 and 1994–5.
9. *Strategic Pragmatism,* op. cit., pp. 59–70.
10. *Strategic Pragmatism,* op. cit., p. 104.
11. EDB Yearbook, 1993–4. Also *Strategic Pragmatism,* op. cit., pp. 108–111.
12. *American Competitiveness,* op. cit. See rank orderings of industry by knowledge intensity.
13. See C. Hampden-Turner and F. Trompenaars (1993) *The Seven Cultures of Capitalism.* London: Piatkus, pp. 181–183.

Chapter 4

1. M. Mohamad and S. Ishihara (1995) *The Voice of Asia.* Tokyo: Kodensha Int., p. 121.
2. See *Charting the Corporate Mind,* op. cit., p. 29.
3. E. Jantsch (1980) *The Self-Organising Universe.* New York: Pergamon Press, pp. 48–50.
4. M. Porter (1990) *The Competitive Advantage of Nations.* New York: Free Press.
5. Ibid.
6. See S. Aizonwa (1985) 'Japan's Technology Agenda', *High Technology,* 11–15.
7. See M. J. Wolk (1983) *The Japanese Conspiracy.* London: NEL, for a somewhat xenophobic account of how Japan took over the global machine-tool business. A more sober account is in M. L. Dertouzos *et al.* (1989) *Made in America.* Cambridge, MA: MIT Press. The MIT Commission on Industrial Productivity reveal that most US machine-tool makers were held by conglomerates and were simply ceded to Japan after they became unprofitable!
8. *High Technology,* op. cit.
9. See I. Magaziner and P. Pantinkin (1989) 'Japan: Race for the Sun', in *The Silent War.* New York: Random House.
10. Ibid., p. 229.
11. EDB Yearbook, 1994, p. 9.
12. See S. Tatsuno (1990) *Created in Japan.* New York: Harper, p. 64–66.
13. EDB Yearbook, 1994, op. cit.
14. Ibid.
15. EDB Yearbook, 1992–3, op. cit.
16. See C. M. Hampden-Turner (1993) 'The Castle of Care: North American Tool and Die', in *Corporate Culture: Vicious and Virtuous Circles.* London: Piatkus.
17. See (1986) 'Developer/Adopter Relationships in New Industrial Product Situations', *Journal of Business Research,* 501–517.

18. N. Oliver *et al.* (1994) *World Wide Manufacturing Competitiveness Study*. London: Andersen Consulting.

Chapter 5

1. See S. P. Huntingdon (1996) *The Clash of Civilisations and the remaking of World Order*. New York: Simon & Schuster, pp. 96–99.
2. See K. Mahbubani (1993) 'The Dangers of Decadence', in *The Clash of Civilisations* (A Foreign Affairs Reader). New York.
3. See A. M. Brandenburger and B. J. Nalebuff, *Co-opetition*. New York: Doubleday, pp. 98–109.
4. Ibid., pp. 11–39.
5. R. A. Cloward (1959) 'Illegitimate Means, Anomie and Deviant Behavior', *American Sociological Review*, **24**(2).
6. *Strategic Pragmatism*, op. cit., p. 30.
7. B. Ouchi (1986) *The M-Form Society*. Reading, MA: Addison-Wesley.
8. R. Dore (1987) *Taking Japan Seriously*. Stanford, CA: Stanford University Press.
9. *The Competitive Advantage of Nations*, op. cit., p. 412.
10. A. Morito, *Made in Japan*, New York: Signet, p. 176.
11. *Strategic Pragmatism*, op. cit., p. 180.
12. Ibid., pp. 181–182.
13. P. Senge (1990) *The Fifth Discipline*. New York: Doubleday, Anchor.
14. Personal communication.
15. For a description see *Harvard Business School Case Clearing House*, Motorola.

Chapter 6

1. *An Essay on the Nature and Significance of Economic Science*, op. cit., p. 36.
2. C. Handy (1989) *The Age of Unreason*. London: Century Hutchinson.
3. Peters and Waterman (1982) *In Search of Excellence*. New York: Harper & Row.
4. C. Handy (1993) *The Age of Paradox*. Boston, MA: Harvard Business School Press. In the UK it is called *The Empty Raincoat*.
5. A. Kaplan (1964) *The Conduct of Inquiry*. Scranton, PA: Chandler.
6. J. B. Rotter (1966) 'Generalised Experiences of Internal vs. External Control of Reinforcement', *Psychological Monographs*, 609.
7. D. Goleman (1995) *Emotional Intelligence*. London: Bloomsbury.
8. K. Lux *(1990) Adam Smith's Mistake*. Boston, MA: Shambhala.
9. *Tales of a New America*, op. cit., p. 126.
10. Ibid., p. 184.
11. M. Maruyama (1963) 'The Second Cybernetics', *American Scientist*, **51**, 164–179, 250–256.
12. See H. Mintzberg (1987) 'Crafting Strategy', *Harvard Business Review*, March/April, 66–75. Strategies are not necessarily designed in advance and then imposed.
13. *The Knowledge Creating Company*, op. cit., pp. 127–129.
14. Ibid., pp. 86–87.
15. Ibid., pp. 96–113.
16. Ibid., pp. 65–66.

17. W. Edwards Deming (1986) *Out of the Crisis*. Cambridge, MA: Technology Center for Advanced Engineering Study.
18. P. Watzlawick, J. H. Beavin and D. D. Jackson (1967) *Pragmatics of Communication*. New York: W. W. Norton.
19. *Strategic Pragmatism*, op. cit. See also D. Ashton and F. Green (1996) *Education, Training and Global Learning*. Cheltenham: Edward Elgar.

Chapter 7

1. Discussed by Bruce Scott in *American Competitiveness*, op. cit., p. 24.
2. Ibid., p. 53.
3. *Education, Training and the Global Economy*, op. cit. See the chapter 'High Skills Route', pp. 137–149.
4. T. Ohno (1978) *The Toyota Production System*. Cambridge, MA: Productivity Press, p. 73.
5. Personal communication. Barbara can be reached through the Global Business Network, Emeryville, CA.
6. Lester Thurow (1996) *The Future of Capitalism*. New York: William Morrow, pp. 282–286.
7. Ibid., pp. 290–298.
8. *Asia Rising*, op. cit., pp. 58–59.
9. D. Ashton and F. Green (1996) *Education and Training and the Global Economy*. Cheltenham: Edward Elgar.
10. *The M-Form Society*, op. cit., pp. 207–214.
11. *Education and Training in the Global Economy*, op. cit., pp. 154–156.
12. Ibid., p. 173.
13. See *The Seven Cultures of Capitalism*, op. cit., pp. 155–157.
14. See *The Age of Paradox*, op. cit.

Chapter 8

1. Personal communication at Motorola University.
2. The details of this conversation have been altered to preserve confidences.
3. See C. M. Hampden-Turner (1993) 'Malaysia on the March', in *Corporate Culture: Vicious and Virtuous Circles*. London: Piatkus.
4. The incident is described well by R. M. March (1988) *The Japanese Negotiator*. Tokyo: Kondanshi.
5. Ibid., p. 224.
6. K. Kurokawa (1994) *The Philosophy of Symbiosis*. London: Academy Editions, pp. 55–57.
7. D. Tannen (1990) *You Just Don't Understand*. New York: Ballantine Books.
8. For synergy between toughness and tenderness, see A. Maslow (1954) *Motivation and Personality*. New York: Harper & Row; and more recently, R. Fisher and B. Ury (1987) *Getting to Yes*. London: Penguin, who argues for being 'tough on the problem, tender on the relationship'.
9. Menthe (1993) *Japanese Etiquette and Ethics in Business*. Lincolnwood, IL: NTC, p. 186.
10. See, for example, R. C. Christopher (1984) *The Japanese Mind*. London: Pan.

11. See D. McNeil and P. Frieberger (1993) *Fuzzy Logic*. New York: Simon & Schuster.

12. For example, the Japanese *Kanji* (ideogram) for opinion or theory reads literally 'elder brother with horns telling younger brother off'.

13. *Japanese Etiquette and Ethics in Business*, op. cit., p. 143.

14. *The M-Form Society*, op. cit., p. 141.

15. M. Maruyama (1994) *Mindscapes of Management*. Singapore: Dartmouth, pp. 30–33.

16. *The M-Form Society*, op. cit., p. 144.

17. *Mindscapes of Management*, op. cit., p. 72.

18. See, for example, R. B. Reich and E. D. Mankin (1996) 'Joint Ventures with Japan Give Away America's Future', *Harvard Business Review*, March–April. American negotiators aimed for profits and innovative opportunities. Japanese negotiators aimed for learning opportunities and development of core competencies.

19. M. Boisot and J. Child (1988) 'The Iron Law of Fiefs and The Problem of Governance in Chinese Economic Reforms', *Administrative Science Quarterly*, **33**, 507–527.

20. M. Boisot (1995) *Information Space*. London: Routledge, pp. 171–172.

21. *The Knowledge Creating Company*, op. cit., p. 16.

22. Personal communication in a Malibu restaurant.

23. P. Slater (1974) *Earthwalk*. New York: Anchor, Doubleday.

Chapter 9

1. E. Jaques (1982) *The Form of Time*. New York: Crane Russak, Chapter 1.

2. R. B. Reich (1983) *The Next American Frontier*. New York: Time Books, pp. 56–59.

3. F. W. Taylor *The Principles of Scientific Management*, New York: W. W. Norton, p. 249.

4. *The Next American Frontier*, op. cit., p. 74.

5. This metaphor is used by L. Thurow (1980) *The Zero-Sum Society*. New York: McGraw-Hill.

6. For example, E. T. Hall (1983) *The Dance of Life*. New York: Anchor, Doubleday.

7. *The Voice of Asia*, op. cit., p. 111.

8. E. Vogel (1991) *The Four Little Dragons*. Cambridge, MA: Harvard University Press.

9. Global Business Network, Emeryville, CA Conference on Educational Futures.

10. *The Toyota Production System*, op. cit., pp. 29–30.

11. *Worldwide Manufacturing Competitiveness*, op. cit., pp. 29–30.

12. *Kommunikation*, in-house journal, Motorola, Penang.

13. J. Abegglen and G. Stalk (1985) *Kaisha: The Japanese Corporation*. New York: Basic Books, pp. 240–243.

14. *Worldwide Manufacturing Competitiveness*, op. cit., p. 33.

15. The point is well made by J. Sculley (1987) *Odyssey: From Pepsi to Apple*. New York: Harper & Row. See 'Tutorials' at the end of Chapters 7, 8 and 9.

16. See 'Korea: Winning with Microwaves' in *The Silent War*, op. cit., pp. 21–44.

17. See (1993) *The Art of the Long View*. New York: Currency Books, Doubleday.

18. *Mindscapes in Management*, op. cit., p. 7.
19. Ibid.
20. *World Competitiveness Report*, 1996, op. cit.
21. T. Umehara (1990) *New Perspectives Quarterly*, **7**(3), 31.

Chapter 10

1. A point made eloquently by R. Bellah (1985) *Habits of the Heart*. Berkeley, CA: University of California Press, p. 182.
2. David K. Hurst and Sir Adrian Cadbury, personal communication. See also D. K. Hurst (1995) *Crisis and Renewal*. Boston, MA: Harvard Business School Press, pp. 77–95.
3. See Chapter 11, 'Self Constructed Lands', in *The Seven Cultures of Capitalism*, op. cit., pp. 292–294.
4. Proposed by Michael Howard, Home Secretary.
5. K. P. Easson and R. R. Easson (eds) (1978) *Milton*. New York: Random House.
6. NAL (1949) 'The Crack-Up', in *The Essays of Scott Fitzgerald*. New York.
7. M. Buber and P. Tillich (1959) *The Courage to Be*. New Haven, CT: Yale University Press, p. 165.
8. J. D. Watson (1969) *The Double Helix*. New York: Academic Press.
9. P. Watzlawich (1981) *How Real is Real?* New York: Vintage.
10. C. Argyris (1978) *Organisational Learning: A Theory of Action Perspective*. Reading, MA: Addison-Wesley.
11. D. Schon (1988) *The Reflective Practitioner*. New York: Basic Books.
12. F. C. Lesieur (1958) *The Scanlon Plan*. Cambridge, MA: MIT Press.
13. 'The Parenting Deficit' in *Life After Politics*, op. cit., pp. 199–212. See also the journal *The Responsive Community: Rights and Responsibilities*.
14. H. Williams (1962) in A. R. Vidler (ed.), *Soundings*. Cambridge: Cambridge University Press, 1962.
15. K. Pribam (1971) *Languages of the Brain*. Englewood Cliffs, NJ: Prentice Hall.

Bibliography

Abegglen, James C. and George Stalk Jr, *Kaisha: The Japanese Corporation*, New York: Basic Books, 1985.

Addis, Stephen and Audrey Yoshiko Seo, *How to Look at Japanese Art*, New York: Harry N. Abrams, 1996.

Adler, Nancy J., *Competitive Frontiers*, Oxford: Blackwell Business, 1994.

Aizawa, Susumu, 'Japan's Technology Agenda', *High Technology*, August, 1985.

Albert, Michel, *Capitalism Contre Capitalism*, Paris: Edition de Seuil, 1991.

Allinson, R. E., *Understanding the Chinese Mind*, Hong Kong: Oxford University Press, 1989.

Anderson Consulting, 'The Second Lean Enterprise Report', in *Worldwide Manufacturing Competitiveness Study*, Manchester: Arthur Anderson, 1994.

Argyris, Chris and Donald Schon, *Organisational Learning: A Theory of Action Perspective*, Reading, MA: Addison-Wesley, 1978.

Ashton, David and Francis Green, *Education, Training and The Global Economy*, Cheltenham: Edward Elgar, 1996.

Axelrod, Robert, *The Evolution of Co-operation*, New York: Basic Books, 1984.

Barber, Benjamin R., *Jihad vs. McWorld*, New York: Times Books, 1995.

Bartlett, Christopher A. and Sumantra Ghoshal, *Managing Across Borders*, Boston, MA: Harvard Business School Press, 1991.

Bateson, Gregory, *Steps to an Ecology of Mind*, New York: Ballantine, 1975.

Bateson, Mary Catherine, *Our Own Metaphor*, Washington, DC: Smithsonian Institution Press, 1993.

Bedi, Hari, *Understanding the Asian Manager*, Sydney: Allen & Unwin, 1991.

Bellah, Robert N., *Tokugawa Religion—The Cultural Roots of Modern Japan*, New York: Free Press, 1985.

Bellah, Robert N. *et al.*, *Habits of the Heart*, Berkeley, CA: California University Press, 1985.

Blenkhorn, David L. and A. Hamid Noori, 'What it Takes to Supply Japanese OEMs' in Siew Men Leong *et al.* (eds), *Marketing Insights for the Asian Pacific*, Singapore: Heinemann, 1996.

Bohm, David, *On Dialogue*, New York: Pegasus Communications, 1993.

Boisot, Max, *Information and Organisation*, London: Fontana, 1987.

Boisot, Max, *Information Space*, London: Routledge, 1996.

Boisot, Max and John Child, 'The Iron Law of Fiefs and the Problem of Governance in Chinese Economic Reforms', *Administrative Science Quarterly*, **33**, December 1988.

de Bono, Edward, *Lateral Thinking*, London: Penguin, 1982.

de Bono, Edward, *Water Logic*, London: Penguin, 1994.

Brandenburger, Adam M. and Barry J. Nalebuff, *Co-opetition*, New York: Doubleday, 1996.

Briggs, J. and F. D. Peat, *The Turbulent Mirror*, New York: Harper & Row, 1989.

Capra, Fritjof, *The Tao of Physics*, Berkeley, CA: Shambhala, 1975.

Capra, Fritjof, *The Web of Life*, New York: Harper Collins, 1996.

Carse, James B., *Finite and Infinite Games*, New York: Ballantine Books, 1986.

Cheng, Chung-yuan, *Creativity and Taoism*, New York: Harper & Row, 1963.

Choate, Pat, *Agents of Influence*, New York: Simon & Schuster, 1990.

Christopher, Robert C., *The Japanese Mind*, London: Pan, 1984.

Chua, Beng-Huat, *Communitarian Ideology and Democracy in Singapore*, London: Routledge, 1995.

Cleary, T., *The Essential Tao*, San Francisco, CA: Harper, 1961.

Cohen, Stephen and John Zysman, *Manufacturing Matters*, New York: Basic Books, 1987.

Collins, James C. and Jerry I. Porras, *Built to Last*, London: Century, 1994.

Corning, Peter A., *The Synergism Hypothesis: A Theory of Progressive Evolution*, New York: McGraw-Hill, 1983.

Corning, Peter A. and Susan Corning, *Winning with Synergy*, New York: Harper & Row, 1986.

Connors, Michael, *The Race for the Intelligent State*, Oxford: Capstone, 1997.

Cottle, Tom J., 'The Location of Experience: A Manifest Time Orientation', *Acta Psychologica*, **28**, 129–149, 1968.

Craig, JoAnn Meriwether, *Singapore Culture Shock!*, Portland, OR: Graphic Arts, 1994.

Davies, Howard, T. K. P. Leung, S. T. K. Luki and Yiu-Hing Wong, 'The Benefit of Guanxi', in *Marketing Insights for the Asia Pacific*, Singapore: Heinemann, 1996.

Deming, W. Edwards, *Out of the Crisis*, Cambridge, MA: Technology Centre for Advanced Engineering Study, 1986.

Dertouzas, Michael L., Richard K. Lester and Robert M. Solow, *Made in America: Regaining the Productive Edge*, Cambridge, MA: MIT Press, 1989.

Doi, Takeo, *The Anatomy of Dependence*, New York: Kondansha / Harper, 1976.

Dore, Ronald, *Taking Japan Seriously*, Stanford: Stanford University Press, 1987.

EDB, *Towards a Global City*, Singapore: Yearbook 1991–2.

EDB, *Singapore Unlimited*, Singapore: Yearbook 1994.

Engholm, Christopher, *Doing Business in Asia's Booming 'China Triangle'*, Engelwood Cliffs, NJ: Prentice Hall, 1994.

Etzioni, Amitae, 'The Parenting Deficit', in Geoff Mulgan (ed.), *Life After Politics*, London: Harper-Collins, 1997.

Findlay, R., 'The New Political Economy: Its Explanatory Powers for LDCs', in Gerald M. Meier (ed.), *Politics and Policy Making in Developing Countries*, San Francisco, CA: ICEG, 1991.

Frank, Robert H. and Philip J. Cook, *The Winner-Take-All Society*, New York: Free Press, 1993.

Fung, Yu-Lan, *A Short History of Chinese Philosophy*, New York: Free Press, 1918.

Garratt, Bob, *The Learning Organization*, London: Fontana, 1987.

Garratt, Bob, *Learning to Lead*, London: Fontana, 1990.

Gazzaniga, Michael S., 'The Split Brain in Man', *Scientific American*, Jan. 1964.

de Geus, Arie P., 'Planning as Learning', *Harvard Business Review*, March / April 1988.

George, Robert Lloyd, *The East–West Pendulum*, New York: Woodhead-Faulkner, 1992.

Goleman, Daniel, *Emotional Intelligence*, London: Bloomsbury, 1995.

Gudykunst, William B. and Tsukasa Nishida, *Bridging Japanese/North American Differences*, London: Sage, 1994.

Gurvitch, G., *The Spectrum of Social Time*, Reidel: Dordrecht, 1964.

Halberstam, David, *The Reckoning*, New York: Avon, 1988.

Hall, Edward T., *The Silent Language*, New York: Doubleday, 1959.

Hall, Edward T., *Beyond Culture*, New York: Doubleday, 1976.

Hall, Edward T., *Dance of Life: The Other Dimension of Time*, New York: Anchor, Doubleday, 1983.

Hall, Edward T., *Hidden Differences: Doing Business with the Japanese*, New York: Doubleday, 1987.

Hampden-Turner, Charles M., *Radical Man: Towards a Theory of Psycho-social Development*, London: Duckworth, 1973.

Hampden-Turner, Charles M., *Maps of the Mind*, New York: Macmillan, 1981.

Hampden-Turner, Charles M., *Gentlemen and Tradesmen: The Values of Economic Catastrophe*, London: Routledge & Kegan Paul, 1983.

Hampden-Turner, Charles M., 'Approaching Dilemmas', *Shell Guides to Planning*, No. 3, 1985.

Hampden-Turner, Charles M., *Charting the Corporate Mind: From Dilemma to Strategy*, Oxford: Basil Blackwell, 1990.

Hampden-Turner, Charles M. and Fons Trompenaars, *The Seven Cultures of Capitalism*, London: Piatkus Books, 1994.

Handy, Charles, *The Gods of Management*, London: Souvenir Press, 1978.

Handy, Charles, *The Age of Unreason*, London: Century-Hutchinson, 1989.

Handy, Charles, *The Age of Paradox*, Boston, MA: Harvard Business School Press, 1994 (published in the UK as *The Empty Raincoat*).

Harland, Bryce, *Collision Course: America and East Asia in The Past and The Future*, Singapore: Institute of Southern Asia, 1995.

Hofstede, Geert, *Cultures' Consequences*, Beverley Hills: Sage, 1980.

Hofstede, Geert, *Cultures and Organizations: Software of the Mind*, New York: McGraw-Hill, 1991.

Holstein, William J., *The Japanese Power Game: What it Means for Americans*, New York: Charles Scribner and Sons, 1990.

Huizinga, Johan, *Homo Ludens: A Study of the Play Element in Culture*, Boston, MA: Beacon, 1970.

Huntingdon, Samuel P., *The Clash of Civilizations: The Debate. A Foreign Affairs Reader*, New York: Council on Foreign Relations, 1993.

Huntingdon, Samuel P., *The Clash of Civilizations and the Remaking of World Order*, New York: Simon & Schuster, 1996.

Hurst, D.K., 'Of Boxes, Bubbles and Effective Management', *Harvard Business Review*, May/June 1984.

Hurst, D.K., *Crisis and Renewal*, Boston, MA: Harvard Business School Press, 1995.

Ishihara, Shintaro, *The Japan that Can Say 'No'*, Congressional Record, Nov. 14, 1989, also Kubansha/Kapper-Holmes, 1989.

Ishinomori, Shotaro, *Japan Inc.*, Berkeley, CA: University of California Press, 1988.

Jacobs, Michael T., *Short-term America*, Boston, MA: Harvard Business School Press, 1991.

Jantsch, Erich, *The Self-Organising Universe*, New York: Pergamon Press, 1980.

Jaques, Elliott, *Free Enterprise Fair Employment*, New York: Crane Russak, 1982.

Jaques, Elliott, *The Form of Time*, New York: Crane Russak, 1982.

Johnson, Barry, *Polarity Management: Identifying and Managing Unsolvable Problems*, HRD Press, 1994.

Jones, E. L., *Growth Recurring: Economic Change in World History*, Oxford: Oxford University Press, 1988.

Joynt, Pat and Malcolm Warner (eds), *Managing Across Cultures*.

Kao, John, *Entrepreneurship, Creativity and Organization*, London: Prentice Hall, 1991.

Kaplan, Abraham, *The Conduct of Inquiry*, Scranton, PA: Chandler, 1964.

Ketudat, Sippanondham and Robert M. Textor, *The Middle Path for the Future of Thailand*, Hawaii: East-West Center, 1990.

Keynes, John Maynard, 'Economic Possibilities for our Grandchildren', in *Essays in Persuasion*, Cambridge: Cambridge University Press, 1930.

Kluckholn, F. and F. L. Strodtbeck, *Variations in Value Orientations*, Conn.: Greenwood Press, 1961.

Kurokawa, Kisho, *The Philosophy of Symbiosis*, London: Academy Editions, 1994; London: International Thompson, 1996.

Laurent, André, 'The Cultural Diversity of Western Conceptions of Management', *International Studies of Management and Organization*, XIII(1–2), 1983.

Laurent, André, 'The Cross Cultural Puzzle of International Human Resource Management', *Human Resource Management*, 25(1), 1986.

Laurent, André, 'Cross Cultural Management for Pan European Companies', in Spyros Makridakis (ed.), *Europe 1992 and Beyond*, San Francisco, CA: Jossey-Bass, 1991.

Lawler, Edward E., *High Involvement Management*, San Francisco, CA: Jossey-Bass, 1986.

Lebra, Takie Sugiyama, *Japanese Patterns of Behaviour*, Honolulu, HI: University Press of Hawaii, 1976.

Lesieur, Frederick C., *The Scanlon Plan*, Cambridge, MA: MIT Press, 1958.

Leong, Siew Meng, Swee Hoon Ang and Chin Tiong Tan, *Marketing Insights for the Asia Pacific*, Singapore: Heinemann Southeast, 1996.

Lipton, M., *Why Poor People Stay Poor*, Cambridge, MA: Harvard University Press, 1977.

Lodge, George C., *The American Disease*, New York: Knopf, 1984.

Lodge, George C. and Vogel, Erza F. (eds), *Ideology and National Competitiveness*, Boston, MA: Harvard Business School Press, 1987.

Lux, Kenneth, *Adam Smith's Mistake*, Boston, MA: Shambhala, 1990.

McClelland, David, *The Achieving Society*, Princeton, NJ: Van Nostrand, 1961.

McGregor, Douglas, *The Human Side of the Enterprise*, New York: McGraw-Hill, 1960.

McNeill, Daniel and Paul Freiberger, *Fuzzy Logic*, New York: Simon & Schuster, 1993.

Magaziner, Ira and Mark Pantinkin, *The Silent War*, New York: Random House, 1989.

Mahbubani, Kishore, 'The Dangers of Decadence', in *The Clash of Civilizations*, New York: Council on Foreign Relations, 1993.

Makridakis, Spyros (ed.), *Europe 1992 and Beyond*, San Francisco, CA: Jossey-Bass, 1990.

Mant, Alistair, *The Rise and Fall of the British Manager*, London: Macmillan, 1977.

March, Robert M., *The Japanese Negotiator*, Tokyo/New York: Kondanshi Int., 1988.

Marquand, David, *The Unprincipled Society: New Demands, Old Politics*, London: Fontana, 1980.

Maruyama, Magorah, 'The Second Cybernetics', *American Scientist*, **51**, 1963.

Maruyama, Magorah, 'New Mindscapes for Future Business Policy and Management', *Technological Forecasting and Social Change*, **21**, 1982.

Maruyama, Magorah, 'Epistemological Sources of New Business Problems in the International Environment', *Human Systems Management*, **9**, 1989.

Maruyama, Magorah, *Mindscapes of Management*, Singapore: Dartmouth, 1994.

Maslow, Abraham, *Motivation and Personality*, New York: Harper & Row, 1954.

Matson, Floyd, *The Broken Image*, New York: George Braziller, 1964.

Meier, Gerald M. (ed.), *Politics and Policy Making in Developing Countries*, San Francisco, CA: ICEG, 1991.

de Mente, Boye Lafayette, *Japanese Etiquette and Ethics in Business*, Lincolnwood, IL: NTC Business Books, 1993.

Mintzberg, Henry, 'The Manager's Job: Folklore or Fact', *Harvard Business Review*, July/August 1976.

Mintzberg, Henry, 'Planning on the Left Side, Managing on the Right', *Harvard Business Review*, July/August 1976.

Mintzberg, Henry, 'Crafting Strategy', *Harvard Business Review*, March/April 1987, 66–75.

Mintzberg, Henry, *Mintzberg of Management: Inside our Strange World of Organizations*, New York: Free Press, 1989.

Mitroff, Iain, *Business NOT as Usual*, San Francisco, CA: Jossey-Bass, 1987.

Mohamad, Mahathir, 'The Way Forward: Vision 2020', Working Paper, Prime Minister's Office, Kuala Lumpur, Nov. 10 1996.

Mohamad, Mahathir and Shintaro Ishihara, *The Voice of Asia*, Tokyo: Kodensha Int., 1995.

Moore, James F., *The Death of Competition*, New York: Harper Business, 1996.

Morgan, Gareth, *Images of Organization*, Beverley Hills, CA: Sage, 1986.

Morgan, Gareth, *Riding the Waves of Change*, San Francisco, CA: Jossey-Bass, 1988.

Morita, Akio, *Made in Japan*, New York: Signet, 1986.

Mulgan, Geoff (ed.), *Life after Politics*, London: Harper-Collins, 1997.

Ngoh, Chan Lai, *The Penang Journey*, Motorola Malaysia, Sdn. Bhd., 1994.

Nock, S. L. and P. H. Rossi, 'Achievement vs. Ascription in the Attribution of Family Social Status', *American Journal of Sociology*, **84**(3), 1978.

Nonaka, Ikujiro and Hirotaka Takeuchi, *The Knowledge-Creating Company*, New York: Oxford University Press, 1995.

Ogilvy, Jay, *Many Dimensional Man*, New York: Oxford University Press, 1977.

Ogilvy, Jay, *Social Issues and Trends: The Maturation of America*, Menlo Park, CA: VALS, SRI International, 1984.

Ohmae, Keniche, *The Borderless World: Power and Strategy in the Interlinked Economy*, London: Collins, 1990.

Ohno, Taiichi, *Toyota Production Systems*, Cambridge, MA: Productivity Press, 1978.

Oliver, N. and D. T. Jones *et al.*, *Worldwide Manufacturing Competitiveness Study*, Manchester: Arthur Andersen, 1994.

Olsen, Mancur, *The Rise and Decline of Nations*, New Haven, CT: Yale University Press, 1982.

Orstein, Robert, *The Psychology of Consciousness*, San Francisco, CA: W. H. Freeman, 1973.

Ouchi, William, *Theory Z: How American Business Can Meet the Japanese Challenge*, Reading, MA: Addison-Wesley, 1981.

Ouchi, William, *The M-form Society*, Reading, MA: Addison-Wesley, 1986.

Ozbekhan, H., 'Planning and Human Action', in P. A. Weiss (ed.), *Systems in Theory and Practice*, New York: Haffner, 1971.

Parsons, Talcott and Edward A. Shils, *Towards a General Theory of Action*, Cambridge, MA: Harvard University Press, 1951.

Pascale, Richard T., 'Perspectives in Strategy: The Real Story behind Honda's Success', *California Management Review*, **XXVI**(3), 1984.

Pascale, R. T. and A. G. Athos, *The Art of Japanese Management*, New York: Simon & Schuster, 1981.

Peebles, Gavin and Peter Wilson, *The Singapore Economy*, Cheltenham: Edward Elgar, 1996. Penang Skills Development Centre. *Update: Bayan Lepas*, Penang, 1996.

Penang Skills Development Centre, *The Pangkor Review*, Penang, 1996.

Peters, T. and R. H. Waterman, *In Search of Excellence*, New York: Harper & Row, 1982.

Pfeffer, Jeffrey, *Competitive Advantage Through People*, Boston, MA: Harvard Business School Press, 1994.

Porras, Jerry I., *Stream Analysis*, Reading, MA: Addison-Wesley, 1987.

Porter, Michael E., *Competitive Strategy: Techniques for Analyzing Industries and Competitors*, New York: Free Press, 1980.

Porter, Michael E., *The Competitive Advantage of Nations*, New York: Free Press, 1990.

Prestowitz, Clyde V., *Trading Places*, New York: Basic Books, 1989.

Quah, Jon S. T., *In Search of Singapore's National Values*, Singapore: Times Academic Press, 1990.

Quinn, J. B., 'Logical Incrementalism', *Sloan Management Review*, **20**(Fall), 1978.

Quinn, J. B., Henry Mintzberg and Robert M. James, *The Strategy Process*, Engelwood Cliffs, NJ: Prentice Hall, 1988.

Quinn, Robert E., *Beyond Rational Management*, San Francisco, CA: Jossey-Bass, 1988.

Redding, S. G., *The Spirit of Chinese Capitalism*, New York: Walter de Gruyter, 1990.

Reich, Robert B., *Tales of a New America*, New York: Times Books, 1987.

Reich, Robert B., *The Work of Nations*, New York: Alfred Knopf, 1991.

Reich, Robert B. and Eric D. Mankin, 'Joint Ventures with Japan Give Away America's Future', *Harvard Business Review*, March/April, 1986.

Rhinesmith, Stephen H., *Globalisation: Six Keys to Success in a Changing World*, New York: Irwin, 1993.

Robbins, Lionel, *An Essay on the Nature and Significance of Economic Science*, London: Macmillan, 1946.

Rohwer, Jim, *Asia Rising*, London: Nicholas Brealey, 1996.

Rotter, J. B., 'Generalized Experiences of Internal vs. External Control of Reinforcement', *Psychological Monographs*, **609**, 1966.

Schein, Edgar H., *Organization, Culture and Leadership*, San Francisco, CA: Jossey-Bass, 1985.

Schein, Edgar H., *Strategic Pragmatism*, Cambridge, MA: MIT Press, 1996.

Schon, Donald A., *Beyond the Stable State*, New York: Random House, 1971.

Schon, Donald A., 'Creative Metaphor: A Perspective on Problem Setting in Social Policy', in A. Ortny (ed.), *Metaphor and Thought*, Cambridge: Cambridge University Press, 1979.

Schon, Donald A., *The Reflective Practitioner*, New York: Basic Books, 1982.

Schwartz, Peter, *The Art of the Long View*, New York: Currency Books, Doubleday, 1993.

Scott, Bruce R. and George C. Lodge (eds), *American Competitiveness*, Boston, MA: Harvard Business School Press, 1985.

Sculley, John, *From Pepsi to Apple*, New York: Harper & Row, 1987.

Senge, Peter M., *The Fifth Discipline*, New York: Doubleday, 1990.

Sheridan, Greg (ed.), *Living with Dragons: Australia Confronts its Asian Destiny*, St Leonards: Allen Unwin, 1995.

Slater, Phil, *Earthwalk*, New York: Doubleday, 1974.

Sperry, Roger W., 'The Great Cerebral Commissure', *Scientific American*, January, 1964.

Sperry, Roger W., *Science and Moral Priority*, New York: Columbia University Press, 1983.

Stouffer, S. A. and J. Toby, 'Role Conflict and Personality', *American Journal of Sociology*, **1**, V1–5, 1951.

Swee, Goh Keng [Linda Low (ed.)], *Wealth of East Asian Nations*, Singapore: Federal Publications, 1995.

Tannen, Deborah, *You Just Don't Understand*, New York: Ballantine Books, 1990.

Tatsuno, Sheridan M., *Created in Japan*, New York: Harper & Row, 1990.

Taylor, Frederick Winslow, *The Principles of Scientific Management*, New York: W. W. Norton, 1947.

Thurow, Lester C., *The Zero-Sum Society*, New York: McGraw-Hill, 1980.

Thurow, Lester C. (ed.), *The Management Challenge: Japanese Views*, Cambridge, MA: MIT Press, 1985.

Thurow, Lester C., *The Future of Capitalism*, New York: William Morrow, 1996.

Tillich, Paul, *The Courage to Be*, New Haven: Yale University Press, 1959.

Trompenaars, Fons and Charles M. Hampden-Turner, *Riding the Waves of Culture*, London: Nicholas Brealey, 1997.

Tung, Rosalie L., *The New Expatriates*, Cambridge MA: Ballinger, 1988.

Tung, Rosalie L., 'Managing in Asia: Cross-Cultural Dimensions', in Pat Joynt and Malcolm Warner (eds), *Managing Across Cultures*, Singapore: International Thompson, 1996.

Van der Haag, Ernest, 'Of Happiness and Despair we have no Measure', in B. Rosenberg and D. White (eds), *Mass Culture*, New York: Free Press, 1957.

Van Wolferen, Karl, *The Enigma of Japanese Power*, New York: Alfred Knopf, 1989.

Vogel, Ezra F., *Japan as No 1*, New York: Harper & Collins.

Vogel, Ezra F., *One Step Ahead in China*, Cambridge, MA: Harvard University Press, 1989.

Vogel, Ezra F., *The Four Little Dragons*, Cambridge, MA: Harvard University Press, 1991.

Warner, Malcolm, *Comparative Management: A Reader*, London: Routledge (4 vols), 1996.

Watzlawick, Paul, *How Real is Real?*, New York: Vintage, 1981.

Watzlawick, Paul, J. H. Beavin and D. D. Jackson, *Pragmatics of Communication*, New York: W. W. Norton, 1967.

Wenzhong, Hu and Cornelius Grove, *Encountering the Chinese*, Yarmouth, ME: Intercultural Press, 1991.

Williamson, Oliver E., 'Transaction-Cost Economics: Governing Economic Exchanges', *Journal of Law and Economics*, 22, 1979.

Womak, James P., Daniel T. Jones and Daniel Roos, *The Machine that Changed the World*, New York: Harper, 1991.

Yoshikawa, Muneo, *Communicating with the Japanese*, Portland, OR: Summer Institute for Cross Cultural Communication, 1992.

Zohar, Danah, *The Quantum Self*, London: Bloomsbury, 1993.

Zohar, Danah, *The Quantum Society*, London: Bloomsbury, 1995.

Index